Apple Training Series

Mac OS X Security and Mobility v10.6

Robert Kite, Ph.D., Michele Hjörleifsson, and
Patrick Gallagher

Apple
Certified

Apple Training Series: Mac OS X Security and Mobility v10.6
Robert Kite, Ph.D., Michele Hjörleifsson, and Patrick Gallagher

Published by Peachpit Press. For information on Peachpit Press books, contact:
Peachpit Press
1249 Eighth Street
Berkeley, CA 94710
510/524-2178
510/524-2221 (fax)

Find us on the Web at: www.peachpit.com
To report errors, please send a note to errata@peachpit.com
Peachpit Press is a division of Pearson Education

Apple Training Series Editor: Rebecca Freed
Instructional Designers: Shane Ross, John Signa
Production Editor: Danielle Foster
Copyeditor: Gail Nelson-Bonebrake
Tech Editors: Todd Dailey, Shawn Geddis
Proofreader: Suzie Nasol
Compositor: Danielle Foster
Indexer: Valerie Perry
Cover Illustrator: Kent Oberheu
Cover Production: Happenstance Type-O-Rama

ISBN 13: 978-0-321-63535-8
ISBN 10: 0-321-63535-3

9 8 7 6 5 4 3 2 1

Printed and bound in the United States of America

Acknowledgments

Patrick Gallagher First, I would like to thank the team who worked on this at Apple, Peachpit, and our own respective companies. It was certainly a group effort that pulled it through. There are too many people to name, and I suspect there are a number of behind-the-scenes people whom I can't put names to. You are included here, too. Thanks also to my clients and co-workers for tolerating these distractions and for recognizing that what I learn during these endeavors makes us more valuable.

Finally, thanks to all of my family and friends for putting up with the late nights, missing weekends, missed phone calls, late arrivals, cancelled engagements, general distraction, etc. I will do better.

Michele (Mike) Hjörleifsson First, I would like to thank the development team for being so helpful to a first-timer. To Shawn Geddis, John Signa, and Shane Ross at Apple for being a great help and resource through the project. To my friends at PrimeKey for their insights into PKI. To my best friend Ed Volz and my wife Dawn for tolerating my crazy hours, canceled engagements, etc.

Robert Kite, Ph.D. This project could not have been completed without the help of friends, colleagues and family. Darcy, Kelly, Alex, and Kate—I realize the hours were long and I missed a lot. Jan and George Barton: Thanks!

Arek Dreyer, Kevin White, Ben Greisler, Andrew Johnson, and Steve Cervera: Your assistance and participation were greatly appreciated. My colleagues at SARCOM were instrumental in the successful completion of this project. Earl Greer: Thanks for the brainstorming sessions. Tip Lovingood: Once again, thanks for the lab work; I couldn't have done it without you. Shane Ross and John Signa from Apple, as always, were amazing to work with. Rebecca Freed from Peachpit: Thanks for the hard work. Bob Lindstrom: Thanks for jumping in. Once again, I am grateful for your insight and ability to make what I write readable. And lastly, LeRoy Dennison and Judy Lawrence: Your advice and support was very helpful throughout this project.

Contents at a Glance

Contents

Part 3   **Working with Mobile Devices**

Getting Started

This book is based on the same criteria used for Apple's official training course, Mac OS X Security and Mobility 10.6, an in-depth exploration of providing secure access to important network resources from mobile clients using Mac OS X Server. The first section deals with Providing Network Services and covers the common network services: DNS, DHCP, and NAT. The second section deals with Securing Systems and Services and focuses on firewalls, VPNs, certificates, and 802.1x. The final section, Working with Mobile Devices, covers the basics of web and native application development for iPhone OS devices, managing deployment of iPhone OS devices, and configuration and use of the Mobile Access Server.

The primary goal is to help technical coordinators, system administrators, and others who support Macintosh users secure their resources using a variety of tools and know which security and mobility tools are applicable to which circumstances.

Whether you are an experienced system administrator or just want to dig deeper into Mac OS X v10.6 and Mac OS X Server v10.6, you'll learn in-depth technical information and procedures used by Apple-certified technicians to choose, configure, troubleshoot, and maintain these services and resources.

This book assumes a basic level of familiarity with Mac OS X. Unless otherwise specified, all references to Mac OS X refer to Mac OS X v10.6.2, the most current version available at the time of writing. Due to subsequent updates, some screen shots, features, and procedures may be slightly different from those presented on these pages.

Learning Methodology

This book is based on lectures and exercises provided to students attending Mac OS X Security and Mobility 10.6, a three-day, hands-on course that provides an intense and in-depth exploration of services related to network use, security, and mobility, especially with iPhone OS devices. For consistency, we follow the basic structure of the course material, but you may complete it at your own pace.

Each chapter is designed to help experienced users become experts who support other Mac OS X users by:

▶   Providing *knowledge* of how the covered services work

▶   Showing how to use configuration and troubleshooting *tools*

▶   Explaining configuration and troubleshooting *procedures*

For example, in Chapter 1, "Understanding the Domain Name System," you'll learn the basic networking concepts (knowledge) behind DNS. You'll acquire DNS configuration and troubleshooting techniques using Server Admin and other utilities (tools). And you'll explore methods for troubleshooting DNS issues (procedures). In addition, each chapter includes troubleshooting techniques and security information for dealing with common issues.

Each chapter focuses on a different aspect of Security and Mobility:

▶   Chapter 1, "Understanding the Domain Name System"—Understanding the purpose and structure of the DNS; configuring a DNS service on Mac OS X Server; managing DNS zones; creating DNS records; understanding BIND configuration files; troubleshooting DNS problems.

▶ Chapter 2, "Using DHCP"—Understanding DHCP's purpose and how it works; con-figuring a DHCP service on Mac OS X Server; assigning static IP addresses through DHCP (reservations or static maps); troubleshooting common DHCP failures.

▶ Chapter 3, "Network Address Translation/Gateway"—Understanding the purpose and use of NAT; configuring NAT and other services with the Gateway Setup Assistant; configuring NAT manually; configuring port forwarding on Mac OS X Server; trou-bleshooting NAT.

▶ Chapter 4, "Using a Firewall"—Understanding the Mac OS X application firewall; understanding the Mac OS X Server firewall, `ipfw`; configuring the Mac OS X Server firewall using graphical and command-line tools; troubleshooting the firewall service.

▶ Chapter 5, "Virtual Private Networks"—Understanding the VPN protocols supported by Mac OS X; configuring the Mac OS X Server VPN service; configuring Mac OS X clients to use VPN service; configuring the iPhone OS VPN client; troubleshooting common VPN issues.

▶ Chapter 6, "Keys and Certificates"—Understanding and using SSH key-base login; understanding the basics of public key infrastructure (PKI); understanding common uses of certificates; managing certificates on Mac OS X and Mac OS X Server; config-uring 802.1x on Mac OS X.

▶ Chapter 7, "Providing iPhone Applications"—Understanding the iPhone Developer Program and iPhone SDK; creating web applications for iPhone OS devices; creating native applications for iPhone OS devices; managing iPhone OS devices and applica-tions with iPhone Configuration Utility.

▶ Chapter 8, "Using Mobile Access Server"—Understanding how Mobile Access Server (MAS) works; understanding features and limitations of MAS; configuring MAS for the supported protocols; configuring clients to use MAS.

Chapter Structure

Each chapter begins with an opening page that lists the learning goals for the chapter and an estimate of the time needed to complete the chapter. The explanatory material is aug-mented with hands-on exercises essential to developing your skills. For the most part, all you need to complete the exercises is a Macintosh computer running Mac OS X v10.6 or later and a computer running Mac OS X Server v10.6 or later. If you lack the equipment necessary to complete a given exercise, you are still encouraged to read the step-by-step instructions and examine the screen shots to understand the procedures demonstrated.

NOTE ▶ Some of these exercises can be disruptive—for example, they may turn off network services temporarily—and some exercises, if performed incorrectly, could result in data loss or damage to system files. Given this, it's recommended that you perform these exercises on a Macintosh that is not critical to your daily productivity. Apple Inc. and Peachpit Press are not responsible for any data loss or any damage to any equipment that occurs as a direct or indirect result of following the procedures described in this book.

We refer to Apple Knowledge Base documents throughout the chapters, and close each chapter with a list of recommended documents related to the chapter's topic. The Knowledge Base is a free online resource (www.apple.com/support) containing the very latest technical information on all of Apple's hardware and software products. We strongly encourage you to read the suggested documents and search the Knowledge Base for answers to any problems you encounter.

You'll also find "More Info" resources throughout the chapters, and summarized at the end of each chapter, that provide ancillary information. These resources are merely for your edification, and are not considered essential for the coursework or certification.

At the end of each chapter is a short "Chapter Review" that recaps the material you've learned. You can refer to various Apple resources, such as the Knowledge Base, as well as the chapters themselves, to help you answer these questions.

Apple Certification

After reading this book, you may wish to take the Mac OS X Security and Mobility 10.6 Exam as part of the Apple Certified System Administrator 10.6 or the Apple Certified Specialist—Security and Mobility 10.6 certification. These are upper and middle certifications for Mac OS X professionals:

▶   Apple Certified Support Professional 10.6 (ACSP)—Ideal for help desk personnel, service technicians, technical coordinators, and others who support Mac OS X customers over the phone or who perform Mac OS X troubleshooting and support in schools and businesses. This certification verifies an understanding of Mac OS X core functionality and an ability to configure key services, perform basic troubleshooting, and assist end users with essential Mac OS X capabilities. To receive this certification, you must pass the Mac OS X Support Essentials 10.6 Exam.

▶ Apple Certified Technical Coordinator 10.6 (ACTC)—This certification is intended for Mac OS X technical coordinators and entry-level system administrators tasked with maintaining a modest network of computers using Mac OS X Server. Since the ACTC certification addresses both the support of Mac OS X clients and the core functionality and use of Mac OS X Server, the learning curve is correspondingly longer and more intensive than that for the ACSP certification, which addresses solely Mac OS X client support. This certification is not intended for high-end system administrators or engineers, but may be an excellent step to take on an intended career path to system administration. This certification requires passing both the Mac OS X Support Essentials 10.6 Exam and the Mac OS X Server Essentials 10.6 Exam.

▶ Apple Certified System Administrator 10.6 (ACSA)—This certification verifies an in-depth knowledge of Apple technical architecture and an ability to install and configure machines; architect and maintain networks; enable, customize, tune, and troubleshoot a wide range of services; and integrate Mac OS X, Mac OS X Server, and other Apple technologies within a multiplatform networked environment. The ACSA certification is intended for full-time professional system administrators and engineers who manage medium-to-large networks of systems in complex multiplatform deployments. ACSA 10.6 certification requires passing the Mac OS X Server Essentials 10.6 Exam, Mac OS X Directory Services 10.6 Exam, Mac OS X Deployment 10.6 Exam, and Mac OS X Security and Mobility 10.6 Exam.

▶ Mac OS X 10.6 certification offerings now include new Specialist certifications for the ACSA-level Directory Services, Deployment, and Security and Mobility exams. These certifications build on the Apple Certified Technical Coordinator 10.6 (ACTC) certification by adding the corresponding ACSA material.

Apple hardware service technician certifications are ideal for people interested in becoming Macintosh repair technicians, but also worthwhile for help desk personnel at schools and businesses, and for Macintosh consultants and others needing an in-depth understanding of how Apple systems operate:

▶ Apple Certified Macintosh Technician (ACMT)—This certification verifies the ability to perform basic troubleshooting and repair of both desktop and portable Macintosh systems, such as iMac and MacBook Pro. ACMT certification requires passing the Apple Macintosh Service exam and the Mac OS X Troubleshooting Exam.

About the Apple Training Series

Apple Training Series: Mac OS X Security and Mobility v10.6 is part of the official training series for Apple products developed by experts in the field and certified by Apple. The chapters are designed to let you learn at your own pace. You can progress through the book from beginning to end, or dive right into the chapters that interest you most.

For those who prefer to learn in an instructor-led setting, Apple also offers training courses at Apple Authorized Training Centers worldwide. These courses are taught by Apple Certified Trainers, and they balance concepts and lectures with hands-on labs and exercises. Apple Authorized Training Centers have been carefully selected and have met Apple's highest standards in all areas, including facilities, instructors, course delivery, and infrastructure. The goal of the program is to offer Apple customers, from beginners to the most seasoned professionals, the highest-quality training experience.

To find an Authorized Training Center near you, please visit http://training.apple.com.

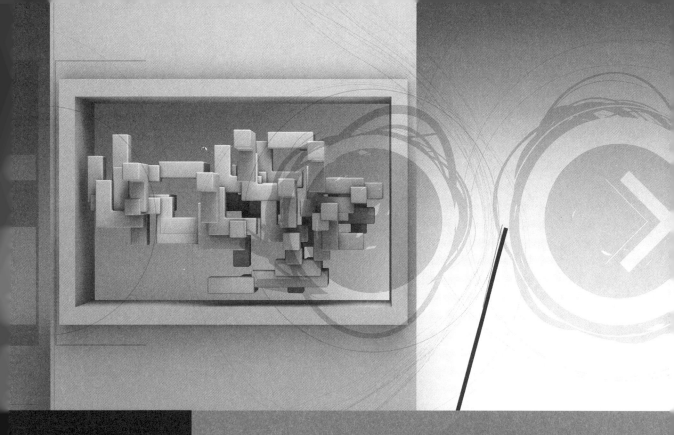

Part 1   Providing Network Services

1

Time This lesson takes approximately 60 minutes to complete.

Goals Understand the purposes of a DNS server

Learn how a DNS server uses a hierarchy of DNS servers to resolve a domain name that's not stored locally

Describe DNS zones and zone records

Identify the three types of DNS zones

Examine the record types in the DNS and their purposes

Learn the differences between a fully qualified domain name and a relative domain name

Locate and use the official BIND documentation

Become familiar with the underlying configuration and directory file structure of DNS services

Understand the impact of a preexisting DNS service on initial server setup

Learn how the DNS associates computer host names with IP addresses

Configure a new DNS service for an organization

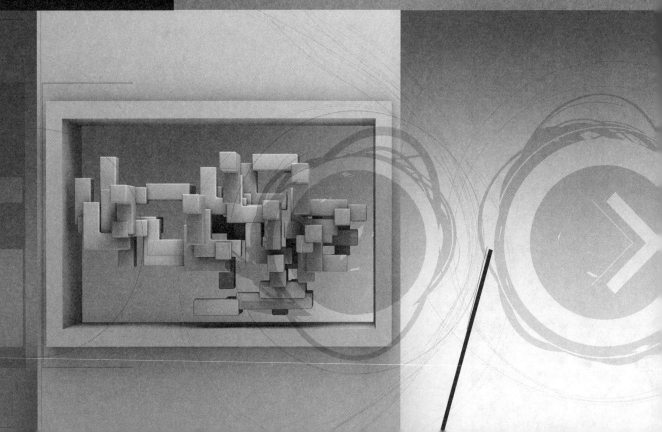

Chapter 1

Understanding the Domain Name System

The Domain Name System (DNS) is arguably the most important network service. The DNS is the method computers use to map IP addresses to domain names. For example, if you were to launch your browser and navigate to 17.149.160.10, you would be presented with the home page for one of our favorite sites, www.apple.com. However, remembering all of the IP addresses for often-visited sites would take some doing. The DNS alleviates that problem by associating domain names (www.apple.com) with IP addresses (17.149.160.10).

In this chapter, you will look at the DNS and how it works. You will also learn to configure and troubleshoot your own DNS server in Mac OS X Server v10.6.

Using the DNS: The Big Picture

The main purpose of the DNS is to convert easy-to-remember names into the harder-to-remember numbers that computers require, and to reduce the response time for name resolution queries. On smaller networks, it is typical, and perfectly acceptable, to rely on the DNS servers supplied by your Internet service provider (ISP). However, in larger installations, a site should host some level of in-house DNS service. Furthermore, it may be necessary to host the DNS internally because of the high number of services that rely on a functioning DNS.

Of the services listed in Server Admin, a fully functioning DNS is required for Open Directory and Mail, while the rest of the services benefit from having a DNS available. For example, the web service will answer requests made by a straight IP address, but the HTTP v1.1 protocol can access and serve multiple websites from the same IP address, based on the DNS name passed to it.

All these considerations require a system administrator who fully understands the DNS and has the skills to maintain a reliable, secure, and accurate DNS service. The graphical configuration tools for the DNS provided in Server Admin have never exposed the full spectrum of options available in the Berkeley Internet Name Domain (BIND), which is the open source DNS product that Apple uses. As a result, anyone with advanced configuration needs must use the command-line interface.

About the DNS

The primary purpose of the DNS is to convert domain names to IP addresses and to convert IP addresses to domain names, so it is important to understand how a DNS server works in the overall system and how IP addresses fit into that context. To that end, this section reviews the implementation of DNS servers throughout the Internet and explores how IP addresses identify the correct locations or paths to deliver and receive information.

Root-Level DNS Servers

At the top of the DNS sit 13 Root Servers. These servers act as traffic cops, directing Internet requests to the servers responsible for gTLDs such as .com, .edu, or .uk. The Root Servers are located throughout the world and are actually multiple systems grouped to provide DNS services. The Internet Assigned Numbers Authority (IANA) has the authority for the day-to-day administration of the Internet DNS.

TLD Servers

The top-level domain (TLD) servers are responsible for directing requests for each of their domains. In the 1980s, generic top-level domains (gTLDs) were created (.com, .edu, .gov, .int, .mil, .net, and .org). Anyone can register a domain in the .com, .net, or .org domains, but the other four domains are restricted. Since then, more gTLDs have been added. Generic TLDs are not country specific and are managed by the IANA.

The gTLD system is not responsible for the country-code top-level domains (ccTLDs) associated with specific countries. Each country is responsible for managing its own ccTLD and has some latitude in how secondary-level domains are deployed within it. For example, in the URL (Uniform Resource Locator) www.bbc.co.uk, .uk is the TLD for the United Kingdom. The responsible party in the UK would determine the policies for assigning the secondary-level domain, .co.

However, consider the URL www.bt.com. The TLD is .com, and the secondary-level domain is .bt. In this URL, British Telecom is responsible for managing the secondary-level domain and all domain levels beneath it. The third-level domain, in this example, is the host name of the machine, www. A domain can have up to 127 levels.

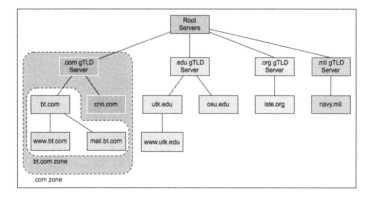

The figure above details the composition of the DNS. The Root Servers communicate with the TLD servers, and the TLD servers communicate with the secondary-level domain servers.

IP Addresses

An IP (Internet Protocol) address can be thought of as a personal identification number for a specific computer. No two computers have the same IP address, although multiple computers can have the same host name. (IPv4 addresses are 32-bit numbers usually shown as four *octets* in a dotted decimal number, such as 17.149.160.10). The four numbers in an IPv4 address are called octets because they each have eight positions when viewed in binary form (01100110.10011001.01011001.10011001). If you add all the individual positions for each number, you arrive at 32 individual positions. IPv6 addresses are longer and thus provide for a larger number of connected devices, but IPv6 addresses are not currently in widespread use. Mac OS X supports both IPv4 and IPv6 addresses, but a detailed discussion of IPv6 is beyond the scope of this book.

The IANA manages IP address allocations globally and in cooperation with five Regional Internet Registries (RIRs) that then allocate blocks of IP addresses to a Local Internet Registry (LIR), such as an ISP, and other groups. Should an organization be large enough to need a sizeable block of IP addresses, it can request an address block directly from an RIR.

Although all computers on the Internet have an IP address, not every computer will have the same IP address each time it goes online. Some are assigned a Dynamic Host Configuration Protocol (DHCP) address by their ISP. Computers with DHCP addresses typically do not have DNS entries because their IP addresses are subject to change at startup.

NOTE ▶ DHCP and IP addresses are discussed in greater detail in Chapter 2.

Computer systems and other online devices that do not regularly restart or provide services to other people or systems will probably have a static IP address that never changes. Examples of these types of devices include servers, routers, and other network appliances. These typically have a DNS entry assigned to their specific IP address.

Domain Names

OK, you now understand how the DNS is put together and how the domain levels are organized. You also know how IP addressing is derived. Now let's examine how the DNS and IP addresses come together to create a massive distributed database that millions of people access billions of times a day.

When you register a domain name with a registrar, you must also define the authoritative DNS servers for your domain—the servers that the root servers will query for your domain. The major registrars also generally provide DNS service for domains registered with them.

After you have registered your domain name and identified your DNS servers, you can add *zones* to your domain and *machine records* to your zones. A zone is the basic organizational unit of DNS and holds the DNS records for a domain. A machine record creates a relationship between a computer's IP address and its host name. For cxample, 17.149.160.10 becomes related to www.apple.com. Once this relationship is created, Internet users can find the server at 17.149.160.10 using its domain name in addition to its IP address.

About the DNS Query Path

A DNS server can be configured in several ways. The configuration a particular organization uses should match its performance and security needs. This section focuses on the path of a typical DNS query within an organization operating behind a firewall. Although this example represents a typical corporate LAN deployment, it doesn't represent every corporate LAN. Therefore, in the next section, you'll also examine other common DNS server configurations.

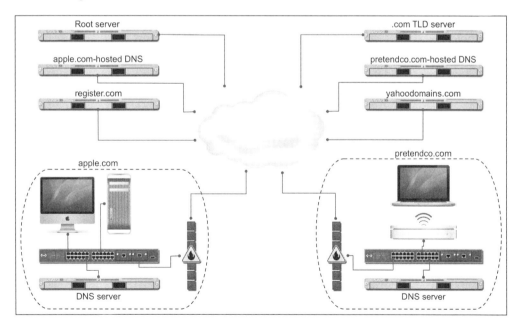

In the system shown in the figure above, all devices at the apple.com site are configured to use the local DNS server. Similarly, all devices on the pretendco.com network are configured to query the local DNS server of that site.

Keeping this structure in mind, imagine that Apple has registered its domain name with register.com, and the pretendco.com domain is registered with yahoodomains.com. When a device on the pretendco.com network needs to perform a DNS lookup, it queries its onsite DNS server. If that server can answer the query in some way—from its cache, or because it is authoritative for the domain in question—it passes the answer back to the client, and the lookups are completed.

If, however, the local DNS server does not have the answer, it performs a *recursive query* to fetch the answer. A recursive query sends the query up the DNS hierarchy and allows other servers to perform the query on the initial server's behalf. The response to the query ultimately passes back to the originating DNS server, which passes it on to the client.

If a device on the pretendco.com network needs to look up partners.apple.com, the device on pretendco.com won't find the IP address of partners.apple.com on its local DNS server or among the domains listed by its registrar, yahoodomains.com. To find the correct IP address, the local DNS server must query one of the Root Servers.

The Root Server, in effect, says, "Ah—you're looking for information about a server in the .com domain? I know just the server for you to talk to." From there, the Root Server refers pretendco.com's local DNS server to the gTLD server for the .com zone. This server, in turn, returns a reference to the specific DNS server responsible for the apple.com domain.

Pretendco.com's local DNS server can now query the server that is authoritative for the apple.com domain and that can actually answer the question. It retrieves the answer to the query, using a forward or reverse lookup, from the hosted DNS service and passes it to the client that made the original query. The local DNS server also caches this result, allowing it to directly answer this question for any future clients, until the expiration of that record.

This caching technique accelerates response to the same requests because the local DNS server already has the information necessary to resolve the query. Caching is especially important in an environment with many users because any DNS request that goes outside the local network can negatively impact the performance of the Internet connection.

About DNS Server Configurations

The previous example discussed several DNS servers, each running with a particular configuration specifically designed to match its function. Here are some common DNS server configurations:

▶ Authoritative name server—The servers responsible for a specific domain are called "authoritative," which means that they contain all the required information for a given domain. For instance, in the previous example, the apple.com domain has multiple authoritative name servers containing all the information regarding the apple.com domain. Therefore, when a name resolution request comes from the Internet, one of the authoritative name servers responds to that query.

There are three primary types of authoritative name servers:

▶ Primary master—The primary master is the specific server that has the primary zone or master file of that specific domain.

▶ Secondary server—The secondary server has an exact duplicate of the specific zones hosted on specific primary masters. Not all master zone files must be hosted on all secondary servers of that particular master. Furthermore, a secondary server can act as a master of some zones while serving as a secondary for another.

▶ Stealth server—A stealth server is an authoritative server that is not visible to the public. Therefore, the primary zone file does not include DNS information regarding this server. An example of this type of server is a split-DNS name server. This configuration will be discussed later in this chapter.

▶ Caching name server—A caching name server is not authoritative; therefore, it is not responsible for any zone files. The sole purpose of this server type is to speed up the resolution of queries and to cache responses.

▶ Split-DNS name server—In a split-DNS setup, the local internal DNS server is configured to be authoritative for the company domain or domains. Meanwhile, the master authoritative DNS server is still hosted externally, and the local DNS server answers all queries from devices located inside the network. Devices outside the network continue to query the hosted DNS service. This provides an interesting opportunity: The internal DNS server need not mirror the external DNS database exactly. The administrator may choose to augment the local version with internal-only resources. Because devices on the outside cannot access the internal resources, internal-only records do not need to exist in the hosted DNS server database. In essence, this creates one name space behind the local LAN's edge router, and a separate one for the world at large.

In the case of a company such as Apple, with all of its network resources, many internal-only addresses reside behind a security system, accessible only to users on the Apple network or perhaps users accessing the network via a virtual private network (VPN). An internal DNS server could serve the internal network and the internal-only addresses, as well as act as a DNS cache, saving bandwidth on external lookups.

Finally, if an administrator at Apple decided to enter information about the pretendco.com domain on the local internal DNS server, it would only affect devices on the Apple network. Everyone else in the world would still be referred to the hosted pretendco.com DNS server for authoritative DNS information about the pretendco.com domain.

Configuring a DNS Service

Now that you have a basic understanding of how the DNS works and the options available when configuring a DNS server, it is time to actually do it. In this section, you'll set up a DNS server on Mac OS X Server v10.6 using both the Server Admin tool and the command-line interface, BIND. However, before you can configure those DNS servers, you need to spend some time with DNS zones and DNS zone records.

Understanding DNS Zones

DNS zones are the basic organizational units of the DNS. DNS zones contain records and are defined by the way they acquire those records and respond to DNS requests.

There are three kinds of zones:

▶   Master zone—This zone has the master copy of the zone's records and provides authoritative answers to lookup requests.

▶   Slave zone—This is a copy of a master zone stored on a slave or secondary name server. Each slave zone keeps a list of masters that it contacts to receive updates to records in the master zone. Slaves must be configured to request the copy of the master zone's data. Slave zones use zone transfers to get copies of the master zone data. Slave name servers can process lookup requests just as master servers do. By linking several slave zones to one master, you can distribute DNS query loads across several computers and ensure that lookup requests are answered when the master name server is down.

Slave zones also have a refresh interval that determines how often they check for changes from the master zone. You can change this interval by modifying the BIND configuration file. See the BIND documentation for more information.

▶ Forward zone—This zone directs all lookup requests for that zone to other DNS servers. Forward zones do not do zone transfers. Often, forward zone servers are used to provide DNS services to a private network behind a firewall. When this is the case, the DNS server must have access to the Internet and to a DNS server outside the firewall. Also, forward zones cache responses to the queries they pass on. This can improve the performance of lookups by clients that use the forward zone.

Using DNS Zone Records

Each zone contains a number of zone records that are requested when a client computer needs to translate a domain name (such as www.pretendco.com) into an IP number and to describe the characteristics of a zone. Web browsers, email clients, and other network applications rely on zone records to contact the appropriate server. Other computers across the Internet will query your master zone so they can connect to your network services.

There are nine types of DNS records:

▶ IPv4 address (A)—Also known as a machine record, this stores the IP address associated with a domain name. An A record is created for each machine entry added to a zone. IPv4 addresses are 32 bits in length and written in dot-decimal notation, such as 17.45.32.119. The 32-bit length supports a maximum of 4.3 billion available addresses.

▶ IPv6 address (AAAA)—Also known as a machine record, an AAA record, like an IPv4 address, stores the IP address associated with a domain name and is created for each machine entry added to a zone. Unlike IPv4, IPv6 addresses are 128 bits in length and written with hexadecimal digits and colon separators. Furthermore, they are composed of two logical parts: a 64-bit network prefix and a 64-bit host part. A typical address would be 1734:8e3:8je4: :b03q:310:4567. The 128-bit length supports a maximum of 340 trillion trillion trillion addresses.

▶ Canonical name (CNAME)—This stores the "real name" of a server when it's given a nickname or alias. For example, mail.pretendco.com might have a CNAME of mailsrvr1.pretendco.com. A CNAME record is created for each entry in the Alias field when a machine is added to a zone.

▶   Mail exchange (MX)—This stores the name of the computer used for a domain's email. An MX record is created when you specify that a machine is a mail server. You can have multiple MX records for your domain, pointing to different servers. Lower numbers take priority over higher numbers when users attempt to use the mail servers on your network.

▶   Name server (NS)—This stores the authoritative name server for a zone.

▶   Pointer (PTR)—This is created automatically to store the domain name of a given IP address (reverse lookup). A PTR record maps an IP address to a computer's DNS name. The pointer record contains the four octets of the IP address in reverse order, followed by in-addr.arpa. (For example, 10.1.0.1 becomes 1.0.1.10.in-addr.arpa.) Pointer records have become increasingly important as a means for ISPs and service providers (AOL, financial institutions, mail servers, and so on) to confirm user identities. For example, your machine host name may be john.bbc.co.uk. However, your PTR record may resolve to hacker.anywhere.org. When these mismatches occur, many ISPs and service providers will not allow the Internet traffic.

▶   Text (TXT)—This stores a text string as a response to a DNS query, such as "This machine is located at John Wolfe's desk."

▶   Service (SRV)—This stores the information about various services, such as LDAP, Jabber, and Simple Mail Transfer Protocol (SMTP). These services are then mapped to the proper IP address and resolved to their respective domain names.

▶   Hardware info (HINFO)—This stores information about a computer's hardware and software, and appears in a format such as Apple-MacBook – 5000MHz "Mac OS X 10.6".

Mac OS X Server simplifies the creation of these records by focusing on the computer name added to the zone rather than the records themselves. As you add a computer record to a zone, Mac OS X Server creates the correct pointer zone record, which resolves to a specific computer IP address. This action creates a fully qualified domain name (FQDN), and only one machine in the name space (apple.com) can resolve to that IP address.

NOTE ▶ The term FQDN refers to the entire address of a host computer. For example, sales.apple.com is an FQDN, whereas "sales" is a relative domain name and is valid only from a machine in the apple.com domain. To indicate that a domain name is fully qualified, add a trailing dot to it (Mac OS X Server v10.6 automatically does so when you select the Fully Qualified checkbox). For example, sales.apple.com. indicates that this is not a relative domain name.

Configuring the DNS with Server Admin

Assuming that you've already registered a domain name or that you're setting up a DNS server for a small network behind a firewall or network address translation (NAT) gateway, you can begin to configure a DNS server to provide DNS services to client systems. In this section, you will use Server Admin to set up a DNS server for a small office. The table below illustrates the systems that will have DNS entries in the pretendco.com domain.

Table 1.1   IP and Host Information for DNS Configuration

Host Name	IP Address
mainserver	10.1.0.1
mail	10.1.0.6
earlgreerserver	10.1.0.7
ravi	10.1.0.10
andrewjohnson	10.1.0.11
tiplovingood	10.1.0.12
leroydennison	10.1.0.13

Turning On a DNS Service

During the initial configuration of the server, you were asked to enter its IP address and DNS information. If a DNS entry for the server was already present on the DNS server that you entered in the Network Interface settings, your server should have automatically pulled the host name and domain name. If this server did not do so, the DNS service is already running and a default zone is present based on the host name and domain name you entered. For example, the primary zone would be ns.pretendco.com.

The default zone might work fine for a home office server, but in this exercise you are building a DNS server for a private LAN with a primary zone that should be pretendco.com. If you leave this default zone in place, the machines' fully qualified domain names will be *xxx*.ns.pretendco.com, where *xxx* is the machine's name. If your DNS service has this default zone, you will remove it after you have created, populated, and saved the pretendco.com zone. However, if you initially set up your server on a network where it was able to resolve its IP address to a host name, the DNS service will not be running.

To turn on the DNS service, follow these steps:

1   In Server Admin, click the Add (+) button in the lower-left corner, and from the pop-up menu choose Add Service.

2   Select the DNS checkbox and click Save.

If necessary, to display the list of services your server offers, in the Servers list, click the triangle to the left of your server's name.

Server Admin should appear as in the figure below. You will notice that the DNS service is now listed as a service under the server name and that a gray dot appears to the left of the name. This dot indicates that you've enabled but not started the service. After you start it, a green dot will appear to the left of the name.

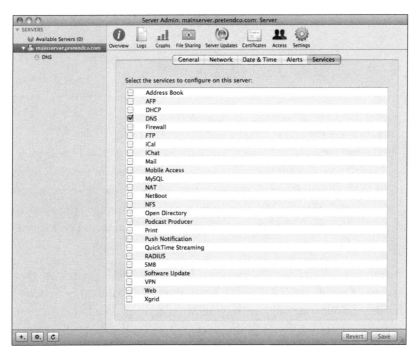

3   Select the DNS service.

4   Click Start DNS.

5   Close Server Admin.

Creating a Primary DNS Zone

Now that you've enabled and started the DNS service, you will configure the primary
DNS zone.

1   In Server Admin, select the DNS service for your server.

2   Click Zones.

3   Click Add Zone, then choose "Add Primary Zone (master)."

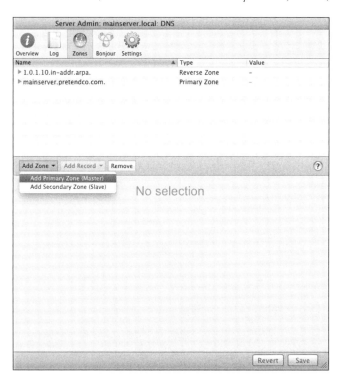

4   Select the new zone.

5   In the Primary Zone Name field, enter `pretendco.com`.

6   Enter the mail address for the zone administrator.

7   Verify that "Allows zone transfer" is deselected.

> **NOTE** ▶ Selecting "Allows zone transfer" permits secondary zones to get copies of the primary zone data. If you had a secondary DNS server, you would select this option.

8   Add a name server for this zone by clicking the Add (+) button and entering a name in the Nameservers field.

> **NOTE** ▶ If you are choosing the server you are configuring as the name server for this zone, the host name should appear automatically. If you are choosing a different server as the zone's name server, you will need to use the host name for that specific server.

9   Add mail exchangers for this zone by clicking the Add (+) button and entering the name in the Mail Exchangers field.

> **NOTE** ▶ The Mail Exchangers field is the basis for the computer's MX record.

10   In the Priority field, specify a mail server priority number.

> **NOTE** ▶ The mail server priority number identifies the first server to which an external mail server will attempt to deliver mail. Delivering mail servers will first attempt to deliver mail to the server with the lowest priority.

11 Click Expiration and enter the number of hours for each setting.

For this exercise, you'll use the defaults.

12 Click Save.

Adding Machine Records

With the primary zone properly configured, you are ready to start adding machine records to that zone.

1 Select the pretendco.com zone and click the disclosure triangle to the left of the zone.

2 Click Add Record and, from the pop-up menu, choose Add Machine (A).

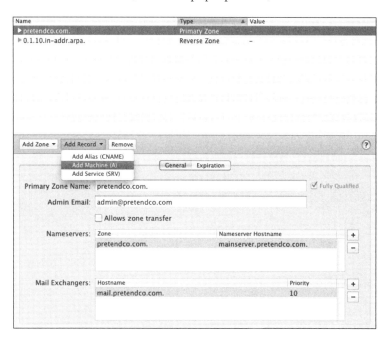

3   Under the primary zone, select newMachine, then enter the following machine
information:

▶   In the Machine Name field, enter the host name of the first computer in Table 1.1
earlier in this chapter (mainserver).

NOTE ▶ The Machine Name field is the basis for the computer's A record. Reverse
Lookup Pointer records are created for the computer.

▶   Click the Add (+) button, then enter the IP address of the first computer in
Table 1.1 (10.1.0.1).

▶   You may optionally also enter information regarding the software and hardware
of the computer in the Software Info and Hardware Info text boxes.

NOTE ▶ These two fields are the basis for the HINFO record of the computer.

▶   You also have the option to enter additional comments regarding the computer in
the Comments text box.

NOTE ▶ The Comments field is the basis for the computer's TXT record. It can contain almost any text string but is limited to 255 ASCII characters.

4   Click Save.

5   Continue adding machine records for computers listed in Table 1.1.

▼ pretendco.com.	Primary Zone	–
mainserver	Machine	10.1.0.1
mail	Machine	10.1.0.6
earlgreerserver	Machine	10.1.0.7
ravi	Machine	10.1.0.10
andrewjohnson	Machine	10.1.0.11
tiplovingood	Machine	10.1.0.12
leroydennison	Machine	10.1.0.13
▼ 0.1.10.in-addr.arpa.	Reverse Zone	–
10.1.0.11	Reverse Mapping	andrewjohnson.pretendco.com.
10.1.0.7	Reverse Mapping	earlgreerserver.pretendco.com.
10.1.0.13	Reverse Mapping	leroydennison.pretendco.com.
10.1.0.6	Reverse Mapping	mail.pretendco.com.
10.1.0.1	Reverse Mapping	mainserver.pretendco.com.
10.1.0.10	Reverse Mapping	ravi.pretendco.com.
10.1.0.12	Reverse Mapping	tiplovingood.pretendco.com.

The Reverse Zone (PTR) records are automatically created and can be viewed by tog-
gling the triangle next to the Reverse zone.

Adding an Alias (CNAME) Record

A CNAME or alias record is a nickname given to a machine record. For example, main-
server.pretendco.com is also a web server. Therefore, it may be given an alias or nickname
of www.pretendco.com. A single machine can have many aliases. However, it can have
only one PTR record.

In this exercise, you will create a www alias for the mainserver.pretendco.com machine record.

1   Select the pretendco.com zone.

2   Click Add Record and choose Add Alias (CNAME).

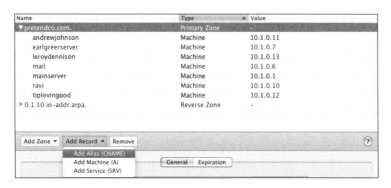

3   From the list of records in the zone, select the newAlias line.

When you do so, the bottom pane of the window changes to reflect what you have chosen.

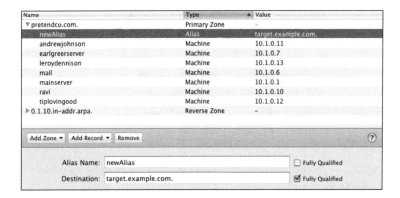

4   In the Alias Name field, enter www, and in the Destination field, enter mainserver. It's not necessary to select the Fully Qualified checkboxes because they will deselect themselves when you enter the data.

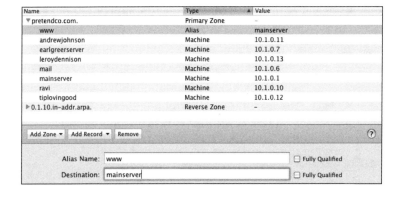

5   Click Save.

After you click Save, look at the Alias record in the list above (under the pretendco.com zone) within Server Admin. You will notice that the Fully Qualified box is now selected. This box indicates how the name is shown where mainserver is the name but mainserver. pretendco.com. is the FQDN.

Adding a Service Record

A DNS service record (SRV) is an entry in DNS that informs client computers a service is in the domain. For example, you may have an Apple file server that uses TCP port 548. For this record, you will use the earlgreerserver listed in Table 1.1.

1   Select the pretendco.com zone.

2   Click Add Record and choose Add Service (SRV).

3   Enter the following service information:

▶   Service name—EarlGreerServer (the name that will appear in Bonjour)

▶   Service type—_afpovertcp.tcp

NOTE ▶ If the service type for the service you are providing is not listed in the pop-up menu, you can enter the specific service directly into the Service Type field. The service you are providing should use a syntax similar to application protocol name.tcp |udp, such as ichat.-tcp.

▶   Host—earlgreerserver

▶   Port—548

> **NOTE ▸** Enter the port number for the service you are providing. For example, if you were providing HTTP service, you would use port 80. You can find port numbers for common services in the Service tab of the Firewall service.

▶ Priority—0

> **NOTE ▸** The priority field is used to determine which machine responds first when multiple machines are configured to provide the same service.

▶ Weight—0

> **NOTE ▸** The weight number is used as a relative weight for records with the same priority.

▶ TXT—optional; used for any additional comments regarding the service

4   Click Save.

After you've added the Service record, you will notice the following entry in the expanded pretendco.com. zone entry.

▼ pretendco.com.	Primary Zone	-
mainserver	Machine	10.1.0.1
mail	Machine	10.1.0.6
earlgreerserver	Machine	10.1.0.7
ravi	Machine	10.1.0.10
andrewjohnson	Machine	10.1.0.11
tiplovingood	Machine	10.1.0.12
leroydennison	Machine	10.1.0.13
EarlGreerServer (_afpovertcp._tcp)	Service	earlgreerserver.pretendco.com.:548

Configuring Logging

Setting the log level and viewing the log is probably the most overlooked feature of a DNS server deployment. A large number of DNS servers are configured by adding the zones, clicking Save, and starting the service with little or no thought given to logging. However, when things break, a log is usually the best place to find out what happened. Therefore, we will devote some time to the DNS service log named.log.

When configuring the log level for a DNS server, you have six options:

▶   Critical records critical errors only, such as hardware errors.

▶   Error records errors only and does not include warning messages.

▶   Warning records warnings and errors.

▶   Notice records important messages, warnings, and errors.

▶   Information records most messages.

▶   Debug records all messages.

When first configuring your DNS server, it is best to set the log level to Debug. After the server is functioning correctly, you can set the log level to something more appropriate for your environment. The Warning level is a good place to start. To change the Log Level from the default of Information, take the following steps:

1   Open Server Admin and connect to the server.

2   In the Servers list, click the disclosure triangle to the left of the server name.

    The list of currently enabled services appears.

3   Select the DNS service and click Settings.

4   From the pop-up menu, choose the required log level. Click Save.

Removing the Default Zone

This section is optional. As discussed earlier, you may already have a default zone in your DNS Zones listing. If you do, follow these steps to remove it.

1   Select the name of the default zone and click Remove.

2   Select the reverse of the default zone and click Remove.

These steps remove both the forward and reverse zone entries for the default zone, which were created when you first set up your server.

Configuring DNS with BIND

The primary interface for configuring DNS services on Mac OS X Server is the graphical Server Admin utility. Similar to many other subsystems on Mac OS X Server, and on Mac OS X in general, DNS is handled by a freely available, open source product: the Internet Systems Consortium's BIND DNS server. You can configure BIND via Server Admin in Mac OS X Server, or manually in Mac OS X.

BIND is the most widely deployed DNS server on the Internet. Mac OS X includes a full installation of BIND, as well as essential utilities such as the named name daemon, which is responsible for handling all queries, and rndc, a utility to control the name server. You can configure and run the DNS service entirely from a command-line shell. By basing this service on a standard, Mac OS X easily interoperates with other DNS name servers, both BIND and non-BIND.

The DNS record types form the database files for each zone. Database files are created in the /var/named hierarchy in the file system. In Snow Leopard, Apple has chosen to allow a mixed approach. The changes made in Server Admin are written to one set of files, but you can also make manual changes to a different set of files. Manual changes update the canonical files, while Server Admin edits some Apple-specific files. Interestingly, this situation shows off Server Admin's ability to interpret these files. Where previous Mac OS X Server versions had a more straightforward graphical user interface–to–config file relationship, new capability is evident in the main configuration file for BIND, /etc/named.conf.

> **NOTE** ▶ Before continuing with this section, it is important that you have access to the BIND 9 Administrator Reference Manual, which you'll find at https://www.isc.org/software/bind/documentation. If you have any questions regarding BIND while reading the next section, refer to the official documentation.

Using Views in BIND

The latest version of BIND, version 9, supports a concept called *views*. Views allow a BIND server to present different zones and zone data to different viewers of the data based on several criteria—all from a single BIND instance. While Mac OS X Server v10.5 was the first version of Mac OS X Server to explicitly use views, the graphical user interface doesn't expose this functionality.

This is still the case with Mac OS X Server v10.6. In fact, all zones are contained in one master view called com.apple.ServerAdmin.DNS.public. To more clearly understand this, look at /etc/named.conf:

```
include "/etc/rndc.key";
controls  {
        inet 127.0.0.1 port 54 allow     {any;   }
        keys    { "rndc-key";    };
    };
options  {
        include "/etc/dns/options.conf.apple";
};
logging {
        include "/etc/dns/loggingOptions.conf.apple";
};
include "/etc/dns/publicView.conf.apple";
```

The comments and hard returns from this file have been stripped out to show how minimal the code is and to conserve space in print. Previous Mac OS X Server versions wrote all configuration options directly into the named.conf file. However, beginning with Leopard (Mac OS X Server v10.5), Mac OS X Server started putting the "real" directives in external files that are then pulled into the main file via `include` statements. This same method is used for the database files, as discussed below.

Notice that the previously listed code has three separate `include` statements:

▶   `include "/etc/dns/options.conf.apple";`

▶   `include "/etc/dns/loggingOptions.conf.apple";`

▶   `include "/etc/dns/publicView.conf.apple";`

The options.conf.apple file is automatically generated and should not be modified. Changes impacting this file should be made in Server Admin or by editing the named. conf file. This file contains the following statements:

▶   `directory "/var/named";`

This statement sets where `named` should find any zone files references in the remainder of the config file.

▶   `forwarders {};`

The `forwarders` statement is empty because no forwarders have been configured. A forwarder is the IP address of the DNS server to which your DNS server will send any query for which it does not have an answer. For example, should a client submit a query for www.apple.com to your DNS server, your server would send that query to a forwarder because your server is not authoritative for the apple.com zone and may not have that information in its cache.

▶   `allow-transfer { none; };`

The `allow-transfers` statement is empty, as the "Allows zone transfer" checkbox was not selected when the zone was created.

NOTE ▶ The "Allows zone transfer" checkbox was selected by default in Mac OS X Server v10.5. This is no longer the case.

The loggingOptions.conf.apple file consists of the following lines:

```
category default {
        apple_syslog;
};
channel apple_syslog {
        file "/Library/Logs/named.log";
        severity info;
        print-time yes;
};
```

These lines ensure that all named logging information is logged to the /Library/Logs/ named.log file and the logging level is set to Information.

Finally, named.conf includes /etc/dns/publicView.conf.apple. Its contents vary with the zones configured in Server Admin. Also, Server Admin generates a globally unique identifier (GUID), specific to each server installation, for this file. Here is a sample named.conf file (stripped of any comments to conserve space in print):

```
acl "com.apple.ServerAdmin.DNS.public" {localnets;localhost;};
view "com.apple.ServerAdmin.DNS.public" {
allow-recursion {"com.apple.ServerAdmin.DNS.public";};
        zone "pretendco.com." {
                type master;
                file "db.pretendco.com.";
                allow-transfer {none;};
                allow-update {none;};
        };
        zone "0.1.10.in-addr.arpa." {
                type master;
                file "db.0.1.10.in-addr.arpa.";
                allow-transfer {none;};
                allow-update {none;};
        };
        zone "." {
                type hint;
                file "named.ca";
        };
        zone "localhost" IN {
                type master;
                file "localhost.zone";
                allow-update { none; };
        };
        zone "0.0.127.in-addr.arpa" IN {
                type master;
                file "named.local";
                allow-update { none; };
        };
    };
```

The first line, `acl "com.apple.ServerAdmin.DNS.public" {localnets;localhost;};`, defines an access control list (ACL) named com.apple.ServerAdmin.DNS.public to be used with a view, and allows the ACLs localnets and localhosts. This corresponds to the list in the Server Admin DNS Settings pane. While BIND allows very fine-grained use of ACLs, Server Admin does not press them into service, which limits their use to defining recursion abilities.

The built-in ACLs in BIND are as follows:

▶   None matches no hosts.

▶   Any matches all hosts.

▶   Localhosts matches the IP address of the server on which BIND is running, as well as the loopback address: 10.1.0.1 and 127.0.0.1, for example.

▶   Localnets matches all of the IP address(es) and subnet masks of the server on which BIND is running: 10.1.0.1 to 10.1.255.255, and 127.0.0.1, for example.

The second line, `view "com.apple.ServerAdmin.DNS.public" {` defines a view. Views in BIND are all-or-nothing propositions. Once in use, all zones must be defined in a view. This named.conf file takes the simple approach: It creates one master view and defines all zones inside it.

The next line, `allow-recursion {"com.apple.ServerAdmin.DNS.public";};` permits recursive lookups for clients matching the ACL for this view—that is to say, "all clients"—which matches the setting in Server Admin.

The definitions for each zone as defined in Server Admin are:

▶   Allow-update defines a match list of the IP addresses that are allowed to submit dynamic updates to the master zone.

▶   Allow-transfer defines a match list of the IP addresses that are allowed to copy the zone information for the master or slave of the specific zone.

▶   File defines the file used by the zone.

▶ Type describes the primary function of the server in relation to a specific zone. There are five types:

  ▶ Master—a server that gets its zone information for a local source

  ▶ Slave—a server that gets its zone information from a zone master

  ▶ Stub—similar to a slave except that it replicates only the NS records of a master zone, not the entire zone

  ▶ Forward—a server that forwards all requests to another server and caches the results

  ▶ Hint—a server that provides caching services and recursive queries

Several definitions are required without which `named` would not function properly. The first required definition is `zone "."`—the root zone. This allows the name server to contact one of the Root Servers on the Internet. /var/named/named.ca contains the names and IP addresses of all Root Servers. It is important that this file be kept up to date, because the information about the root servers changes from time to time. Fortunately, this is easy to do using the `dig` utility:

```
dig . ns > /var/named/named.ca
```

Ideally, you should run this simple utility periodically from a `cron` or `launchd` job. The root servers do not change often; scheduling this update to run once a month is adequate.

The next and final two zone definitions in the named.conf example file define a primary and reverse zone for pretendco.com, respectively. The db.pretendco.com zone is the forward zone, while db.0.1.10.in-addr.arpa is the reverse zone. However, this is a little misleading. Neither of these files actually contains machine names or IP addresses. In fact, each of them contains a single `include` statement, added by Server Admin, which instructs `named` to refer to the file located at /var/named/zones with the same name and .apple extension.

The figure below shows the contents of the db.pretendco.com zone file. You will notice the reference to the actual zone file as configured by Server Admin.

```
;THE FOLLOWING INCLUDE WAS ADDED BY SERVER ADMIN. PLEASE DO NOT REMOVE.
$INCLUDE /var/named/zones/db.pretendco.com.zone.apple
db.pretendco.com. (END)
```

The primary zone contains information relating machine records to IP addresses.

```
;GUID=C4CA00B7-32E5-4A66-B40E-573A1A04A090
;selfResolvingHostname=0

$TTL 10800
pretendco.com. IN SOA mainserver.pretendco.com. admin.pretendco.com (
        2010020600      ;Serial
        86400           ;Refresh
        3600            ;Retry
        604800          ;Expire
        345600          ;Negative caching TTL
    )

pretendco.com. IN  NS mainserver.pretendco.com.
leroydennison IN  A 10.1.0.13
mainserver IN  A 10.1.0.1
tiplovingood IN  A 10.1.0.12
ravi IN  A 10.1.0.10
andrewjohnson IN  A 10.1.0.11
mail IN  A 10.1.0.6
earlgreerserver IN  A 10.1.0.7
pretendco.com. IN  MX 10 mainserver.pretendco.com.
db.pretendco.com.zone.apple (END)
```

The reverse zone contains information relating IP addresses to machine records.

```
                        Terminal — bash — 80×24
;GUID=25FE329B-8561-4021-8013-BAAF3D8CB86D

$TTL 10800
0.1.10.in-addr.arpa. IN SOA mainserver.pretendco.com. admin.pretendco.com (
        2010010306      ;Serial
        86400           ;Refresh
        3600            ;Retry
        604800          ;Expire
        345600          ;Negative caching TTL
    )

0.1.10.in-addr.arpa. IN  NS mainserver.pretendco.com.
11.0.1.10.in-addr.arpa. IN  PTR andrewjohnson.pretendco.com.
13.0.1.10.in-addr.arpa. IN  PTR leroydennison.pretendco.com.
12.0.1.10.in-addr.arpa. IN  PTR tiplovingood.pretendco.com.
7.0.1.10.in-addr.arpa. IN  PTR earlgreerserver.pretendco.com.
6.0.1.10.in-addr.arpa. IN  PTR mail.pretendco.com.
1.0.1.10.in-addr.arpa. IN  PTR mainserver.pretendco.com.
10.0.1.10.in-addr.arpa. IN  PTR ravi.pretendco.com.
db.0.1.10.in-addr.arpa.zone.apple (END)
```

Editing and Importing BIND Files

If you already have BIND files from another DNS server, you can import those files into a BIND instance on Mac OS X Server v10.6. You may also edit files that are currently in place.

However, should you edit named.conf and zone files manually using Terminal, BIND will use that information but it will not appear in the DNS Zones pane in Server Admin. Furthermore, after you make changes to the named.conf and zone files, changes made in Server Admin are not made to named.conf. Therefore it is recommended that you use Server Admin to make these changes.

Importing a zone file is a good example of this issue. Imagine that a company is migrating from Linux servers to a Mac OS X Server setup. Because DNS is already configured on the Linux servers, the company currently has valid and accurate DNS files. These can be used as is on Mac OS X Server.

To import one or more of these files, take the following steps:

1 Update named.conf.

Using root-level access, add the zone definition to /etc/named.conf. Because views are in play, the zone must be wrapped in a view. A sample entry with view and zone definition is:

```
view "MyView" {
zone "example.com" IN {
        type master;         // Primary zone
        file "db.example.com";  // Zone info stored in /var/named/d.example.com
        allow-update { none; };
};
};
```

2 Copy the zone file into place.

Copy the zone file from the original system into the /var/named directory, giving it the same name specified in the zone definition.

3 Restart `named`.

4 Again, as root, issue the following two commands:

```
serveradmin stop dns
serveradmin start dns
```

Alternatively, `rndc` is available for this task and reduces the work to a single statement:

```
rndc -s 127.0.0.1 -p 54 reconfig
```

Creating Secure and Private DNS Servers

The accuracy and security of a network DNS system cannot be undervalued. Not only do zone files require constant maintenance to reflect a changing reality, but the system must be secured so that responses to DNS queries cannot be altered, intentionally or unintentionally. Out-of-date or incorrect zone files may point users or services to incorrect or nonexistent hosts. Also, because data in a DNS server represents a map of a network, it is important that a DNS server provide protection from attackers. Finally, as with any service, a DNS server uses other system resources (such as CPU and bandwidth) and therefore has finite capacity.

Understanding DNS Security Attacks

DNS servers are often targeted by malicious computer users (hackers) because they are susceptible to several kinds of attacks. By taking extra precautions, you can prevent the problems and downtime associated with computer vandalism.

Several kinds of security attacks are associated with DNS service:

- ▶ DNS cache poisoning
- ▶ Server mining
- ▶ DNS service profiling
- ▶ Denial of service (DoS)
- ▶ Service piggybacking

DNS Cache Poisoning

DNS cache poisoning (a form of DNS spoofing) is the addition of false data to the DNS server's cache, which enables hackers to do the following:

- ▶ Hackers can redirect real domain name queries to alternative IP addresses.

  For example, a falsified A record for a bank could point a user's browser to a different IP address that the hacker controls. A duplicate website could fool users into revealing a bank account number and password.

  Also, a falsified mail record could enable a hacker to intercept mail sent to or from a domain. If the hacker forwards that mail to the correct mail server after copying it, this intrusion can go undetected.

▶ Hackers can prevent proper domain name resolution and access to the Internet.

This is the most benign of DNS cache poisoning attacks. It makes a DNS server appear to be malfunctioning.

The most effective method for preventing these attacks is vigilance, which includes maintaining up-to-date software.

If exploits are uncovered in the current version of BIND, the exploits are patched and a security update is made available for Mac OS X Server v10.6. Apply all such security patches.

Server Mining

Server mining is the practice of retrieving a copy of a complete primary zone by requesting a zone transfer. In this exploit, a hacker pretends to be a secondary zone to another primary zone and requests a copy of the primary zone's records.

With a copy of your primary zone in hand, the hacker can see which services a domain offers, along with the IP addresses of the servers that offer them. The hacker can then try specific attacks based on those services. This is reconnaissance before another attack.

To prevent this attack, disable zone transfers. If you require zone transfers, specify only those IP addresses that should have permission to request zone transfers (your secondary zone servers) and deny all others.

Zone transfers are accomplished over TCP on port 53. To limit zone transfers, block zone transfer requests from anyone but your secondary DNS servers.

> **NOTE ▶** Creating advanced firewall rules is discussed in Chapter 4, "Using a Firewall."

DNS Service Profiling

Another common reconnaissance technique of malicious users is to profile your DNS service. First, a hacker makes a BIND version request. The server reports which version of BIND is running. The hacker then compares the response to known exploits and vulnerabilities for that version of BIND.

To prevent this attack, configure BIND to respond with something other than what it is. To alter BIND's version response, do the following:

1   Open a command-line text editor (such as vi, emacs, or pico).

2   Open named.conf.

3   To the options brackets of the configuration file, add the following:

    version "[your text, maybe we're not telling!']";

4   Save named.conf.

Denial of Service (DoS)

This kind of attack is common and easy. A hacker sends so many service requests and queries that a server uses all of its processing power and network bandwidth trying to respond. The hacker prevents legitimate use of the service by overloading it.

It is difficult to prevent this type of attack before it begins. Constant monitoring of the DNS service and server load enables an administrator to catch the attack early and mitigate its damaging effect.

The easiest way to prevent this attack is to block the offending IP address with your firewall. Unfortunately, this means the attack is already under way and the hacker's queries are being answered and the activity logged.

Service Piggybacking

This attack is done not so much by malicious intruders as by common Internet users who learn the trick from other users. They might feel that the DNS response time with their own ISP is too slow, so they configure their computer to query another DNS server instead of their own ISP's DNS servers. Effectively, there are more users accessing the DNS server than were expected.

You can prevent this type of attack by limiting or disabling DNS recursion. If you plan to offer DNS service to your LAN users, they need recursion to resolve domain names—but don't provide this service to Internet users.

Configuring Private DNS Servers

This section describes some standard DNS configurations. Protected by a firewall and inaccessible from the public Internet, these configurations are also secure. Standard configurations include:

- ▶ Caching-only name servers
- ▶ Forwarding name servers
- ▶ Nonrecursive authoritative name servers

Using Caching-Only Name Servers

One common configuration is a caching-only name server. Placing a DNS server inside a network firewall allows caching of DNS lookups for later use, speeding queries and limiting the number of slower links to the outside world. This server is not responsible for any DNS zones and passes all requests to another server. The caching server then caches the information for use on the local network.

To prevent unauthorized access to the DNS server, the default configuration of a caching server allows recursion only on localnets and localhosts. For private LANs that do not require the support of local zone files, this type of server would likely provide for the needs of the users and network administrators.

Although a strict caching name server would not have any zones of its own, in practice this is usually not the case. Typically a caching name server will be a master or slave for one or more zones and a cache server for all other requests.

Configuring Forwarding Name Servers

A forwarding name server, also commonly referred to as a proxy name server, forwards all requests it receives to another DNS server and caches all responses. This sounds similar to the caching name server, but there is a difference. A forwarding name server does not provide any recursion, thereby reducing the amount of traffic on the network, as only a single query crosses it.

A forwarding name server typically contains a primary or secondary zone, allowing it to quickly answer queries about the records in its local database, while it sends all others to a separate server. There are several reasons for deflecting queries. One simple reason is security. If a Mac OS X Server is acting as an Open Directory master and DNS server, this server can be locked down from an access perspective, with no external access, not even to return DNS queries. To resolve queries about outside entities, the server can forward those requests to another internal DNS server that does have access.

For example, in the following figure, client computers are configured to use the DNS server at 10.1.0.5, which is configured as a forwarding name server. The forwarding server is configured to forward queries that it cannot answer to 192.168.1.10.

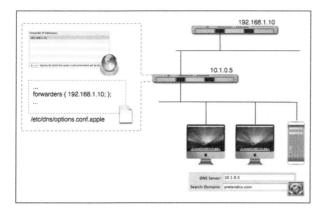

Restricting Zone Transfers

Another way to keep a primary or secondary DNS server secure is to restrict zone transfers to authorized sources only. By default, the "Allows zone transfer" checkbox is not selected for each zone created, which means that users can issue queries against the server but they cannot request a copy of the entire zone file. You should allow zone transfers only to authorized secondary DNS servers. Locking down zone transfers also prevents DoS attacks by zone transfer to unexpected hosts.

If you decide that you must allow zone transfers, you have two ways to manage unauthorized transfers—by using the named configuration or by using the firewall. The method you choose depends on your needs and policies.

Using a configuration file will unfortunately require moving the zone into the /etc/named. conf file (as shown in "Editing and Importing BIND Files"), and losing the ability to manage this zone via Server Admin. Once the zone is configured in /etc/named.conf, add the following line to the zone definition:

```
allow-transfer { 192.168.55.22; 192.168.32.18; };
```

The `allow-transfer` statement creates a whitelist of IP addresses that are allowed to transfer the entire zone to themselves. You should add addresses for all secondary DNS servers that need to transfer the zone.

You can also restrict transfer using a host-based firewall (such as the ones built into Mac OS X Server) or using router-based ACLs. For example, you can restrict inbound access from the secondary zone needing to transfer a zone to TCP port 53 on the DNS server, and deny all others. Because standard client queries use User Datagram Protocol (UDP), zone transfers can be limited in this way.

Providing Authoritative-Only Services

Another option for a DNS server is to provide authoritative-only services, a configuration also known as a *nonrecursive server*. For security reasons, it may be desirable to have a name server that can answer queries about its primary or secondary zones and no others. Such a configuration restricts certain networks from recursion access to the server.

This setup is easy to implement in Mac OS X Server: Simply set up zones as usual, and then remove all recursion from the DNS Settings pane in Server Admin, including local-nets and localhosts, as shown:

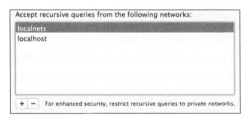

Configuring for Scale

As sites grow to include remote offices accessed via wide area network (WAN) links, DNS infrastructure can become strained. Most of the configurations discussed previously in this chapter may come into play.

Consider using forward servers when you need to build up a sitewide cache. By routing all DNS queries through a single host—or a set of hosts on a large network—you can save bandwidth by reducing outbound queries.

When several sites share a common infrastructure, keep in mind that secondary servers can also provide zone transfers. So you needn't mercilessly pound a single DNS server for zone transfers of a particular zone. Secondary DNS servers across a WAN link can provide zone updates to other secondary DNS servers that are closer on the network. Do whatever makes sense for a particular topology.

As a final note, remember that you can set up a secondary DNS server as a primary server to a network device. In other words, all clients do not have to first query a primary name server. Ensure that the load is spread among all DNS servers.

Necessary Steps to Configure DNS Services

This chapter has discussed the configuration of the DNS on a private LAN in detail, dissecting the DNS and presenting possible configuration schemes. However, it is important to note that the entire process of configuring a DNS really breaks down to four simple steps:

1. Register your domain name.

    You can do this at sites such as www.godaddy.com or www.yahoodomains.com.

2. Create your DNS zones.

    You may be thinking, "Wait, what about installing the software and so on?" It is likely that when you first publish your domain, you will not host your own DNS server. You will probably use a DNS server provided by your domain registrar. It is important to know that this step remains the same, regardless of who manages the DNS server.

3. Add DNS records to your zones.

4. Start the service.

    If you are managing your own DNS server, this is a simple task. If you are not managing your own DNS server, it is even simpler, as the service is almost always running.

Troubleshooting a DNS

The DNS system can fail you in subtle and not-so-subtle ways; however, it is typically the administrator that fails the DNS system. First and foremost, zone records must remain accurate and in sync with reality. Dropping sensitive files on the wrong host because DNS mismapped a name (enabled by a common ID and password on all internal systems) can create a serious problem. More frustrating is a DNS record that simply points to nowhere, leaving no route to a host. Troubleshooting DNS involves knowledge of the system, testing, and sleuthing. Follow log files, look for clues, and *test*.

Isolating and Resolving DNS Issues

DNS is a complicated and subtle protocol. Its distributed nature often makes it difficult to discern where a problem lies. Is it within the client, the local DNS server, or some remote DNS server on the Internet? Advanced DNS issues will probably require the investigation of an experienced system administrator. However, a few quick checks can help you isolate a problem.

Perform DNS Lookups

The best graphical tool for troubleshooting DNS issues is Network Utility. The real test of the success of any DNS change is when your DNS clients can use the new entry. Because of the limited number of services available, you will use both `ping` and `lookup` from a client computer to see if DNS is properly configured. You have a variety of ways to ensure that DNS is working. You can consult both the Ping and the Lookup panes of Network Utility to test the DNS service on your server.

Perform the following checks when you troubleshoot DNS problems:

▸ Check hardware and network issues.

▸ Verify that network settings are correct in the Network pane of System Preferences.

▸ Use Network Utility's Lookup pane to test your DNS server.

▸ Use Network Utility's Ping pane to test direct IP connectivity, bypassing DNS.

▸ `ping` another computer on your subnet to test for basic IP connectivity, but also be sure to test the IP address that is listed as the DNS server in Network preferences.

▸ Check with a network administrator to ensure that the DNS servers are configured properly.

   NOTE ▸ In most cases, DNS problems stem from a local configuration issue (hardware, network, or software) or from a recently installed DNS server. DNS servers that have been in place for some time are typically not the source of problems.

When performing DNS lookups from a client computer, you need to follow these steps:

1   Configure a client computer's Ethernet interface to be on the same subnet as mainserver.pretendco.com.

2   On the client computer, open /Utilities/Network Utility and click the Ping tab.

3   In the address field, type `mainserver` and click the Ping button.

The `ping` command should execute properly and resolve to 10.1.0.1. This confirms that you have successfully created the zone record and initial machine record.

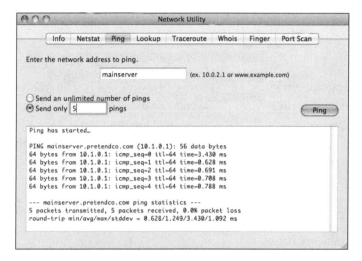

4   Click the Lookup tab of Network Utility, and enter the same information that you entered in the Ping field.

▶ Entering `mainserver` should return a machine (A) record of 10.1.0.1.

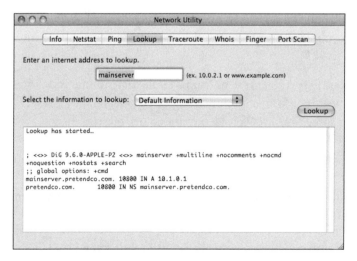

Testing at the Server

When DNS issues arise, the easiest place to start troubleshooting is often at the DNS server itself. If things are not right there, the client has no chance of retrieving correct information, or any information at all.

Use direct login or secure shell (`ssh`) to access a root shell on the primary DNS server—the server that clients will query. Use the `ps` command to check whether `named` is running:

```
# ps ax | grep named
16029   ??  Ss     0:04.17 /usr/sbin/named -f
```

(And yes, the process is `named` and not `bind`.)

If `named` is not running, see the next section, "Checking the Logs and the Process" for further troubleshooting steps. If it is running, ensure that you can actually perform lookups:

```
dig @127.0.0.1 mainserver.pretendco.com
```

If everything works as expected, the issue most likely lies with the client or the network. Perhaps a firewall or router ACL that sits between the client and the DNS server is preventing access. If a client uses DHCP for configuration, ensure that the DHCP server is also supplying a (correct) DNS server.

Checking the Logs and the Process

There are many reasons that `named` may refuse to start, but only one place to look: the logs to /Library/Logs/named.log. Unfortunately, Server Admin sometimes gives DNS the green light, even though `named` is *not* running. The most common reason that `named` does not start properly is bad syntax in one of the configuration files. While you cannot predict what this bad syntax will be, here is an example:

```
20-Oct-2009 12:32:28.710 loading configuration from '/private/etc/named.conf'
20-Oct-2009 12:32:28.713 /etc/dns/publicView.conf.apple:31: zone '0.1.10.in-addr.
arpa': already exists previous definition: /etc/dns/publicView.conf.apple:23
20-Oct-2009 12:32:28.713 reloading configuration failed: failure
20-Oct-2009 12:32:28.715 shutting down
20-Oct-2009 12:32:28.715 stopping command channel on 127.0.0.1#54
20-Oct-2009 12:32:28.716 no longer listening on 127.0.0.1#53
20-Oct-2009 12:32:28.716 no longer listening on 10.1.0.1#53
20-Oct-2009 12:32:28.723 exiting
```

The log shows exactly what the problem is (zone `'0.1.10.in-addr.arpa'`: already exists previous definition: `/etc/dns/publicView.conf.apple:23`) and where to look (/etc/dns/ publicView.conf.apple, line 31).

You may also see a line like this in your log:

```
20-Oct-2009 12:36:29.632 checkhints: view com.apple.ServerAdmin.DNS.public:
L.ROOT-SERVERS.NET/A (199.7.83.42) missing from hints
```

This tells you that the root server cache (/var/named/named.ca) has a bad entry—in this case, for L.ROOT-SERVERS.NET—and needs updating. Update this file as shown earlier in "Using Views in BIND."

On a server that acts as a secondary DNS server, you may see this in the named.log file:

```
20-Oct-2009 17:53:02.588 zone pretendco.com/IN/com.apple.ServerAdmin.DNS.public:
refresh: failure trying master 10.1.0.1#53 (source 0.0.0.0#0): operation canceled
```

For some reason, the DNS server could not contact the master to load the zone. Its own network interface may be down, the master may be down, or a network issue may be causing the failure. This lack of connectivity may cause a secondary DNS server to serve DNS requests from its cached copy of the zone, which is now out of sync with the master and serving incorrect results.

Checking the Configuration File Syntax

This step is an extension of the previous troubleshooting tip, "Checking the Logs and the Process." The BIND config file syntax is exacting and sometimes nonintuitive. If there has been any hand editing, double-check edits if BIND will not load a particular zone or pick up its changes, or if it will not load at all.

Syntax errors will be pointed out in the named.log file.

Testing the Client Service

If all of the above tests come back clean, the issue is most likely on the client side. Simple things to check include the following:

▶ Is the client making requests of the *correct* name server?

▶ Is DHCP pushing out the correct name server?

▶ Is a DNS server entry set at all?

▶ Does the client have a stale entry in its cache?

This last point is important. Just like DNS servers, clients cache results. This way, once an entry is looked up, further requests do not need to take up resources on the server. However, if the DNS is updated after a client caches the result, the two will be out of sync. Typically this does not cause a problem, but sometimes it does. A client can flush its local cache by restarting mDNSResponder:

```
# sudo killall -HUP mDNSResponder
```

If these suggestions do not work, you should investigate whether the DNS server set on the client is actually reachable. Use the dig utility to test lookups from the client:

```
$ dig mainserver.pretendco.com
; <<>> DiG 9.6.0-APPLE-P2 <<>> mainserver.pretendco.com
;; global options: +cmd
;; Got answer:
;; ->>HEADER<<- opcode: QUERY, status: NOERROR, id: 25350
;; flags: qr aa rd ra; QUERY: 1, ANSWER: 1, AUTHORITY: 1, ADDITIONAL: 0

;; QUESTION SECTION:
;mainserver.pretendco.com.            IN   A

;; ANSWER SECTION:
mainserver.pretendco.com.     10800   IN   A    10.1.0.1

;; AUTHORITY SECTION:
pretendco.com.          10800         IN   NS   mainserver.pretendco.com.

;; Query time: 0 msec
;; SERVER: 10.1.0.1#53(10.1.0.1)
;; WHEN: Tue Oct 20 06:24:10 2009
;; MSG SIZE  rcvd: 64
```

Two important things should happen here: An answer should be returned in the ANSWER SECTION, and the server should answer the question (in the statistics section at the bottom of the output). If the output of dig is too dense, you can use the +short flag:

```
$ dig mainserver.pretendco.com +short
10.1.0.1
```

Alternatively, use nslookup:

```
$ nslookup mainserver.pretendco.com
Server:  10.1.0.1
Address: 10.1.0.1#53


Name:    mainserver.pretendco.com
Address: 10.1.0.1
```

Many services that depend on DNS require that both forward and reverse DNS entries resolve correctly. You can test the forward lookup using dig or nslookup, and the reverse using the host or dig command:

```
$ dig mainserver.pretendco.com +short
10.1.0.1
$ host 10.1.0.1
1.0.1.10.in-addr.arpa domain name pointer mainserver.pretendco.com.
```

What You've Learned

▶ The main purpose of a DNS server is to convert easy-to-remember names into the harder-to-remember numbers that computers require to identify machines and to enhance the response time for name resolution queries.

▶ To resolve a domain name that's not listed locally, a local DNS server sends a query to a Root Server. The Root Server returns the IP address for the TLD server for the correct TLD (.com, for example). The local DNS server then queries the TLD for the correct zone. The TLD server responds to the local DNS server with the IP address for the server that is authoritative for the domain not listed locally.

▶ DNS zones are the basic organizational units of the DNS. Zones contain records and are defined by how they acquire those records and how they respond to DNS requests. Zone records describe the characteristics of a zone.

▶ There are three types of DNS zones. The master zone has the master copy of the zone's records and provides authoritative answers to queries. The slave zone is a copy of a master zone and is stored on a slave or secondary name server. The forward zone directs all queries for a particular zone to other DNS servers.

▶ There are nine record types available in Mac OS X Server v10.6.

▶ An FQDN is the full location of the specific machine that has that name and is fully reversible to its specific IP address. A relative domain name is typically only the name of the specific machine without any other domain information. For example, ns.pretendco.com is an FQDN, whereas ns is not. However, should you attempt to look up the ns host while on the apple.com domain, you will receive resolution.

▶ The official BIND documentation can be found at http://oldwww.isc.org/index.pl?/ sw/bind/arm94/index.php.

▶ If a server does not have a DNS entry in a DNS server during initial configuration, it will create a default zone for itself in the DNS server and turn on that service.

▶ There are generally four steps necessary to configure a DNS server for an organization: Register the domain, create the zones, populate the zones, and start the service.

▶ Five major types of security attacks are related to DNS: DNS cache poisoning, server mining, DNS service profiling, DoS, and service piggybacking.

References

For more information, see the following documents:

Administration Guides

Network Services Administration v10.6 Snow Leopard

Mac OS X Server Essentials v10.4 Student Guide

Mac OS X Server: Security Configuration for v10.5 Leopard, 2nd Edition

Books

Albitz, Paul, and Liu, Cricket. *DNS and BIND* (O'Reilly Media, 5th edition, 2006).

Dreyer, Arek and Greisler, Ben. *Apple Training Series: Mac OS X Server Essentials v10.6* (Peachpit Press, 2010).

Marczak, Edward R. *Apple Training Series: Mac OS X Advanced System Administration v10.5* (Peachpit Press, 2009).

Regan, Schoun, and Pugh, David. *Apple Training Series: Mac OS X Server Essentials v10.5* (Peachpit Press, 2008).

URLs

BIND 9 Administrator Reference Manual: www.isc.org/software/bind/documentation

DNS for Rocket Scientists: www.zytrax.com/books/dns

Man Pages

named

Chapter Review

1. How does caching increase the performance of a DNS server?

2. How many root-level name servers are there?

3. How do zone records describe the characteristics of a zone?

4. Of the three types of DNS zones, which type would not include zone records?

5. What is the character limit of the TXT record type?

6. At what level in the domain name hierarchy is .com in the domain ns.pretendco.com?

7. How can you prevent the automatic configuration of the DNS service on a Mac OS X Server v10.6 system?

8. How does the DNS service in Mac OS X Server v10.6 associate computer host names with IP addresses?

Answers

1. Caching increases the performance of a DNS server by storing local copies of DNS resolutions. This allows the server to respond to queries for which it is not authoritative without forwarding those queries through the DNS hierarchy.

2. There are 13 root-level name servers.

3. Zone records describe the machines and services found in a zone.

4. The forward zone does not have any zone records. All requests for resolutions relating to the specific zone are forwarded to another server for resolution.

5. The TXT record type is limited to 255 ASCII characters.

6. The domain .com is at the top level of the domain name hierarchy.

7. It is possible to prevent the automatic configuration of the DNS service on a Mac OS X Server v10.6 system. However, to do this you need to make sure you have a fully functioning and accurately configured DNS server with a record for the new server.

8. The DNS service in Mac OS X Server v10.6 associates computer host names with IP addresses through the configuration of machine records. During the configuration of the machine record, a host name and IP address are assigned to each machine.

2

Time   This lesson takes approximately 60 minutes to complete.

Goals   Learn the function of DHCP

Use Server Admin to configure and manage the DHCP service

Identify whether a network port has a DHCP IP address or a link-local address

Understand static mapping of IP addresses

Identify current clients of Mac OS X Server DHCP services

Display the log files for a DHCP service

Interpret the log files to determine if a DHCP client acquired a lease from a DHCP server

Chapter 2
Using DHCP

Dynamic Host Configuration Protocol (DHCP) dynamically configures a host machine. While most people associate DHCP with assigning an IP address, the configuration information provided to a machine is far more extensive. Typically, DHCP provides an IP address assignment along with a valid subnet mask, router, DNS server, and domain name. DHCP can also provide other host configuration information, such as the search domain—a default domain used for domain name searches.

Understanding How DHCP Works

The process followed when a DHCP server grants an address to the client is well documented. As shown in the following figure, the interaction occurs in this order:

1. A host computer on the network, a MacBook in this case, is set to obtain network configuration information via DHCP. It sends a request to the network to see if a valid DHCP server is available.

2. A DHCP server receives the request from the MacBook and responds with the appropriate information. In this case, the DHCP server sends an IP address of 10.1.0.100, a subnet mask and router, a DNS server address of 10.1.0.1, and an LDAP server of ldap. pretendco.com. The MacBook then formally requests what the DHCP server offers. At this time, the MacBook has a valid IP address and can start using the network.

3. As other devices come on the network and request configuration information via DHCP, they receive the appropriate information. In this example, an iMac receives the next available IP address of 10.1.0.101 as well as the same DNS and LDAP information.

    NOTE ▶ On Mac OS X v10.6-based systems, the LDAP server specified via DHCP option 95 (LDAP) is no longer added to the search base by default. This reduces the possibility that an unauthorized DHCP server will be used to add an LDAP directory domain to the authentication search path on a client. The new behavior locates LDAP servers via Bonjour and then places any DHCP-supplied LDAP servers at the top of the list of servers available for binding.

4. As the MacBook Air joins the network, it also receives appropriate DHCP information.

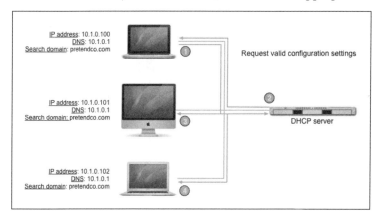

A key benefit provided by the DHCP server in this example is the assignment of configuration information to each host on the network. This negates the need to configure the information manually on each machine. When the DHCP server provides this configuration information, it guarantees you that users will not enter incorrect information when configuring their network settings. In a properly engineered wired or wireless network, a user can take a new Macintosh out of the box, connect it to the network, and automatically configure the computer with an IP address, DNS, search domain, and LDAP information. The user can then authenticate against an LDAP directory and access network services without any manual intervention. This capability provides a simple way to set up and administer computers.

Configuring a DHCP Service

Now that you have a basic understanding of how DHCP works and know some of the configurable components of a DHCP server, let's set one up. This section details the necessary steps for configuring Mac OS X Server v10.6 using both Server Admin and the command-line interface. However, before you can begin the actual configuration, you need to devote some time to planning.

Planning the Configuration

Before stepping into the configuration of the DHCP server, it is important to consider the following:

▶ Subnets

▶ IP addresses

▶ DHCP servers

▶ Multiple DHCP servers

Subnets

The subnet is the foundation of the DHCP service in Mac OS X Server. Subnets are groupings of computers on a network that help make the network and machines on that network more manageable by separating machines in one subnet group from machines in another. Multiple subnets can be configured for different workgroups within an organization or used to identify separate floors or units within a business. For example, you may have one subnet for your public wireless network and another subnet for your conference rooms. Your DHCP server can distribute IP addresses on each of these subnets using multiple network interfaces on the server.

As part of your planning process, you should decide whether you need multiple DHCP subnets or whether a single subnet will suffice.

> **NOTE** ▶ The new Mac mini with Snow Leopard Server is ideal for this role, as it can serve DHCP to many subnets using a USB Ethernet adapter for each subnet.

IP Addresses

IP addresses on a network can be dynamically or statically assigned to individual machines.

▶ Dynamic address—This setup automatically assigns an IP address to a machine on a network. The address is typically "leased" to the machine for a specific period of time, after which the DHCP server either renews the lease of the address to that machine or makes the address available to other machines on the network.

▶ Static address—This configuration assigns an IP address to a specific machine on the network, and that address rarely changes. Static addresses can be applied manually or by configuring the DHCP server to provide a Media Access Control (MAC) address the same IP address every time the machine with that MAC address logs in to the network.

It is likely that you will have a combination of statically and dynamically assigned addresses on your network. One of the indicators for choosing the most appropriate address type is the machine's primary use. For example, if it's a server or network machine, you should consider a static address. In contrast, you're probably best off assigning a dynamic IP address to laptops that come and go on the network.

DHCP Servers

The location of the DHCP server has a direct impact on the viability of a DHCP implementation. If you have separate subnets in your organization, it is important to place the DHCP server on the physical subnet shared by the machines that will be requesting DHCP addresses, or to configure the network switches or routers to relay Bootstrap Protocol (BOOTP) communications between subnets. BOOTP is a network protocol that a network client uses to obtain an IP address from a DHCP server.

Multiple DHCP Servers

If multiple DHCP servers will be providing IP addresses to multiple subnets, you must make sure those servers do not serve the same IP address ranges on the same subnets. For example, make sure the IP range for subnet A is 10.1.0.1 to 10.1.0.254, while the IP range for subnet B is 10.1.1.1 to 10.1.1.254. By providing separate ranges on each subnet, you'll avoid IP conflict errors and guarantee that you can customize the various settings (router, DNS, LDAP, and so on) for each subnet.

Configuring DHCP Using Server Admin

The process for configuring DHCP with Server Admin involves the following steps:

1. Enable the DHCP service.

2. Create subnets.

3. Configure the DHCP log settings.

4. Start the DHCP service.

Enabling the DHCP Service

During the initial configuration of the server, you were asked which services you wanted to deploy on the server. If you selected DHCP, you can skip this section. If you did not enable DHCP during initial configuration, do so by following these steps:

1   In Server Admin, click the Add (+) button in the lower-left corner and, from the pop-up menu, choose Add Service.

2   Select the DHCP checkbox and click Save.

Server Admin should look similar to the following figure. You will notice that the DHCP server is now listed in the Servers list as a service under the mainserver.pretendco.com server, and that it has a gray dot to the left of its name (DHCP). This dot indicates that the service has been enabled but not started. A green dot will appear next to the name of the service after you've started it.

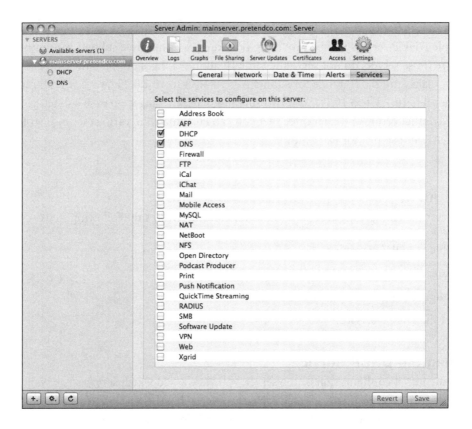

Creating a DHCP Subnet

After enabling the DHCP service, your next step is to create one or more subnets. This process includes the configuration of any optional settings such as DNS, LDAP, and Windows Internet Name Service (WINS) information. In the following exercise, you will configure the DHCP service to provide DHCP addressing to a private workgroup within an organization. Assume the following configuration details:

▶   Subnet name—Private Subnet

▶   Private Subnet DHCP range—10.1.0.100 to 10.1.0.200

▶   Subnet mask of Private Subnet—255.255.0.0

▶   Network interface of Private Subnet—Ethernet 2 (en2)

▸   Router for Private Subnet—10.1.0.1

▸   Lease time—1 hour

▸   DNS server for Private Subnet—10.1.0.1

▸   Search domain for Private Subnet—pretendco.com

▸   LDAP server for Private Subnet—ldap.pretendco.com

▸   LDAP search base—dc=ldap,dc=pretendco,dc=com

To create the DHCP subnet, follow these steps:

1   In Server Admin, from the left column select the DHCP service for your server.

2   Click Subnets.

    You may already see a subnet. This subnet was created when the server was config-
    ured. You will delete that subnet and create a new one.

3   If you need to remove an existing subnet, select the subnet created during initial
    server configuration, and click the Delete (–) button.

4   Click the Add (+) button to add a new subnet to the DHCP service.

    The General information pane will appear by default. In the General pane, you can
    configure the IP settings that the DHCP server provides for a specific subnet: Enter an
    appropriate name for the subnet and select the network interface to be used for the
    range of addresses, and enter the appropriate IP addresses to define the IP range in
    the Starting IP Address and Ending IP Address fields. This IP range must be unique
    and may not overlap with another DHCP subnet range being served on the network.
    This range also should not overlap any addresses used by VPN services or by static IP
    addresses not set by static maps (such as routers, printers, and so on). Also, here you
    can enter the appropriate Subnet Mask and Router settings.

5   Configure the subnet by entering the following information in the General pane.

    ▸   Subnet Name: `Private Subnet`

    ▸   Starting IP Address: `10.1.0.100`

▶ Ending IP Address: 10.1.0.200

▶ Subnet Mask: 255.255.0.0

▶ Network Interface: en2

▶ Router: 10.1.0.1

▶ Lease Time: 1 Hour

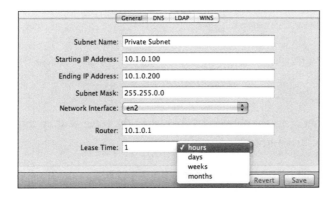

The Lease Time field is one of the key options to consider when implementing a DHCP service. DHCP servers use a range of IP addresses to *lease* an IP address to computers for a temporary period, the *lease time*. Leasing allows an organization to support a larger number of computers than the number of available IP addresses available, by reusing IP addresses over time.

A host receives an IP address for the assigned lease time and relinquishes the address when the network interface is no longer in use, such as when the machine is shut down. If a machine is still using the IP address, it can request an extended lease time. The lease time is configurable based on the needs of the organization.

6   Click the DNS tab to view the DNS settings for the subnet.

In addition to providing an IP address, DHCP can also provide network configuration information, such as the addresses for the DNS server. In the DNS pane, you can set the DNS information that the DNS server will provide to DHCP clients.

7   Configure the DNS pane with the following information:

   ▶ DNS Servers: `10.1.0.1` (may already be in place)

   ▶ Search Domains: `pretendco.com` (may already be in place)

8   Click the LDAP tab to configure the LDAP settings for the subnet.

LDAP is a network-based directory service designed to provide information to the client. Mac OS X Server simplifies LDAP configuration by sending configuration information to clients using the DHCP response.

NOTE ▶ Mac OS X v10.6 clients will not see these settings in their network configurations.

In the LDAP pane, the administrator can enter LDAP configuration information that will be sent to clients. Clients receiving this information can connect to the LDAP server and will automatically be configured to use that server's directory services.

9   Configure the LDAP pane with the following information:

   ▶ Server Name: ldap.pretendco.com

   ▶ Search Base: dc=pretendco,dc=com

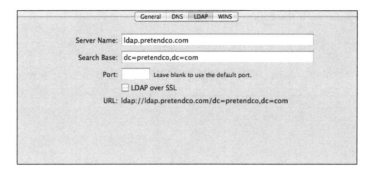

10 Leave the default values in the remaining fields.

11 Select the Enable checkbox next to Private Subnet, then click Save.

In the Subnets pane, you can configure multiple subnet ranges on Mac OS X Server. For example, an additional subnet range could be added for a second range on an existing port or for a range on a different Ethernet interface. However, when you create multiple subnets, make certain that those subnets do not overlap.

12 To create a subnet on multiple network interfaces, repeat the previous steps, entering information specific to the new subnets.

Configuring Logging

Logging is always turned on by default with the DHCP service. However, the level of logging is configurable using Server Admin. The following options are available:

▶ Low—Errors only

▶ Medium—Errors and warnings

▶ High—All events

To configure the log level, do the following:

1   In Server Admin, select the DHCP service for your server.

2   Click Settings.

Within the Settings pane, you will find only an option to change the log level of the DHCP service. Because this is a new DHCP server, you should change the log level to High while you're verifying that it will work correctly.

3   Select High from the drop-down menu and click Save.

Starting the DHCP Service

To complete your setup, you have only to start the DHCP service:

1   In Server Admin, select the DHCP service for your server.

2   Start the DHCP service by clicking the Start DHCP button in the lower-left corner.

Assigning Static IP Addresses Using DHCP

DHCP allows the assignment of specific IP addresses to network computers. This allows you to benefit from the ease of using DHCP to configure computers while assigning static addresses to key equipment (such as servers, printers, and switches).

To assign a static IP address to a computer, you first need to know its Ethernet address (sometimes called its MAC address or hardware address). Each network interface has a unique Ethernet address. You can assign a static address to a computer in Mac OS X Server in either the Static Maps pane or the Clients pane.

To assign a static address to a computer using the Static Maps pane, follow these steps:

1   In Server Admin, select the DHCP service for your server.

2   Click Static Maps.

3   Click Add Computer.

4 Enter the name of the computer.

5 In the Network Interfaces list, click the appropriate column to enter the following information:

▶ The MAC address of the computer to which you are assigning a static IP address.

▶ The IP address you want to assign to the computer.

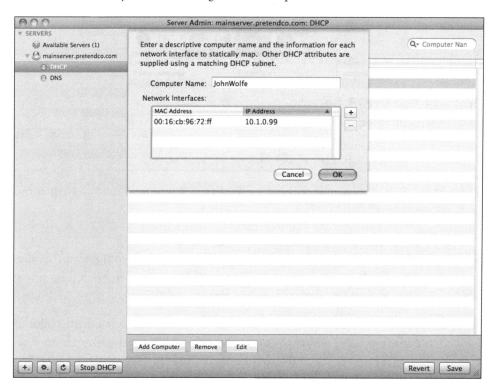

6 If the computer you are configuring has more than one network interface that needs a static IP address, click the Add (+) button and enter the IP address you want to assign to each interface.

NOTE ▶ If you have a computer that moves between wired and wireless status on the network, it require two different Ethernet addresses—one for the wired connection and one for the wireless connection—so be sure to create two entries for that computer.

7   Click OK, then click Save.

NOTE ▶ If DHCP is running, you will be prompted to restart DHCP to put your change into effect. Otherwise, your changes take effect the next time you start DHCP.

If your DHCP server is already running and assigning IP addresses to DHCP clients, you can apply a static IP address to a client that already has a DHCP address by using the Clients pane.

1   In Server Admin, select the DHCP service on your server.

2   Click Clients.

You should see a list of the machines currently provided a DHCP address by the server.

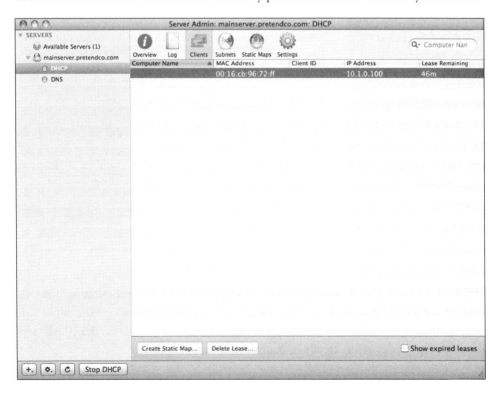

3   Click the MAC address of the computer that will receive a static address.

4   Click the Create Static Map button.

     You are notified that a static map will be generated with the client's current network configuration. The IP address can be changed in the next steps.

5   Click the Create Map button.

     You will be taken to the Static Maps pane. Notice that the computer has been added to the list of static maps. However, no name has been assigned to the computer.

Computer Name	▲	MAC Address	IP Address
▶ new computer		00:16:cb:96:72:ff	10.1.0.100

6   Double-click the name of the computer.

     A dialog appears in which you can enter a computer name and change the IP address of the machine.

7   Click OK, then Save.

Computer Name	▲	MAC Address	IP Address
▶ JohnWolfe		00:16:cb:96:72:ff	10.1.0.99

NOTE ▶ When the DHCP address for that computer expires, the DHCP server will provide the address as configured in the Static Maps pane. The computer will no longer be listed as a client of the DHCP server.

Troubleshooting DHCP

As with many network services, it is sometimes difficult to locate exactly the causes of DHCP failures. At times, configuration errors will crop up on client systems. Other times, problems with the network infrastructure will prevent the machines on the network from communicating with the DHCP server. On occasion, issues arise when the DHCP server has not been configured correctly or is not behaving as expected.

To think through the troubleshooting process, imagine that a specific machine on your network is unable to obtain a DHCP address from your server. First you'll troubleshoot the client, then you'll troubleshoot the server.

Ask the following questions when you are troubleshooting DHCP issues for Mac OS X:

▶ Is the machine configured correctly on the network? Check physical network issues, such as cabling, broken routers or switches, and limitations of the physical subnet.

▶ Can you establish any network connection? Can you `ping` another host? Can you see another host over Bonjour?

▶ Is the configuration properly set up? Are you using addresses dynamically assigned via DHCP or manually assigned static address? If the problem is with DHCP, would a static address work?

▶ Is an IP address assigned via DHCP or is the address self-assigned (169.254.*x.x* range)? Can you `ping` another host via both IP address and host name? Can you perform a DNS lookup?

In this imaginary situation, you were able to connect to an external website by manually configuring the network interface with a static address, so you have concluded that the issue must lie with the server.

Ask the following questions when you are troubleshooting DHCP issues for Mac OS X Server:

▶ Is the DHCP server configured correctly on the local network? Is the server reachable on the network via ping? Is a static address properly assigned to the server?

▶ Is the DHCP service configured properly? Is the DHCP service turned on?

▶ Does Server Admin show the expected DHCP client activity?

▶ Do the DHCP log entries match the expected DHCP client activity?

Verifying the DHCP Service

You can determine if the DHCP service is actually running using Server Admin or the Terminal application. We will look at Server Admin first.

1   In Server Admin, select the DHCP service for your server.

2   Click Overview to see whether the service is actually running.

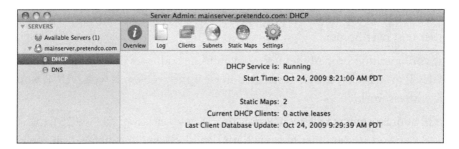

3   If the service is not running, click the Start DHCP button.

Using the command line, you can view two status reports. The first reports whether the service is running, and the second displays specific details including external and internal ports.

4   To view a DHCP status overview in Terminal, type:

```
$ sudo serveradmin status dhcp
```

The command will return RUNNING or STOPPED.

5   To view a detailed DHCP status overview:

```
$ sudo serveradmin fullstatus dhcp
```

The command will return a response similar to this:

```
dhcp:state = "RUNNING"
mainserver:~ root# sudo serveradmin fullstatus dhcp
dhcp:backendVersion = "10.5"
dhcp:dhcpLeasesArray = _empty_array
```

```
dhcp:state = "RUNNING"
dhcp:numDHCPActiveClients = 0
dhcp:timeOfSnapShot = "2009-10-24 09:35:15 -0700"
dhcp:servicePortsRestrictionInfo = _empty_array
dhcp:numDHCPLeases = 0
dhcp:logPaths:systemLog = "/var/log/system.log"
dhcp:numConfiguredStaticMaps = 2
dhcp:readWriteSettingsVersion = 1
dhcp:setStateVersion = 1
dhcp:servicePortsAreRestricted = "NO"
dhcp:timeServiceStarted = "2009-10-24 08:21:00 -0700"
dhcp:timeOfModification = "2009-10-24 09:34:39 -0700"
```

Viewing Assigned IP Addresses

You can use Server Admin to view detailed information about the DHCP clients associated with a DHCP server. To view the DHCP client information, do the following:

1 In Server Admin, select the DHCP service for your server.

2 Click Clients to display a list of clients.

The DHCP Clients pane provides the following information:

▸ Computer name

▸ MAC address

▸ DHCP client ID

▸ IP address assigned

▸ Lease time remaining

NOTE ▸ A DHCP client can have a client ID. The client ID may provide an administrator more information about which host is assigned a specific IP address. Some service providers may require a valid client ID before providing an IP address from their DHCP server. Use the Network pane of System Preferences in Mac OS X to configure the client ID.

You can also determine whether a client has received an IP address from a DHCP server. If the DHCP server has run out of available network addresses, or if no DHCP service is available, the client will automatically generate a self-assigned link-local address. Link-local addresses are always in the IP address range of 169.254.*x.x* and have a subnet mask of 255.255.0.0. The network client will automatically generate a random link-local address and then check the local network to make sure no other network device is using that address. Once a unique link-local address is established, the network client will only be able to establish connections with other devices on the local network.

Examining the Logs

DHCP log entries are contained in the main System Log file. You can view the System Log using other utilities such as Console or System Profiler, but if you use the Log pane for the DHCP service in Server Admin, it will only display the DHCP entries.

Apple's implementation of DHCP relies on BOOTP. BOOTP was available before DHCP and is the basis for Apple's DHCP implementation. That's why the DHCP process that runs on the server is listed as the `bootpd` process, as shown in the following figure.

1   In Server Admin, select the DHCP service for your server.

2   Click Log to display the system.log file.

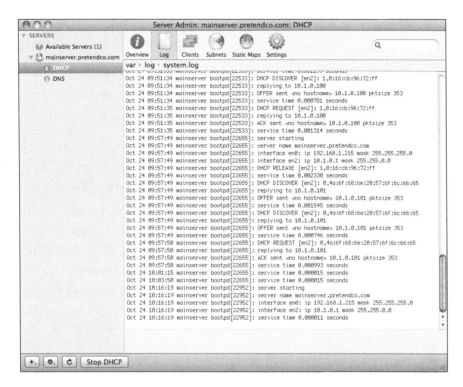

You can look for specific events by entering them in the search box at the top right of the pane. Note the specific DHCP entries and the general flow of events for DHCP:

▶ DHCP DISCOVER—A DHCP client sends a discover message to look for DHCP servers.

▶ OFFER—A DHCP server responds to a client's DHCP DISCOVER message.

▶ DHCP REQUEST—A DHCP client requests DHCP configuration information from the DHCP server.

▶ ACK—A DHCP server responds with DHCP configuration information for the DHCP client.

```
Oct 24 09:57:49 mainserver bootpd[22655]: DHCP DISCOVER [en2]: 0,4a:6f:68:6e:20:57:6f:6c:66:65
Oct 24 09:57:49 mainserver bootpd[22655]: replying to 10.1.0.101
Oct 24 09:57:49 mainserver bootpd[22655]: OFFER sent <no hostname> 10.1.0.101 pktsize 353
Oct 24 09:57:49 mainserver bootpd[22655]: service time 0.000746 seconds
Oct 24 09:57:50 mainserver bootpd[22655]: DHCP REQUEST [en2]: 0,4a:6f:68:6e:20:57:6f:6c:66:65
Oct 24 09:57:50 mainserver bootpd[22655]: replying to 10.1.0.101
Oct 24 09:57:50 mainserver bootpd[22655]: ACK sent <no hostname> 10.1.0.101 pktsize 353
```

You can remember this chain of events with the acronym DORA: Discover, Offer, Request, Acknowledge.

The client sends a DHCP RELEASE message to the server when it shuts down. This message notifies the server that it can reassign the address to another client.

Understanding DHCP Security

Using DHCP is not recommended. Assigning static IP addresses eases accountability and mitigates the risks posed by a rogue DHCP server. If DHCP use is necessary, only one system should act as the DHCP server and the service should be disabled on all other systems.

If you decide to use Mac OS X Server v10.6 as a DHCP server, be sure to configure the DHCP service to *not* distribute DNS, LDAP, and WINS information unless absolutely necessary. This security measure is meant to protect client systems. When client systems accept dynamically assigned DNS, LDAP, and WINS addresses, they become vulnerable to certain forms of network-based attacks from rogue DHCP servers. Users may unknowingly be redirected to malicious websites or servers.

What You've Learned

▶   The primary function of DHCP is the dynamic configuration of IP information on a host machine. However, DHCP can also be used to provide other host configuration information, such as the default information for connecting to an LDAP server.

▶   When using Server Admin to configure a DHCP server, you follow these steps:

1.   Enable the DHCP service.

2.   Create the subnet.

3.   Enable the interface.

4.   Start the DHCP service.

▶   You can identify whether a host has a DHCP address or a link-local address by looking at its IP address. All link-local addresses are in the 169.254.*x.x* range. If a client's IP is not in that range, the client does not have a link-local address.

▶   Static mapping is the process of assigning a specific IP address to a specific host via the host's MAC address.

▶ You can view the current client list of a DHCP server in the Client pane.

▶ Log files that only show information regarding the DHCP service can be viewed in the Log pane.

▶ When viewing the DHCP log entries, you can determine whether a specific host has received a DHCP lease by looking for DORA: Discover, Offer, Request, and Acknowledge.

▶ DHCP is not secure and should be used only after you've evaluated all security considerations. If you must use DHCP, it is advisable not to provide DNS, LDAP, or WINS.

References

For additional information, see the following resources:

Administration Guides

Network Services Administration v10.6 Snow Leopard

Mac OS X Server Essentials v10.4 Student Guide

Mac OS X Server: Security Configuration for v10.5 Leopard, 2nd Edition

Books

Dreyer, Arek, and Greisler, Ben. *Apple Training Series: Mac OS X Server Essentials v10.6* (Peachpit Press, 2010).

Regan, Schoun, and Pugh, David. *Apple Training Series: Mac OS X Server Essentials v10.5* (Peachpit Press, 2008).

White, Kevin M. *Apple Training Series: Mac OS X Support Essentials v10.6* (Peachpit Press, 2010)

RFC Documents

Access the RFC (Request for Comment) documents at: www.ietf.org/rfc*nnnn* (where *nnnn* is the RFC number).

RFC 2131—Dynamic Host Configuration Protocol

RFC 1632—The IP Network Address Translator (NAT)

RFC 3022—Traditional IP Network Address Translator (Traditional NAT)

Man Pages

bootpd

Apple Knowledgebase Articles

HT3844—DHCP-provided LDAP not used for authentication in Mac OS X v10.6, Mac OS X Server v10.6.

Chapter Review

1. When configuring the LDAP option in DHCP, in what format do you present the URL?

2. How many subnets can a single DHCP server manage?

3. If a host machine is on an active network with other clients receiving DHCP addresses, why might this specific machine not get an IP address?

4. How can you determine whether a host has a routable IP address or a link-local address?

5. Before you can statically map an IP address to a specific client, what must you know about that client?

6. Where would you find log entries related only to the DHCP service?

7. When viewing log entries for the DHCP service, how can you filter those entries to show you only the information regarding a specific host?

Answers

1. The URL for the LDAP server must be in the ldap://host.pretendco.com format, where host.pretendco.com is the fully qualified domain name of the LDAP server.

2. A given server can manage any number of subnets. Limitations are based on other resources of the server, such as available RAM, CPU power, and so on.

3. If other machines on a given network are able to secure DHCP addresses, it is likely that the server has run out of DHCP leases.

4. Because a link-local address must fall in the 169.254.*x.x* range, checking the current IP address of the client will provide the answer.

5. You must know the client's MAC address.

6. You would find log entries related only to the DHCP service in the Log pane of the DHCP service.

7. You can enter specific host information in the search field in the upper right corner of the Log pane to search for information related to a particular host.

3

Time   This lesson takes approximately 120 minutes to complete.

Goals   Learn the types of address translation

Understand how an outbound NAT connection works

Use Server Admin to manage IP traffic filtering in Mac OS X Server v10.6

Understand the relationship between IP ports and services on an IP host

## Chapter 3

Network Address Translation/Gateway

Network address translation (NAT), sometimes referred to as *IP masquerading* or *IP aliasing*, is a technique that allows a group of network devices in a private network to use a single IP address to communicate with devices on other networks. NAT alleviates the shortage of IP addresses available to ISPs and businesses and provides some security to private networks, because hosts inside the private network are not directly addressable from the Internet.

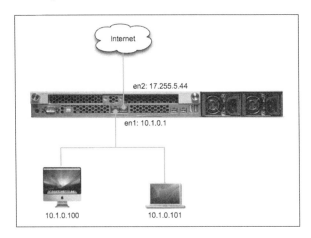

Using NAT

A Mac OS X Server system running NAT reviews all the requests that originate within your private network and remembers which internal address made each request. When the NAT service receives a response to a request, it forwards that response to the originating computer. Traffic that *originates* from the Internet does not reach any of the computers behind the NAT system unless port forwarding is enabled. Port forwarding lets you reroute packets sent to specific ports on the NAT system to other hosts in the private network.

With Mac OS X Server, you can use NAT to protect a private network. For example, you could connect an Xserve or Mac Pro computer to your network using one of its Ethernet interfaces, and connect it to the Internet (via a T1 or other high-speed connection) using its second Ethernet interface. With this configuration, the NAT service would shield the private network behind the Xserve's or Mac Pro's IP address. The computers in your network could access the Internet by sharing the Xserve's or Mac Pro's Internet connection while remaining private—that is, other computers on the Internet could not directly access them.

NAT has several forms, including:

► Static NAT maps a private IP address to a public IP address (one-to-one mapping).

► Dynamic NAT maps a private IP address to the first available address from a list of public IP addresses.

► Port address translation (PAT) maps multiple private IP addresses to a single public IP address by using different ports. This is also known as *port overloading, single-address NAT,* or *port-level multiplexed NAT.*

How NAT Works

The following figure shows a typical NAT transaction using a computer running
Mac OS X Server:

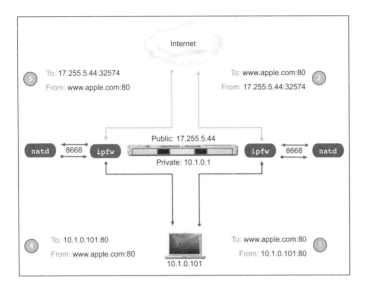

1. The MacBook user requests a page on the Internet—the Apple home page, in this
   example. The request goes to the default router address (10.1.0.1), which is the
   address of the en1 Ethernet interface of an Xserve running NAT.

2. This outbound request is redirected to natd (the NAT daemon) by the divert rule
   in the firewall configuration. This rule diverts any packet on the external interface,
   incoming or outgoing, to the natd port, 8668.

   In an internal table, natd notes the IP address of the MacBook that sent this request
   (10.1.0.101) and adds an internal port number (32574) to identify the table entry
   applying to this request. Then natd sends the request back to the firewall service and
   forwards this request to the appropriate host on the Internet using the address of the
   Xserve's en2 Ethernet interface (17.255.5.44), which is connected to the Internet, as
   the new source (the "from" address). Also, the natd port number is added to the external IP address.

3. The Apple web server receives a request for a page and returns the page requested. In this
   example, the server returns the page to the requesting address 17.255.5.44 at port 32574.

4. The Xserve receives the response page from www.apple.com and the firewall forwards the response to natd for processing. Packets that are received with a target IP of the Xserve are checked against the internal table. If an entry is found, it is used to determine the correct target IP address and port of the host on the private network.

After processing, natd sends the response back to the firewall for delivery to the MacBook, and the MacBook displays the resulting webpage from www.apple.com.

Configuring a NAT Gateway

The process of configuring a NAT gateway can be as simple or as complicated as the LAN that you're managing. You can configure a NAT gateway two ways using Server Admin. First, you can individually configure each required service. Second, you can use the Gateway Setup Assistant to complete the process in eight steps. However, if the LAN behind the gateway has multiple subnets, external services that need access to internal resources, or a more robust DNS configuration, you must configure each service individually.

Depending upon the current LAN and which services are already provided elsewhere, these services may be configured on the gateway server:

▶ DHCP—DHCP may be configured to provide IP addressing and other network services. Some routers also provide this service, as may other systems on the LAN. It is not required that the gateway server provide DHCP addressing to the LAN.

▶ DNS—DNS may be configured to support the needs of the LAN as, for example, a caching server, an authoritative domain server, or even a split-DNS server.

▶ Firewall—The Firewall service must be configured on the gateway server because an essential part of NAT is the divert rule. That rule is added to the firewall when NAT service is enabled, but the Firewall service must be turned on for the packet divert rule, or any firewall rule, to have an effect.

▶ NAT—The NAT service must be configured on the gateway server. The external and internal network interfaces are determined through this service.

▶ VPN (virtual private network)—VPN is optional. If the service is desired, it can be configured on the gateway server. VPN allows authorized external clients to connect to the private LAN.

Configuring NAT Using the Gateway Setup Assistant

The Gateway Setup Assistant allows you to efficiently set up and configure the NAT, DHCP, VPN, Firewall, and DNS services on Mac OS X Server v10.6 when sharing an Internet connection on a private network. During the setup process, you'll make choices that customize the server configuration to meet the needs of your local environment.

After you've successfully completed the gateway setup process, the following features will be configured on your server:

▶ The network interface chosen to be the internal interface will have an IP address in the 192.168.*x*.1 range.

> **NOTE** ▶ When using the Gateway Setup Assistant, this is the only available IP range. If you need a different IP range, you should configure NAT manually. This option is presented later in "Using Server Admin to Configure NAT."

▶ The DHCP server will be configured and started to provide IP addresses on the internal interface in the 192.168.*x*.2 to 192.168.*x*.254 range.

▶ The NAT service will be configured and started to share the external network interface with the private LAN.

▶ The Firewall service will be configured and started to block all Internet traffic except traffic resulting from internal requests or traffic required for connections to this host (such as VPN).

▶ The DNS service will be configured and started to provide DNS services to the LAN as a caching server.

▶ If selected during gateway configuration, VPN will be configured and started to allow authorized external connections via the L2TP protocol. The DHCP service will set aside IP addresses for those connections.

Before running the Gateway Setup Assistant, make sure that the external (WAN) network connection is attached to Ethernet 1 (en0) and the internal (LAN) network connection is attached to Ethernet 2 (en1).

The Gateway Setup Assistant is accessed via the NAT service overview. However, before you can access that option, you must enable the NAT service.

1   Open Server Admin and connect to the server.

2   Click the name of the server. Click Settings, then click Services.

> **NOTE** ▶ After the services appear, you will notice that the DNS service is already enabled. That's because the DNS service was enabled, configured, and started during the initial setup of the server because all computers running Mac OS X Server require DNS. New to Mac OS X Server v10.6 is the autoconfiguration of the DNS service, which allows the server to function correctly. If you were setting up the server on a LAN with a functioning DNS server and the appropriate machine records already configured, this service would not be preconfigured.

3   Select the NAT checkbox and click Save.

4   Click the disclosure triangle to the left of the server name. A list of the currently
    enabled and/or active services will appear.

5   From the expanded Servers list, select NAT.

6   Click Overview.

7   Click the Gateway Setup Assistant button.

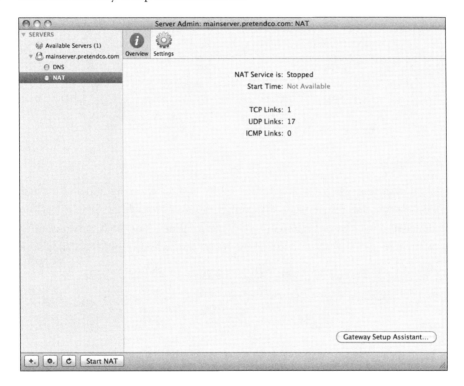

You'll see information about the Gateway Setup Assistant and what it is about to do.
If you click the More Info button, a dialog appears that details how the assistant will
configure each of the services.

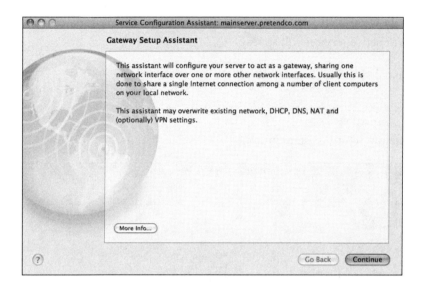

8 Click Continue.

A dialog now appears stating that a DHCP subnet is already configured and the assistant wants permission to overwrite this configuration. Although the DHCP service was not enabled and you did not manually configure a subnet, Mac OS X Server automatically configured a DHCP subnet during the initial setup. As a result, this dialog appears.

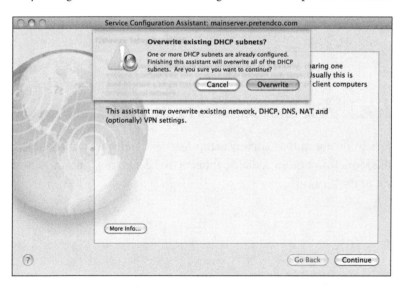

9   Click the Overwrite button to continue.

10 From the Gateway: WAN Interface pop-up menu, choose Ethernet 1 (en0) for your WAN interface, then click Continue.

11 From the list of network interfaces, select the Ethernet 2 checkbox for your LAN interface. Click Continue.

12 If you decide not to configure VPN, leave the "Enable VPN for this server" checkbox unchecked and do not enter a shared secret.

You don't have to configure VPN settings to enable a gateway server. However, if the environment requires VPN configuration and you choose to enable VPN, you will have to use the L2TP protocol and you must enter a shared secret.

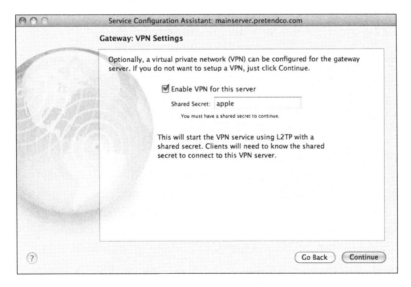

13 Click Continue.

14 Confirm the configuration and click Continue.

The following services are now configured: DHCP, DNS, Firewall, NAT, and—if you chose to do so—VPN.

15 Click Close.

Notice that all of the configured services listed in step 14 have been enabled, configured, and started.

From this base configuration, it is possible to further customize your gateway by entering additional DNS information, more DHCP subnets, other firewall settings, or Point-to-Point Tunneling Protocol (PPTP VPN connections. See Chapter 1, "Understanding the Domain Name System"; Chapter 2, "Using DHCP"; Chapter 4, "Using a Firewall"; or Chapter 5, "Virtual Private Networks" for more information.

However, you may find that even the base NAT gateway configuration will not provide the foundation your specific environment requires. The next section will present the configuration of a gateway server, service by service.

Using Server Admin to Configure NAT

Although the Gateway Setup Assistant easily creates a robust NAT environment in minutes, it may not be the best solution for many organizations. For example, the assistant allows the creation of a LAN network only in the 192.168.*x.x* range. This can be problematic in some situations, especially if your organization already has a network in a 10.*x.x.x* or 172.16.*x.x* range. Modifying the base NAT configuration created by the assistant requires reconfiguring the DHCP range, DNS, the firewall, and the internal Ethernet interface. Therefore, it is usually more effective to configure the gateway manually using Server Admin.

In this exercise, you are going to set up a gateway server that will sit on your network between the Internet and your LAN. Furthermore, you have been given a single IP address from your Internet service provider (ISP) and you need to share that single address with your entire LAN.

Assume the following configuration details:

▶ Ethernet interface names and functions—Ethernet 1 (connected to the Internet), Ethernet 2 (connected to the private LAN)

▶ Internet IP information (Ethernet 1)—IP address (17.255.5.44), subnet mask (255.255.255.0), router (17.255.5.1), DNS server (17.255.1.253)

▶ Private LAN IP information (Ethernet 2)—IP address (10.1.0.1), subnet mask (255.255.0.0), router (10.1.0.1), DNS server (10.1.0.1)

▶ Private LAN IP range—10.1.0.0 to 10.1.255.255

▶ Private LAN DHCP range—10.1.0.100 to 10.1.0.200

▶ Private file server IP address—10.1.0.5

> **NOTE** ▶ Ordinarily an organization's ISP or its IT department would supply IP information. If you were setting up this configuration at home with the server directly connected to the Internet, DHCP would provide the configuration information for this interface.

Configuring Gateway Network Settings

Before you can configure the server, you must configure the network settings on both the public (Ethernet 1) and private (Ethernet 2) interfaces.

1 Configure the Ethernet 1 (external) interface based on the following settings:

   ▶ IP address—17.255.5.44

   ▶ Subnet mask—255.255.255.0

   ▶ Router—17.255.5.1

   ▶ DNS—17.255.1.253

2 Configure the Ethernet 2 (internal) interface based on the following settings:

   ▶ IP address—10.1.0.1

   ▶ Subnet mask—255.255.0.0

▶   Router—10.1.0.1

▶   DNS—10.1.0.1

3   Confirm that the Ethernet 1 interface is at the top of the interface list. If it is not,
    modify the service order to make it the first interface listed.

    NOTE ▶ The first interface in the interface list is the default route for all network
    traffic. Therefore, the first interface is also the path the system will take when trying
    to route traffic to the external network and the Internet.

4   After you've configured both interfaces, click Apply.

Configuring DHCP Service

With both Ethernet interfaces configured, you can configure the gateway server to provide
DHCP addressing to the private LAN.

1   Using Server Admin, connect to the gateway server.

2   Click the name of the server. Click Settings, and then click Services.

3   Select the checkbox next to the DHCP service to enable it, and click Save.

4   In the Servers list, click the triangle to the left of the gateway server.

5   Under the name of the gateway server, select the DHCP service, and click Subnets.

    You may already see a subnet that was created when the server was configured. You
    will delete that subnet and create a new one.

6   To delete the existing subnet, select the subnet created during initial server configura-
    tion, and then click the Delete (–) button.

7   Click the Add (+) button to add a new subnet to the DHCP service.

8   In the General pane, configure the subnet with the following information:

    ▶   Subnet Name—Private Subnet

    ▶   Starting IP Address—10.1.0.100

▶ Ending IP Address—10.1.0.200

▶ Subnet Mask—255.255.0.0

▶ Network Interface—Ethernet 2

▶ Router—10.1.0.1

▶ Lease Time—1 hour

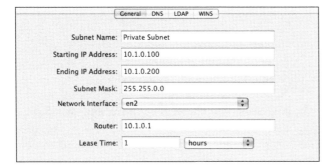

9 Click DNS.

10 Configure the DNS pane with the following information:

▶ DNS Servers—10.1.0.1 (may already be in place)

▶ Search Domains—pretendco.com (may already be in place)

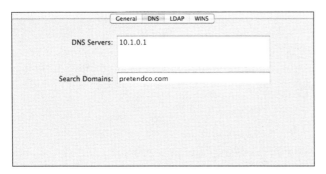

11 Click the Enable checkbox next to Private Subnet, and click Save.

12 In the Servers list, select the DHCP service under the gateway server, and click the Start DHCP button below the Servers list.

Configuring NAT Service

Now that you've configured both network interfaces, you can configure your server to provide NAT from the internal network interface to the external network interface.

1 Using Server Admin, connect to the gateway server.

2 Click the name of the server, click Settings, and then click Services.

3 Select the checkbox next to the NAT service to enable the service, and click Save.

4 In the Servers list, click the disclosure triangle to the left of the gateway server.

5 Select the NAT service under the name of the gateway server, and click Settings.

6 Confirm the following settings:

   ▶   IP forwarding and NAT are selected.

   ▶   The external network interface is Ethernet 1.

   ▶   Enable NAT Port Mapping Protocol is selected.

NOTE ▶ By enabling NAT Port Mapping Protocol, you are allowing systems behind your NAT to configure the NAT service automatically to provide external computers access to those systems. This is a security risk that you should carefully consider when you configure the NAT service.

7 Click Save.

8 With the NAT service under the name of the gateway server still selected, click the Start NAT button below the Servers list.

Configuring Firewall Service

Although the next chapter in this book is dedicated to the configuration and trouble-shooting of the Firewall service, it is important to touch briefly on that service here. As you learned when using the Gateway Setup Assistant, NAT will not function without the Firewall service started because an essential part of NAT is the packet divert rule. That rule is added to the firewall when the NAT service is enabled, but the Firewall service must be started for the packet divert rule, or any firewall rule, to have an effect. Configure the Firewall service by following these steps:

1 Using Server Admin, connect to the gateway server.

2 Click the name of the server. Click Settings, then click Services.

3 Select the checkbox next to the Firewall service to enable it, and click Save.

4 In the Servers list, click the disclosure triangle to the left of the gateway server.

5 Select the Firewall service under the name of the gateway server. Click Settings, and then click Address Groups.

   By default, three address groups will be present.

   For this exercise, you are going to enable all traffic for all three subnets,

   NOTE ► For additional information on firewall configuration, see Chapter 4, "Using a Firewall."

6 Select Services.

7 Set the "Editing services for" pop-up menu to "any," and choose "Allow all traffic."

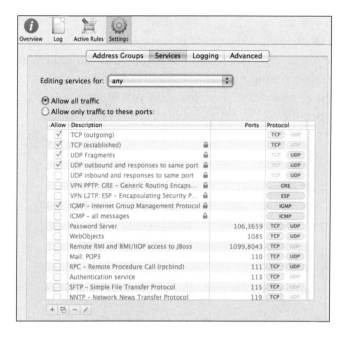

8   Repeat this step for the other two address groups, and click Save.

   NOTE ▶ Remember, the goal of this exercise is to have the Firewall service running so
   that NAT will function, not to configure the Firewall service completely for a secure LAN.

9   With the Firewall service still selected in the Servers list, click the Start Firewall button
   at the bottom of the list.

About Port Forwarding

With DHCP, NAT, and the Firewall service configured, the private LAN now has access to
the Internet. However, you still need to configure NAT to allow Internet users to connect
to the file server on the private LAN. To do this, you need to configure *port forwarding*,
which allows you to provide external users with access to services on the private LAN.
Port forwarding works by using port-to-service relationships created by editing the /etc/
natd/natd.plist file. The following figure shows what happens when a request for TCP port
548 comes to 17.255.5.44.

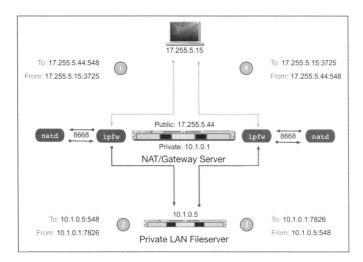

1. The MacBook user requests to be connected to TCP port 548 (AFP) on server 17.255.5.44. The NAT service gets that request. Based on the /etc/natd/natd.plist configuration, the NAT service knows that a relationship exists between that protocol (TCP) and port (548), and forwards that request to the target IP: 10.1.0.5.

2. The NAT service running on the NAT/Gateway server notes the IP address of the MacBook that sent this request (17.255.5.15) and identifies an internal port number (3725) to associate with the specific request. The NAT service forwards this request to the appropriate target IP (10.1.0.5) on the private LAN using the address of the NAT/Gateway server's en2 Ethernet interface (10.1.0.1)—which is connected to the private LAN, as the new source or "from" address. The NAT/Gateway server also supplies its own port number (7826) for this request.

3. The file server receives a request for a connection and an authentication request is passed. In this case, the file server returns the authentication request to the requesting address 10.1.0.1 at port 7826 (NAT/Gateway server).

4. The NAT/Gateway server receives the request for authentication for the file server and forwards the request to the appropriate host on the corporate LAN by changing the destination address to match the address of the MacBook that made the original request. In this case, the port number 7826 informs the NAT/Gateway server that it should send this request to address 17.255.5.15 at port 3725. The MacBook then displays the resulting request for authentication to the file server.

This same process is used to configure port forwarding for all other protocols and services, including web, email, VPN, and so on. You can identify the port numbers associated with specific services by viewing the Services pane in the Firewall service. There you will find a list of the most common services, their protocols (TCP, UDP, ICMP, and so forth), and their port numbers.

Configuring Port Forwarding

In this example, you are providing access to an AFP file server behind your NAT service and forwarding incoming port 548 TCP connection requests to the file server.

First you need to confirm that the natd.plist file (/etc/nat/natd.plist) exists. You will use this file to save the port forwarding settings. The contents of this plist file will be used to generate /etc/nat/natd.conf.apple, which is passed to the NAT daemon when it starts. If you change the natd.plist file in any way, you will have to restart the NAT service before the changes will be active.

1 If the file /etc/nat/natd.plist file does not exist, create a copy of the default NAT daemon plist file and rename it *natd.plist* with the following command:

```
$ sudo cp /etc/nat/natd.plist.default /etc/nat/natd.plist
```

Next, you will populate that plist file with the configuration information to forward port 548 to the file server at 10.1.0.5.

2 Using a Terminal editor (such as vi or picco), add the following lines to the /etc/nat/natd.plist file just before the last </dict> tag in the file.

```
<key>redirect_port</key>
    <array>
        <dict>
            <key>proto</key>
            <string>tcp</string>
            <key>targetIP</key>
            <string>10.1.0.5</string>
            <key>targetPortRange</key>
            <string>548</string>
            <key>aliasIP</key>
```

```
            <string>17.255.5.44</string>
            <key>aliasPortRange</key>
            <string>548</string>
        </dict>
    </array>
```

3 Save the file.

4 Restart NAT. Because you are already in the Terminal application, you can do so by issuing the following commands:

```
$ sudo serveradmin stop nat
$ sudo serveradmin start nat
```

You have now created a private LAN. Should you wish to test this lesson, create a share point on a Mac OS X client or server with the IP address 10.1.0.5.

The next section focuses on troubleshooting tips to assist in tracking down issues during the configuration of NAT with either the Gateway Setup Assistant or Server Admin.

Security Considerations

The NAT service, by design, offers a layer of security between your private LAN and a public network.

▶ Communication from a computer on your private network is translated from a private IP address to a shared public IP address. Multiple private IP addresses are configured using a single public IP address.

▶ Communication to your private network is translated and forwarded to an internal private IP address (IP forwarding). The external computer cannot determine the private IP address, which creates a barrier between your private network and the public network.

▶ Communication from a public network cannot come into your private network unless it is requested. It is allowed only in response to internal communication.

The NAT service takes all traffic from your private network and remembers internal addresses that have made requests. When the NAT service receives a response to a request, it forwards it to the originating computer. Traffic that originates from the Internet does not reach computers behind the NAT service unless port forwarding is enabled.

However, if you choose to enable the Port Mapping Protocol, you have created an environment that diminishes much of the security provided by NAT. For example, a client system can ask the NAT service to create a port map for specific services. The NAT service will create these maps automatically. In this instance, NAT provides the ability to share a single public IP without the security of network isolation. For a secure local network, you should not enable the Port Mapping Protocol.

Troubleshooting NAT on Mac OS X Server

Although the configuration and operation of the NAT service on Mac OS X Server v10.6 is quite a simple affair, you'll find times when things just don't work the way you might expect. In this section, you'll learn some troubleshooting tips and explore the most common problems that occur when running the NAT service on Mac OS X Server.

The first step in troubleshooting the NAT service is to confirm that the service is running. If the service is running and NAT is still not working correctly, you should check the following:

▶ Ethernet cabling and infrastructure

▶ Ethernet interface configuration

▶ NAT service external port configuration

▶ Firewall configuration

Verifying the NAT Service

You can verify that the NAT service is actually running by using Server Admin or Terminal. Let's first look at Server Admin.

1   Open Server Admin and connect to the server.

2   Click the disclosure triangle to the left of the server, and select NAT.

3   Click Overview to determine if the service is running; when it started; and the number of TCP, UDP, and ICMP links.

4   If the server is not running, click the Start NAT button at the bottom of the Servers list.

From Terminal, you can view two status reports. The first simply reports whether the service is running, and the second displays specific details including external ports, internal ports, and so on.

▶ To view NAT status overview in Terminal, issue this command:

```
$ sudo serveradmin status nat
```

It returns the following:

```
"RUNNING" or "STOPPED"
```

▶ To view a detailed NAT status overview in Terminal, issue this command:

```
$ sudo serveradmin fullstatus nat
```

It returns a report similar to this:

```
nat:readWriteSettingsVersion = 1
nat:activeICMP = 0
nat:devices:_array_index:0:device = "en1"
nat:devices:_array_index:0:name = "Ethernet 2"
nat:devices:_array_index:1:device = "en0"
nat:devices:_array_index:1:name = "Ethernet 1"
nat:state = "RUNNING"
nat:setStateVersion = 1
nat:activeUDP = 7
nat:logPaths:natLog = "/var/log/alias.log"
nat:activeTCP = 3
nat:startedTime = "2009-10-15 05:06:04 -0700"
```

Checking Ethernet Cabling and Infrastructure

One common cause of network-related failures is improper cabling and/or infrastructure configuration. Although these issues are beyond the scope of this book, it is important to touch on them as they relate to NAT. The following should be considered:

▶ Is the network appliance from the external network on and configured correctly?

▶ Can you connect another machine to that device and get Internet access?

▶   Is the Ethernet cable in functioning order?

▶   Is the Ethernet cable from the external network plugged into the correct port on the NAT/Gateway server?

Configuring the Ethernet Interfaces

The private and external Ethernet interface configurations can be problematic. IP information may not have been entered correctly, or IP information may have been entered for the incorrect interface. Another common configuration problem is the placement of the external network interface in the list of interfaces in the Network pane of System Preferences.

Remember, the interface for the external network must be the first interface in the list:

The preceding figure shows Ethernet 1 at the top of the interfaces list. You are able to confirm that this is the correct interface for your external network by looking at the IP information for the interface.

When troubleshooting the Ethernet interface configuration, you should ask the following questions:

▶ Is the correct Ethernet port at the top of the list of network interfaces in System Preferences?

▶ Is the IP information correct for the external Ethernet interface on the NAT/Gateway server?

▶ Can the Internet be accessed directly from the NAT/Gateway server?

▶ Can a client system behind the NAT (on the private LAN) connect to the Internet?

If the answer to the third item is "Yes," then your Ethernet interfaces, cabling, and infrastructure are all correctly configured. If the answer to the fourth item is "Yes," then you also have a correctly configured NAT server. However, if you answered "No" to the fourth item, you need to verify the NAT service configuration.

Checking the NAT Service Configuration

Although the NAT service is either running or stopped, a couple configuration options still need to be confirmed.

1 Using Server Admin, connect to the gateway server.

2 Click the name of the server. Click Settings, and then click Services.

3 Select the checkbox next to the NAT service to enable the service, then click Save.

4 In the Servers list, click the disclosure triangle to the left of the gateway server.

5 Select the NAT service under the name of the gateway server, then click Settings.

6 Confirm the following settings:

 ▶ IP Forwarding and NAT are selected.

 ▶ The external network interface is Ethernet 1 (or your external interface).

 ▶ Enable NAT Port Mapping Protocol is selected.

7 Click Save.

If clients on the private LAN still can't access external resources, check the Firewall configuration.

Verifying the Firewall Service Configuration

Remember, the Firewall service must be running for NAT to work. You can check the status of the firewall using Server Admin or Terminal:

1 Using Server Admin, connect to the gateway server.

2 In the Servers list, click the triangle to the left of the gateway server.

If the Firewall service is not present in the list, or if you don't see a green dot to the left of the Firewall service name, refer to "Configuring Firewall Service" earlier in this chapter. If the Firewall service is present and does have a green dot, proceed to step 3.

3 Select the Firewall service under the name of the gateway server. Click Settings, and then click Address Groups.

4 Select Services.

5 Set the "Editing services for" pop-up menu to "any," and choose "Allow all traffic."

6 Repeat step 5 for the other address groups, and click Save.

NOTE ▶ This is a serious security faux pas and should be resorted to only for troubleshooting. If the issue does lie in the firewall configuration, you should identify the specific port blocking your workflow, then lock everything else back down.

What You've Learned

▶ There are three types of NAT: static NAT, dynamic NAT, and port address translation (PAT).

▶ Port forwarding lets you reroute packets sent to specific ports on the NAT system to other hosts in the private network.

▶ The Gateway Setup Assistant automatically configures the DHCP, DNS, Firewall, and NAT services and provides an option for configuring the VPN service.

▶ In addition to the NAT service, only the Firewall service needs to be running on the NAT/Gateway server for NAT to function.

▶ The NAT service, by design, provides a level of security between your private network and a public network. Traffic from the public network only reaches your private network in response to an internal request or through port forwarding.

References

For additional information, see the following resources:

Administration Guides

Network Services Administration v10.6 Snow Leopard

Mac OS X Server Essentials v10.4 Student Guide

Mac OS X Server: Security Configuration for v10.5 Leopard, 2nd Edition

RFC Documents

Access the RFC (Request for Comment) documents at: www.ietf.org/rfc*nnnn* (*nnnn* is the RFC number).

RFC 1918—Address Allocation for Private Internets

RFC 1632—The IP Network Address Translator (NAT)

RFC 3022—Traditional IP Network Address Translator (Traditional NAT)

URLs

NAT Port Mapping Protocol Internet Draft:

http://files.dns-sd.org/draft-cheshire-nat-pmp.txt

Man Pages

`natd`

`ipfw`

Chapter Review

1. When using the Gateway Setup Assistant, what IP range will it assign to the LAN?

2. The Gateway Setup Assistant allows for the easy configuration of what services?

3. What rule is required to be in place in the Firewall for NAT to function?

4. When configuring Mac OS X Server to provide NAT, which Ethernet interface should be listed first in the Network Interfaces list in Network Preferences?

5. How can unsolicited traffic from a public network reach computers on your private network?

Answers

1. The IP range assigned to the LAN will be in the 192.168.*x*.1/24 range.

2. The assistant can configure the DHCP, NAT, DNS, Firewall, and VPN services.

3. NAT relies on the packet divert rule.

4. When configuring NAT on Mac OS X Server, the public Ethernet interface (the interface facing the Internet) must be listed before all other Ethernet interfaces.

5. Traffic from a public network can reach a machine on your private network if you configure port forwarding to allow it.

Part 2

Securing Systems and Services

4

Time   This lesson takes approximately 30 minutes to complete.

Goals   Control network traffic

Understand the firewall options in Mac OS X and Mac OS X Server

Explore the command line and remote configuration of firewalls

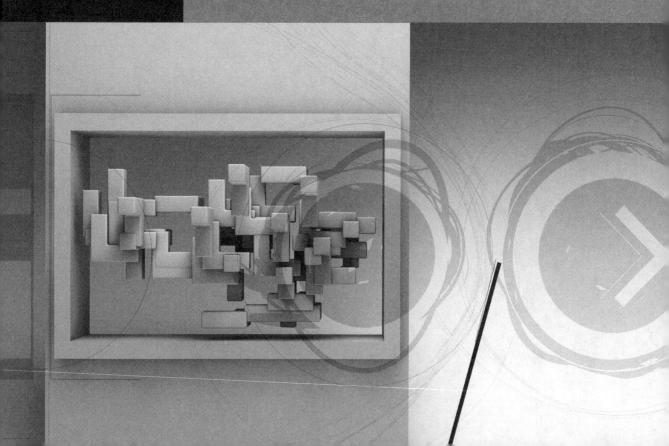

Chapter **4**
Using a Firewall

Security has never been more critical when administrating client and server systems.

Today's external threats range from macro viruses embedded in documents and spreadsheets, to denial of service network attacks. All networked systems are potentially vulnerable to probes and attacks—intentional and unintentional—as assailants constantly scan systems connected to the Internet. However, attacks can also come from internal sources. In 2008 and 2009, the greatest number of reported data breaches actually came from within corporate networks.

To help administrators protect their systems, this chapter focuses on mitigating and controlling access using Mac OS X firewalls on both the client and server. In this chapter, you'll learn how to verify when attack attempts and system failures occur, and how to configure firewalls to guard against them.

Understanding the Mac OS X Firewall

In the days before digital technology, the term *firewall* described an actual fireproof wall designed to contain fires, such as the barrier between a car's engine and its passenger section.

Like those physical walls, computer firewalls work to prevent improper network packets from "burning through" a host or network perimeter. Today's digital firewalls consist of hardware or software that blocks unauthorized network access from sources outside or inside your network.

Mac OS X has two software firewalls: the IP Firewall (ipfw) and the Application Firewall. While ipfw is available in both Mac OS X and Mac OS X Server, Mac OS X Server includes a graphical user interface for detailed configuration, monitoring, and troubleshooting. Mac OS X provides basic, user-oriented service configuration, and optional advanced configuration. Mac OS X Server also includes an Adaptive Firewall, which can add and remove firewall rules based on network events.

> **NOTE** ▶ Technically, the IP Firewall is now in its second generation, and is sometimes called ipfw2. It consists of both the IPv4 and IPv6 programs for restricting IPv4 packets and IPv6 packets, respectively. However, it is commonly referred to as ipfw, as it will be in this book.

Using the Mac OS X Application Firewall

The most common method for securing network services is to configure a firewall at the network perimeter, where the network connects to a remote network such as the Internet. Most networks use a firewall to limit inbound traffic from the Internet or remote connections. In fact, most home and small business routers, such as Apple's AirPort base stations, are designed with built-in firewall software.

While network-level firewalls will block unauthorized traffic trying to enter your network, they will not block traffic that originated inside your network. Also, if your Mac is mobile and frequently joins new wired or wireless networks, your computer will regularly encounter networks with different firewall rules or, possibly, no firewall protection at all. So secure mobile access is an important consideration in designing your overall firewall policies.

To protect against unauthorized network access to your Mac, you can enable the Application Firewall via System Preferences. Administrators can utilize command-line tools to enable and configure the firewall.

Network-based firewalls use a set of rules that target specific service port numbers, such as TCP port 80, the port used for standard HTTP services. However, certain network services—such as iChatAgent (the background process that receives incoming connections for iChat)—use a wide range of dynamically assigned ports. These dynamic multiport services use more than one port to transfer multiple data types. For example, iChat can transmit audio, video, screen sharing, and text all at one time, which requires a multiport approach. This typically causes configuration complications with network-based firewalls because numerous ports need to be open to allow the service to function.

As a solution to this issue, Mac OS X's Application Firewall allows connections based on application and service needs without requiring the user or administrator to know the myriad ports these apps and services may use. For example, you can authorize iChatAgent to allow incoming connections without manually configuring ports or port ranges.

The Application Firewall in Mac OS X version 10.6 includes a new feature that enables administrators to allow signed software to receive incoming connections automatically. Applications that have been digitally signed by their authors can accept inbound network connections without further configuration from the user or administrator, simplifying administration of deployed systems. Digitally signing an application provides reassurance that the application has not been tampered with.

Its adaptive nature means the Application Firewall will open necessary ports only when an application is running. This prevents several types of known attacks on personal systems.

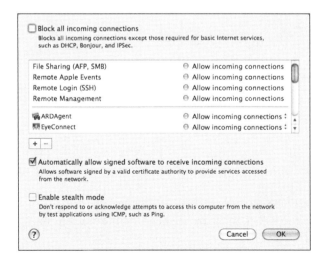

Configuring the Mac OS X Application Firewall

To enable and configure the Max OS X firewall using System Preferences, here's what you do:

1   Open iChat by clicking its icon in the Dock.

2   Choose Apple menu > System Preferences and then click the Security icon to open Security preferences.

3   In the lower-left corner of the security pane, click the lock icon and then authenticate yourself as an administrative user to unlock Sharing preferences.

4   Click the Firewall tab, and then click Start to turn on the Max OS X firewall using its default rules.

    When the firewall is enabled, the Start button changes to a Stop button and the advanced button is enabled.

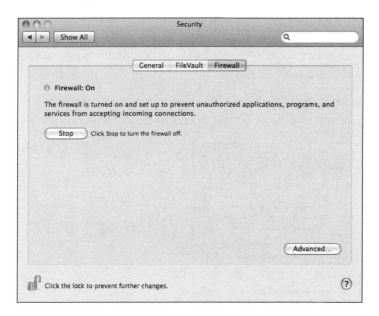

The default firewall configuration allows incoming traffic for established connections (such as a website responding to a click in Safari) and communications from any signed software or enabled services. This default configuration provides a level of security that is adequate for most users.

TIP   Firewall logging is always enabled and can be viewed using the Console. The firewall log is located at /private/var/log/appfirewall.log.

5   To customize the firewall, click Advanced for additional configuration options.

You can see which services are currently enabled from the Sharing preferences. Sharing service ports are enabled by default when a service such as Web Sharing is enabled.

If you want to exercise more control over the configuration, you can manually set which applications and services the firewall allows by selecting or deselecting the checkbox that automatically allows signed software.

With this firewall choice enabled, when a network-aware application such as iChat opens or requests a network connection, a dialog, such as the one shown in the following figure, asks if you want to allow the application access to the network. This dialog will appear as a warning anytime a network-aware application requests incoming access for the first time.

6   Click Allow to create a firewall rule that allows access for the application.

When manually setting firewall access by application or service in the Advanced tab, you can return to the Advanced tab to review and modify or specifically deny connections.

Another option provided by the firewall, *Stealth Mode,* prevents network probing tools that use common discovery tools based on the ICMP protocol (such as ping) from discovering the Mac is even on the network.

7   Select the checkbox to enable Stealth Mode.

8   From Applications > Utilities in Finder, open the Terminal and execute the following command to attempt to `ping` your system:

`ping localhost`

You will see the following timeout message illustrating that your system is not responding to the `ping` request.

Request timeout for icmp_seq

When utilizing your Mac on an unfamiliar network such as at an Internet café or a trade show, you can select "Block all incoming connections" to prevent any access except that required for basic network services, Internet browsing, and email. Selecting this option also will disable access to all shared services hosted on your Mac, but on an unfamiliar network this is highly desirable.

Unlike in Mac OS X Server, in Mac OS X the command-line `ipfw` program is the only interface available to configure port-based rules for a firewall manually.

Understanding the Mac OS X Server Firewall

Though Mac OS X's Application Firewall provides a simplified interface for handling firewall rules based on services and applications, Mac OS X Server administrators require more granular access controls than the Application Firewall provides. Mac OS X Server v10.6 contains a host-based firewall service based on `ipfw` software that was developed as part of the FreeBSD project. This traditional *stateful* packet firewall provides *stateless* or stateful packet inspection.

Stateful packet inspection tracks the state of network connections traveling across it. A stateless firewall looks at packets as individual events. A stateful firewall, on the other hand, can track multipacket communication sessions and more intelligently accept or deny traffic. For example, a stateful firewall can remember that a protected client initiated a request to download data from an Internet server and allow data back in for that connection.

Mac OS X Server can do both stateless and stateful processing. To use stateful processing, Mac OS X Server adds the `keep-state` keyword to rules. Since the release of Mac OS X Server version 10.5 Leopard, an Adaptive Firewall has been present in OS X Server. The Adaptive Firewall will monitor firewall activity and block an IP address that has excessive failed login attempts.

While documentation may make this seem like a second firewall, the Adaptive Firewall is really a monitor that dynamically creates and disables rules in the `ipfw` firewall as needed. The Adaptive Firewall is currently called into action following ten failed login attempts. Such behavior blocks the requesting IP address for 15 minutes, which makes brute-force password attacks virtually impossible. No administrator needs to take action to enable the Adaptive Firewall, as it is enabled by default.

Accessing the Firewall Setup

Some servers will have access to several networks such as an internal network, the Internet, and a management network. To avoid having to configure rules manually for each system on a specific network, you can create an address group to handle network addresses. The Address Groups tab in the Settings pane enables you to group addresses logically and create address ranges to which you can then apply rules. An address group can be a single address, such as 192.168.3.1, or a range of addresses, such as 192.168.3.0–192.168.3.255. You can set up a range of addresses using subnet mask notation (192.168.3.0: 255.255.255.0) or Classless Interdomain Routing (CIDR) notation (192.168.3.0/24).

> **NOTE ▶** If you are accessing your server remotely using Server Admin or the Secure Shell protocol (SSH), you should establish a dead man's switch prior to enabling the firewall to ensure that your firewall rules are properly tested and allow you to administer your server remotely. You may inadvertently disallow ports that are required for Server Admin or SSH essentially locking you out from remote access to that server. Dead man's switch configuration is discussed later in this chapter.

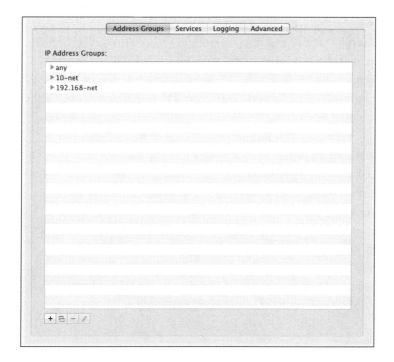

1 From the Dock, open Server Admin.

2 Authenticate, if necessary, and then click the name of the server you want to configure.

3 In the Toolbar, click the Settings button, and then select the Firewall checkbox, if necessary.

4 At the lower right of the Server Admin window, click Save.

5 In the leftmost pane, click the Firewall service.

6 Click the Address Groups tab (as seen in the figure above).

7 Click the Add (+) button located at the bottom of the Server Admin window.

8 In the proceeding dialog box, enter the network address or range (using subnet notation), and then click OK to add the group.

You will now be able to assign rules to this specific address group.

9 Click the pencil button if or when you need to edit existing groups.

Configuring Service Firewall Rules

The Services tab defines the rules for predetermined services for a given address group
selected in the pop-up menu.

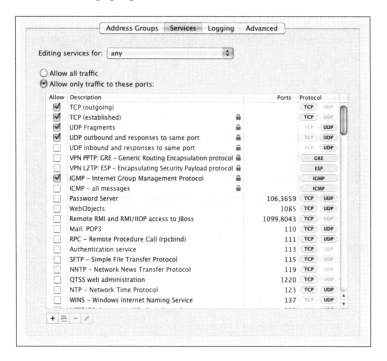

By default, all traffic is allowed out, but only Apple administrative ports and established
traffic are allowed in. Established traffic has validly been sent out and is receiving a reply.
Established traffic may receive reply traffic on ports that are closed, but because the firewall
software tracks established traffic, use of the ports is allowed for established traffic streams.

The Services tab contains a long list of predefined services, any of which may be activated for a given address group. If the service or port range needed has not been predefined, it is easy to add a custom service. To add a custom service like Jabber for the iChat service, do the following:

1   Click the Advanced tab.

2   Click the Add (+) button to display a dialog box in which you can define a custom service to add to the list.

3   Provide a name for the service you are configuring. In this exercise, enter *Jabber*.

4   Enter the port numbers and, from the Protocol pop-up menu, choose a transport type (such as TCP for Jabber).

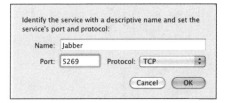

If you are not sure which port to add for a given service, you can get that information from several places. You can find well-known services in the /etc/services file on your local computer.

5   In Applications > Utilities, open the Terminal application.

6   Use the grep command to filter out terms in the services file, which contains a list of known services and their associated ports and transport types:

```
$ grep -i jabber-server /etc/services
jabber-server     5269/udp  # Jabber Server Connection
jabber-server     5269/tcp  # Jabber Server Connection
```

NOTE ▶ Two good sources to refer to when determining port numbers are Apple and the Internet Assigned Number Authority (IANA). For Apple services, see *http://docs. info.apple.com/article.html?artnum=106439*. For general services, see *http://www.iana. org/assignments/port-numbers*.

7   Click OK to save your rule.

8   To view the rules you are currently enforcing with your firewall, in the Toolbar, click the Active Rules button.

This displays the currently active rules for all rule sets and address groups.

Notice that each rule includes a priority number, the number of packets and bytes affected by the rule, and a description of the rule.

As mentioned earlier in "Understanding the Mac OS X v10.6 Server Firewall," the firewall service in Mac OS X Server is built on top of ipfw, a kernel-based application. This means that the actual code for the ipfw service(s) is built into the kernel stack, making it extremely fast and secure from tampering. You can control ipfw via the same-named command-line program.

Verifying current firewall rules is simply a matter of asking `ipfw` to list them. This list corresponds to the list in the Active Rules pane in Server Admin.

9   In Applications > Utilities, open the Terminal application.

10 Execute the `ipfw command` using the `list` argument:

```
# ipfw list
01000 allow ip from any to any via lo0
01010 deny ip from any to 127.0.0.0/8
01020 deny ip from 224.0.0.0/4 to any in
01030 deny tcp from any to 224.0.0.0/4 in
12300 allow tcp from any to any established
12301 allow tcp from any to any out
12302 allow tcp from any to any dst-port 22
12302 allow udp from any to any dst-port 22
12303 allow udp from any to any out keep-state
12304 allow tcp from any to any dst-port 53 out keep-state
12304 allow udp from any to any dst-port 53 out keep-state
12305 allow udp from any to any in frag
12306 allow tcp from any to any dst-port 311
12307 allow tcp from any to any dst-port 625
12308 allow udp from any to any dst-port 626
12309 allow icmp from any to any icmptypes 8
12310 allow icmp from any to any icmptypes 0
12311 allow igmp from any to any
65534 deny ip from any to any
65535 allow ip from any to any
```

Dissecting this output, let's take `ssh tcp` as an example:

```
12302 allow tcp from any to any dst-port 22
```

The first position is the rule number; the second is the action (allow or deny); the third position represents protocol type, TCP in our example. Fourth is the from-to combination explaining the allowed or denied path of traffic. In this case you are allowing TCP from any network to any network (equivalent to allow all), and the final two positions describe the type of rule, in this case a port-based rule, and the port number. So reading this across, you are allowing TCP from any network to any network on port 22.

Using Stealth Mode

In the Server Admin Settings pane, under the Advanced tab, you can set stealth options and create custom rule sets for the firewall service. Stealth options drop denied packets rather than sending the requesting computer an error message.

Once you have completed setup and testing, you should enable the Stealth Mode option for both TCP and User Datagram Protocol (UDP), which makes the job for attackers much more difficult as probing attacks and open port discovery are thwarted.

1   In the Stealth Mode section of the Advanced tab, select the "Enable For TCP" checkbox.

2   Select the "Enable for UDP" checkbox.

3   From Applications > Utilities, open the terminal and type the following command to
ping your system:

```
ping localhost
```

You will receive the following timeout message to indicate that your system is not
responding to the ping request.

```
Request timeout for icmp_seq
```

Understanding Firewall Rule Priority

The rules in the Firewall Settings Services pane operate with the rules shown in the
Advanced tab. Usually, the broad rules in the Advanced tab block (or open) access for all
ports. These broad, lower-priority (higher-numbered) rules apply after the rules in the
Services pane.

The rules created in the Services pane open access to specific services. Higher in priority,
Services rules take precedence over those created in the Advanced tab. For most normal
uses, using the Advanced tab to open access to designated services is sufficient.

If you create multiple rules in the Advanced tab, the rule number determines the precedence for a rule. This number corresponds to the order of the rule in the Advanced pane.
You can reorder rules in the Advanced pane by dragging them up or down in the list. If
necessary, you can add more rules using the Advanced pane.

Using ipfw

Although Server Admin treats the firewall as a service, it does not implement the firewall
by a running process. Implementation is simply a set of behaviors in the kernel, controlled
by the ipfw and sysctl tools. To start and stop the firewall, Server Admin sets a switch
using the sysctl tool. Use the sysctl tool to enable the firewall as follows:

```
$ sysctl -w net.inet.ip.fw.enable=1
```

You can also disable the firewall by changing the setting to 0:

```
$ sysctl -w net.inet.ip.fw.enable=0
```

A successful command will respond with the change made represented after the arrow.

```
$ net.inet.ip.fw.enabled: 1 -> 0
```

Regardless of this setting, the rules loaded in the firewall remain. But they are ignored when the firewall is disabled.

You can also use the `ipfw` command-line program to manipulate firewall rules. This is practical when you're working remotely or over `ssh`, or when a scripted solution is needed.

As an example rule, imagine that an Xserve with multiple network interfaces—physical or virtual—is running AFP (Apple Filing Protocol) for file access. The security team decides that AFP should be available only on the subnets that it is serving. AFP does not have the control to specify which interface it binds to. However, you can use the built-in firewall, `ipfw`, to block AFP on the unwanted ports. For example, to block AFP on the `en0` interface, you can use the following command to add the appropriate rule:

```
ipfw add deny dst-port 548 via en0
```

The keywords to `ipfw` are as follows:

▶ `add`—Denotes adding a rule

▶ `deny`—Indicates what type of rule

▶ `dst-port`—Denotes which port the rule affects and is specified by number or service name

▶ `via`—Applies rules to packets arriving via the specified interface or IP address

If a rule number is not specified, `ipfw` will assign a default number to the added rule. You may want to specify this rule number yourself because the firewall evaluates rules in a sequential order. When a default rule number is assigned, it will be done in such a way that the rule becomes the last rule, prior to the default rule. You can add an equivalent AFP-blocking rule using this command:

```
ipfw add 6000 deny dst-port afpovertcp via 10.10.15.68
```

However, doing so specifies the rule number (`6000`). The command lists the destination port by service name (`afpovertcp`) and gives an IP address rather than an interface name.

If a rule is incorrect or no longer needed, you can remove it with the del (delete) command by executing the following:

```
ipfw del 6000
```

Using Firewall Log Files

The firewall sends log messages to /var/log/ipfw.log. For example, if the AFP service was blocked and a subsequent user request was made to the AFP service from a computer with the IP address of 10.1.17.2, the log might read:

```
Oct 17 09:41:17 mainserver servermgrd[58]: servermgr_ipfilter:ipfw
config:Notice:Flushed IPv6 rules
Oct 17 09:41:19 mainserver servermgrd[58]: servermgr_ipfilter:ipfw
config:Notice:Enabled firewall
Oct 17 09:41:24 mainserver ipfw[1940]: 1040 Deny TCP 10.1.17.2:49232 10.1.0.200:548
in via en0
Oct 17 09:41:59 mainserver ipfw[1940]: 1040 Deny TCP 10.1.17.2:49232 10.1.0.200:548
in via en0
Oct 17 09:42:31 mainserver ipfw[1940]: 1040 Deny TCP 10.1.17.2:49232 10.1.0.200:548
in via en0
Oct 17 09:43:31 mainserver ipfw[1940]: 100 Accept TCP 10.1.0.1:721 192.168.12.12:515
in via en0
```

Each log entry follows a similar form:

▶   Time of entry—In this example, it is Oct 17….

▶   Host name—In this example, it is mainserver.

▶   Process name and ID—In this example, it is ipfw[1940].

▶   Log message—The first two lines in this sample simply state that the firewall is flushing, then rereading its configuration, then starting and enabling.

For the firewall itself, each message follows this pattern:

▶   Matching rule number—Why the firewall took this behavior

▶   Action—The action taken (Deny, Accept, and so on)

▶   Protocol—Which protocol this affected (TCP, UDP, and so on)

▶ Source—The source IP address of packet

▶ Destination—The destination IP address of packet

▶ Interface—The network interface on which this packet appeared; in this example, it is in via `en0`, but it could also be `lo0` (loopback), `en1`, or some other interface.

You can fine-tune logging from the Server Admin graphical user interface (Settings > Logging) or by using the `serveradmin` command-line utility. For example, to log all allowed packets, you can make the following `serveradmin` call:

```
serveradmin settings ipfilter:logAllAllowed = yes
```

Using Firewall Configuration Files

In Mac OS X Server, the firewall is a service that administrators can configure. In contrast, Mac OS X does not support the firewall directly. Its `ipfw`-based firewall has no graphical user interface and you must manipulate it via the command line. However, Mac OS X does contain the Application Firewall, which you can configure in Security preferences.

Mac OS X Server uses several files for its `ipfw`-based firewall. The following configuration files are stored in `/etc/ipfilter`:

```
-r--r--r--@  1 root wheel   281 Oct 17 12:56 ip6fw.conf.apple
-r--r--r--  1 root wheel     0 Oct 17 12:33 ip6fwstate-on
-rw-r--r--  1 root wheel 41219 Oct 17 12:56 ip_address_groups.plist
-r--r--r--  1 root wheel 38243 Sep 23 2009 ip_address_groups.plist.default
-rw-r--r--  1 root wheel  1874 Sep 23 2009 ipfw.conf
-r--r--r--@  1 root wheel  1353 Oct 17 12:56 ipfw.conf.apple
-r--r--r--  1 root wheel  1874 Sep 23 2009 ipfw.conf.default
-r--r--r--  1 root wheel     0 Oct 17 12:33 ipfwstate-on
-r--r--r--  1 root wheel   632 Sep 23 2009
standard_services.plist.default
```

Server Admin writes to these configuration files. Note that:

▶ IPv6 and IPv4 rules are kept in separate files.

▶ Files with a name ending in "state-on" exist only if the service is running. They are flags used at boot time to indicate if the firewall should be enabled.

▶   Plist files contain information presented in Server Admin. They are well commented, and you can customize services and addresses seen in Server Admin. For example, if you have a custom application that communicates with other servers on a particular port, you can add an entry to this file so that this service appears in the list of ports that may be selected via a checkbox.

▶   The .apple files are edited by servermgrd. Changes made in these files may be overwritten by changes in Server Admin and may render Server Admin unable to manage the firewall service. You can make changes in other configuration files, such as ipfw.conf. Rules added to ipfw.conf will be loaded into ipfw at start time. The ipfw.conf file lists rules in the same format as rules added with the ipfw command line, minus the ipfw command itself. For example:

```
add 03000 allow tcp from any to any http
```

When added to ipfw.conf, rule 3000 is appended to the rule list, allowing HTTP on any interface. In addition, two premigration files may exist if the server was upgraded to version 10.6 from an earlier version.

As mentioned in the section "Using Firewall Log Files," the Mac OS X Server ipfw logs messages to /var/log/ipfw.log. The Mac OS X Server Adaptive Firewall is configured by and uses several files:

▶   /etc/af.plist lists Adaptive Firewall preferences.

▶   /var/db/af/whitelist contains addresses that will not be blocked.

▶   /var/db/af/blacklist contains addresses that will always be blocked.

▶   /System/Library/LaunchDaemons/com.apple.afctl.plist contains the launchd plist.

Do not manually edit the whitelist and blacklist files. Rather, you should use the command-line utility afctl to modify these files. The Apple Event Monitoring daemon, emond, performs the actual monitoring and spurs the Adaptive Firewall into action. While emond is an off-limits subsystem, the man page states that "emond accepts events from various services, runs them through a simple rules engine, and takes action." One of its rules is /etc/emond.d/rules/AdaptiveFirewall.plist.

This rule is activated after ten failed login attempts and blocks the offending host attempting the login for a period of 15 minutes.

The Mac OS X Application Firewall also contains configuration files that affect its behavior. The Application Firewall is configured in Security preferences.

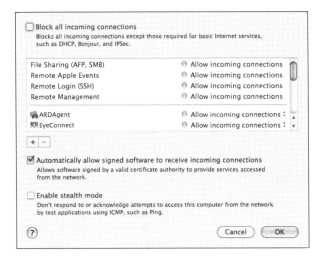

The Application Firewall can also be configured using the command line. The `socketfilterfw` program, which resides in /usr/libexec/ApplicationFirewall, can query and configure the Application Firewall. There is no `man` page for `socketfilterfw`, but a usage statement can be printed when using the `-h` switch.

By default, the Application Firewall is set to allow all incoming connections. The Application Firewall offers two choices for any given application: "Allow incoming connections" and "Block incoming connections."

The Application Firewall logs its activity at /var/log/alf.log and is enabled by default when the Application Firewall is active.

A sample log snippet follows:

```
Sep 29 16:16:00 dhcp-172-26-94-100 Firewall[38]: Deny Microsoft Word data in from
192.168.92.234:52684 uid = 0 proto=17
```

You can set the Application Firewall state from the command line using the `defaults` command to alter preferences:

```
defaults write /Library/Preferences/com.apple.alf globalstate -int 1
```

In this command, the integer passed is one of the following:

- ▶ 0—Off
- ▶ 1—On for specific services
- ▶ 2—On for essential services

The main preference file for the Application Firewall is located in /Library/Preferences/ com.apple.alf.plist.

The executable files for the Application Firewall are located in /usr/libexec/ ApplicationFirewall.

Configuring Client Systems Remotely

Utilizing SSH, ARD (Apple Remote Desktop), or other management tools to deliver shell commands to your remote system, you can enable or disable the default firewall, turn stealth mode on and off, and allow or block signed applications using simple `defaults write` commands.

Using `defaults write` commands to turn on the firewall from the command line without adding any options enables default mode, which allows signed application network traffic and shared services traffic to pass.

Here's how you configure the Application Firewall from the command line:

1 From System Preferences, click the Security icon, click the Firewall tab, and, if locked, click the Lock icon in the lower left corner of the Security pane and authenticate. To turn off the firewall, click Stop.

2 From Applications > Utilities, open the Terminal application and enter the following command to enable the Application Firewall in default mode:

```
sudo defaults write /Library/Preferences/com.apple.alf globalstate -int 1
```

3 Enable the Allow Signed Applications option with the following `defaults write` command:

```
sudo defaults write /Library/Preferences/com.apple.alf allowsignedenabled -int 1
```

4   Enable Stealth Mode from the command line with the following `defaults write` command:

```
sudo defaults write /Library/Preferences/com.apple.alf stealthenabled -int 1
```

5   To reverse any of these commands, simply rerun the command using a `0` as the integer instead of a `1`. Be aware that changing the `globalstate` to `0` will disable the firewall.

Configuring a Dead Man's Switch

When configuring client or server systems, you should take care that the rules you're implementing don't lock you out of the system. Configure an alternate path via a secondary interface—physical or virtual—that is not affected by the firewall, or that has different rules applied to it, to ensure that you can gain access if your rules accidentally deny access to SSH or other remote management tools like ARD.

Another technique you can use to protect yourself against accidental lockout is a *dead man's switch*. This switch gets its name from the railroad industry, where the conductor's throttle had a switch that required pressure at all times to keep the train moving. This was to slow the train to a stop if the conductor had a heart attack or, a more likely scenario, fell asleep.

For your purposes, a dead man's switch enables a service but allows the administrator a temporary back door or other method to remediate an accidental lockout. A simple implementation of the dead man's switch is a one-line set of `bash` commands that runs prior to activating the firewall.

1   From Applications > Utilities, open the Terminal application.

2   Issue the following set of commands on a single line to test a set of firewall rules with a dead man's switch:

```
# sudo ls; sleep 90; sudo serveradmin start ipfilter; sudo serveradmin stop ipfilter
```

This process will enable the firewall and automatically disable the firewall in 90 seconds, allowing you time to verify that your remote access tools (such as `ssh` or ARD) are still working with the firewall enabled. If not, you can correct your firewall settings and test again before going live with the firewall.

Troubleshooting Your Firewall

The firewall services discussed in this chapter provide a point-and-click graphical user interface in Server Admin for simplified configuration. Of course, this simplification makes troubleshooting a little more complicated when things do not run as expected, especially with the firewall service.

The firewall service requires planning. You should make one change at a time and ensure that each change has the intended effect. Implementing too many changes at once makes it difficult to locate the source of a problem. Documenting changes is essential. When several administrators have permission to make changes to the firewall rules, it is imperative that each administrator be kept current with the actions of the others.

When rules are not working and time is not an issue, you can employ several tools and methods—such as ping, telnet, Network Utility, and tcpdump—to troubleshoot the firewall service.

Let's examine a potential firewall configuration issue and the troubleshooting steps necessary to identify and remedy that issue. To simplify the exercise, we will utilize a server that is on an internal network and demonstrate restrictions and permissions on that internal network.

1   Open Server Admin.

2   Select the name of your server in the leftmost pane.

3   In the Toolbar, click the Settings button.

4   Select the Services tab.

5   Select the checkbox to enable configuration of the firewall.

6   In the lower-right corner of the Server Admin window, click Save. The Firewall service will now have an entry in the Services section of the left pane of the Server Admin window as seen in the following figure:

7 In the left pane, click the Firewall service to view its settings, but do not start the service.

8 If necessary, click the Address Group tab.

9 Notice that the default address groups are 192.168-net and 10-net, which may or may not reflect your network settings. You will address these items first.

10 Double-click 192.168-net and change the name to your internal network's IP range. For example, the server used in this exercise has an internal IP address of 172.16.100.130 and a net mask of 255.255.255.0, so 172.16.100-net is appropriate.

11 Enter your internal network range in the "Addresses in group" field.

12 Click the 10-net address group to select it, then delete it by clicking the Delete (−) button at the bottom of the configuration window.

Test the Firewall Using Command-Line Tools

You can test and verify the performance of your firewall using commands in the Terminal application.

1   On your client machine, open the Terminal application.

2   ping your server's IP address using your server's internal IP address instead of the address shown below.

```
ping 172.16.100.130
```

3   Press Control-C to exit the ping. The report should look like this:

```
PING 172.16.100.130 (172.16.100.130): 56 data bytes
64 bytes from 172.16.100.130: icmp_seq=0 ttl=64 time=0.344 ms
64 bytes from 172.16.100.130: icmp_seq=1 ttl=64 time=0.586 ms
64 bytes from 172.16.100.130: icmp_seq=2 ttl=64 time=0.545 ms
64 bytes from 172.16.100.130: icmp_seq=3 ttl=64 time=0.537 ms
64 bytes from 172.16.100.130: icmp_seq=4 ttl=64 time=0.171 ms
64 bytes from 172.16.100.130: icmp_seq=5 ttl=64 time=0.721 ms.
```

This report shows that a ping packet was sent from your client machine (which utilizes the ICMP protocol) to the server, and the server responded. The output of the command displays the number of bytes received, the address received from the sequence (or the order of the ping request), the time to live, and the response time in milliseconds. Enabling stealth mode in the advanced section of the firewall configuration will block ping and other network status requests. Stealth mode does not block these requests from the internal network unless an explicit rule is set in the advanced tab of the firewall configuration.

4   Click the Logging tab and then select "log all denied packets." Click Save.

To test whether a specific port is blocked or allowed, you will test the AFP service using telnet to check if the connection can be established.

5   If the AFP service does not appear in the left pane of your server admin window, repeat steps 1 through 5 of the previous task to add the AFP service. Click the AFP service, and then click the Start button.

6 In the Terminal window on your client machine, use the following telnet command, inserting your server's internal network IP address to replace 172.16.100.130 (note that 548 is added to the command because AFP utilizes port 548):

```
telnet 172.16.100.130 548
```

The command output should resemble the listing below, which shows that telnet was able to establish a connection to the AFP service on port 548:

```
Trying 172.16.100.130...
Connected to 172.16.100.130.
Escape character is '^]'..
```

7 Press `Control-J` to close the connection.

8 At the bottom of the Server Admin window, click Start Firewall to enable the default firewall rules.

9 In the Terminal window on your client machine, type the following telnet command, inserting your server's internal network IP address instead of 172.16.100.130.

```
telnet 172.16.100.130 548
```

The command output should look something like the listing below, illustrating that telnet was able to establish a connection to the AFP service on port 548:

```
Trying 172.16.100.130...
telnet: connect to address 172.16.100.130: Operation timed out
telnet: Unable to connect to remote host
```

10 In the Server Admin toolbar, click the Log button and examine the log.

11 To filter the results and view only the DENY messages, at the right side of the Toolbar, type *DENY* in the filter area. Your output should be similar to this:

```
Nov 22 13:41:43 server ipfw[2086]:  65534 Deny TCP 172.16.100.1:50971
172.16.100.130:548 in via en0
Nov 22 13:41:46: --- last message repeated 3 times ---.
```

Looking at the output from the log the information displayed in order from left to right, you'll see the date, the time, the host name of the server, the firewall component that responded (in this case, `ipfw`), the rule number, the action that was taken on specified ports and Ethernet card. Notice that this action occurred an additional three times and that the server IP address and requested port number is displayed last, not first.

Another method to test whether the firewall allows a port through or denies it is to use the Network Utility application located in /Applications/Utilities.

12 Open Network Utility on your client machine and click the Port Scan tab. Enter your server IP address in the "Enter an internet or IP address to scan for open ports" field and enter *548* in both "Only test ports between" fields. Verify that the "Only test ports between" checkbox is selected, and then click the Scan button.

As seen below, the port scan is initiated and completed with no indication of an error. This is the normal behavior—Network Utility is reporting that it found no open port at the addresses specified.

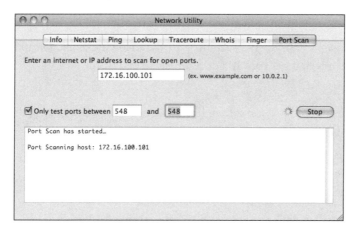

13 Using Server Admin on your server, click the Stop Firewall button and repeat the network scan described in step 12.

This time the output includes a line indicating that the network traffic connected to the server on the specified port.

```
Open TCP Port:    548          afpovertcp
```

Using a Packet Sniffer

If rules look like they should be working, but they are not, and time is not an issue, a packet sniffer will allow you to view the problem from the inside. Mac OS X ships with the tcpdump packet sniffer. This popular open source sniffer can print information in real time for a quick determination, or it can write its dump to a file for later, offline analysis.

1 To dump all packets passing through the en0 interface to stdout, use the following commands:

   NOTE ▶ The configuration and output displayed below may or may not reflect your server and network setup, and command outputs will vary based on your specific configuration.

```
# tcpdump -i en0
tcpdump: verbose output suppressed, use -v or -vv for full protocol decode
listening on en0, link-type EN10MB (Ethernet), capture size 96 bytes
06:42:37.514597 IP mainserver.pretendco.com.ssh > 72.14.228.89.11667: P
3011092458:3011092650(192) ack 3151495640 win 33312 <nop,nop,timestamp 1488505430
575729407>
06:42:37.523288 IP 72.14.228.89.11667 > mainserver.pretendco.com.ssh: .
ack 0 win 65535 <nop,nop,timestamp 575729408 1488505364>
06:42:37.589744 IP 72.14.228.89.11667 > mainserver.pretendco.com.ssh: .
ack 192 win 65535 <nop,nop,timestamp 575729409 1488505430>
06:42:37.637216 IP comproxy2.example.net.53730 > 192.168.1.1.9090:
UDP, length 74
06:42:37.760644 arp who-has 192-168-232-92.in-
addr.arpa.example.com tell 192-168-232-1.in-addr.arpa.example.com
06:42:38.137423 IP comproxy2.example.net.53730 > 192.168.1.1.9090:
UDP, length 74
06:42:38.320315 arp who-has 69-55-228-118.in-
addr.arpa.johncompanies.com tell 69-55-228-1.in-
addr.arpa.johncompanies.com
^C
316 packets captured
349 packets received by filter
0 packets dropped by kernel
```

2   Press Control-C to stop the capture.

Each line displays the time that the packet was received; the protocol; the source of the packet; its destination; and, optionally, any set flags.

3   To limit the tcpdump capture to a specific IP address, specify the host in the tcpdump command:

```
# tcpdump -i en0 host 10.1.0.1
```

4   Perhaps even more useful when troubleshooting a firewall problem is to limit the capture to a specific port—port 80, in this exercise:

```
# tcpdump -i en0 port 80
```

You can also negate a filter using the not keyword. For example, if you are troubleshooting remotely via the Secure Shell protocol (SSH), the SSH traffic that makes up your session is typically noise. Furthermore, you can combine filters with the and conditional.

5   To listen for all traffic from the host at 192.168.55.8, but filter out traffic on port 22, use this command:

```
# tcpdump -i en0 host 10.1.0.1 not port 22
```

Sometimes, analyzing tcpdump on the fly is not enough. For deeper analysis, you can write dumps to a file and analyze them offline using a more powerful program, such as the open source application Wireshark. For deeper analysis, you can also increase the size of the packet capture. By default, tcpdump captures only the first 96 bytes of each packet. For a deeper look, you should capture the entire packet.

6   To capture all traffic of unlimited packet size and write it to a file, you can use the -s (size) and -w (write) switches:

```
# tcpdump -i en0 -s0 -w server_trace.pcap
```

The -s0 ("ess zero") designates unlimited packet size, and the -w switch in this example writes all capture data to the file server_trace.pcap.

A common error when configuring the firewall is accidentally creating conflicting rules. Review your rules and the order in which they are executed to ensure that your configuration is correct. Utilize the tools above to test the traffic through the firewall and adjust your rules accordingly.

In most cases, all you're looking for on a server is any activity getting through the firewall or to the local interface. The more detailed traces are typically more helpful from the client side. In a worst-case scenario, you can document and back up the current firewall rule set, and then flush the current rules entirely. Then you can add half of the rules back in at a time, starting the firewall service each time that you introduce a new set of rules. Incrementally adding back rules will make it easier to determine which rule is causing the undesired behavior.

If you become completely lost with the firewall configuration, you may want to back it up and start from scratch. For instructions on resetting the firewall to default values, see "Resetting the Firewall to the Default Setting" in the Apple Network Services Administration document at: http://images.apple.com/server/macosx/docs/Network_Services_Admin_v10.6.pdf.

Security Considerations

Implementing firewalls at the perimeter of your network is a powerful security tool for thwarting unauthorized access to your internal resources. Some best-practice considerations when deploying the firewall service on Mac OS X or Mac OS X Server are:

▶ On Mac OS X, enable sharing services only as required. Turning on all services just to have them running makes securing your system more difficult. When enabling sharing services, the firewall will automatically open the required ports, providing additional attack points for potential hackers.

▶ Turning off sharing services and enabling the firewall's Stealth Mode when traveling outside an organization-controlled network will allow the firewall to provide the additional blocking required when accessing insecure public networks.

▶ When planning server installations, refer to the planning documents provided by Apple (http://images.apple.com/server/macosx/docs/Worksheet_v10.6.pdf).

▶ Open firewall ports only for services provided to resources and individuals outside your local network.

▶ Utilize address groups to limit allowed access to specified IP addresses or address ranges whenever possible.

▶ Review your firewall logs on a regular basis, note penetration (denied) attempts from the same or similar IP address ranges, and consider blocking the entire range.

▶ Be extremely wary of providing SMB access through your firewall. Crackers attempting to penetrate corporate networks commonly scan and exploit SMB ports. They are also a common vehicle for virus programmers.

▶ Be specific when creating advanced rules. Open only required ports, not ranges of ports, to simplify your initial setup.

▶ Third-party tools are available for threat analysis and detection, such as the open source Snort project and the Nagios monitoring suite.

▶ When configuring a firewall, a good rule of thumb is: Less is more. The less access you provide to the outside world, the more secure you make your internal network.

What You've Learned

▶ Mac OS X and Mac OS X Server contain a built-in stateful packet firewall that keeps track of the state of network connections traveling across it. The packet firewall is based on the open source `ipfw` project.

▶ Mac OS X Server runs a service called `emond` that monitors bad login attempts. Ten consecutive incorrect login attempts cause `emond` to use the Adaptive Firewall to inject a rule into `ipfw`, blocking the offending hosts access entirely for 15 minutes.

▶ The Mac OS X Server packet firewall uses rules to make decisions on which packets to allow or deny. You can modify these rules using the Server Admin graphical user interface, or the `ipfw` command-line tool. `ipfw` logs its messages in `/var/log/ipfw.log`.

▶ Mac OS X contains the Application Firewall. Unlike a traditional stateful firewall, the Application Firewall grants or denies access to specific applications.

▶ `tcpdump` is an excellent utility to use when you're troubleshooting a service that is not connecting and a firewall is a suspected reason.

▶ Mac OS X firewall provides powerful protection for desktop and mobile Mac systems.

▶ Administrators can remotely enable and disable the Mac OS X firewall utilizing standard deployment and management tools.

References
Refer to these resources for updated and in-depth information:

Administration Guides
Network Services Administration v10.6 Snow Leopard

Mac OS X Server Essentials v10.6 Student Guide

Books
Dreyer, Arek, and Greisler, Ben. *Apple Training Series: Mac OS X Server Essentials v10.6* (Peachpit Press, 2010).

Marczak, Edward R. *Apple Training Series: Mac OS X Advanced System Administration v10.5* (Peachpit Press, 2009).

URLs
http://docs.info.apple.com/article.html?artnum=106439

www.iana.org/assignments/port-numbers

http://images.apple.com/server/macosx/docs/Network_Services_Admin_v10.6.pdf

Man Pages
ipfw

tcpdump

telnet

ping

Chapter Review

1. Identify the stateful firewall that is built into Mac OS X and Mac OS X Server.

2. When enabling the default set of firewall rules in Mac OS X Server, what traffic is allowed?

3. In what primary way does the Mac OS X Application Firewall differ from a standard port-blocking firewall?

4. Why is `tcpdump` a good utility for troubleshooting the firewall configuration?

5. Which configuration file is used for the Application Firewall?

6. Which standard OS X configuration command is used to remotely enable or disable firewall services?

Answers

1. The IP Firewall, `ipfw`, is the stateful firewall built into Mac OS X and Mac OS X Server.

2. By default, all traffic is allowed out, and only Apple administrative ports and established traffic are allowed in.

3. The Application Firewall identifies the application that is generating or receiving traffic when choosing which traffic to allow. Port-blocking firewalls use ports only, and do not identify which application is behind the traffic.

4. On the server side, `tcpdump` shows what traffic is going past the firewall and arriving at the application layer. On a client, it informs you if traffic is being generated and accepted on the remote end.

5. The `/Library/Preferences/com.apple.alf.plist` file.

6. The `defaults write` command is used to change parameters in the firewall plist that will enable or disable the firewall or turn Allow Signed Applications or Stealth Mode on and off.

5

Time   This lesson takes approximately 40 minutes to complete.

Goals   Understand virtual private networking (VPN)

Learn the VPN client options in Mac OS X and the iPhone OS

Configure the VPN service on Mac OS X Server

Use the command line to configure the VPN service on Mac OS X Server

Chapter 5
Virtual Private Networks

Remote access has been an information technology requirement for decades. Whether it is linking remote offices or providing data access for roaming employees, remote access is a critical service that IT departments must provide to its internal clients, partners, and vendors. It has evolved from high-priced private data circuits between remote offices to banks of dial-up servers.

The advent of virtual private networking (VPN) was a logical next step in this evolution, and it has become widely used in business, education, and government. Its widespread use can be attributed to widely adopted standards and the secure remote access provided to users from the host organization's infrastructure. VPNs provide almost instantaneous secure access to critical corporate data.

Understanding VPNs

No standardized definition of VPN exists, but it commonly refers to a setup in which a secured network exists within an insecure network—for example, a secured connection to a corporate network through an insecure public network like the Internet.

Early on, these types of networks were called *tunnels:* A client machine connects to a VPN server, negotiates a protocol, provides and establishes authentication, then shares encryption data to a secure connection (the tunnel) within the insecure network. The remote user receives a network address on the desired network, which sees the remote system as a local computer.

Supported VPN Protocols

▶   Point-to-point tunneling protocol (PPTP)—This method uses point-to-point (PPP) dial-up protocol and Microsoft Challenge Handshake Authentication Protocol (MS-CHAP) version 2 for authentication. PPTP also supports public key infrastructure (PKI) certificates via the Extensible Authentication Protocol–Transport Layer Security (EAP-TLS) for a higher degree of authentication security. PPTP is widely supported, works easily with most network address translation (NAT) firewalls, requires little overhead, and is fast and scalable. PPTP clients are built into Mac OS X and Windows systems.

▶   L2TP—More secure than PPTP, Layer 2 Tunneling Protocol (L2TP) leverages the PPP protocol for communication and IPsec for encryption. However, it is not as scalable as PPTP due to the intense cryptographic calculations performed on the traffic traversing the VPN. L2TP works at the second layer (the data link layer) of the Open System Interconnection (OSI) networking model, which allows it to traverse frame relay, ATM, and other non–TCP/IP-based networks. L2TP also provides for data integrity to prevent man-in-the-middle tampering with the data stream. Wide support is available for L2TP, including support in Mac OS X, Windows 2000, Windows XP, Windows Vista, Windows 7, and Linux.

▶   Cisco IPsec—This can be implemented on its own without L2TP. Though it was initially used for site-to-site communications, later developments accommodated user-to-site communications and implemented enforceable network access policies. Mac OS X supports client connections to Cisco IPsec, as does the iPhone OS. Mac OS X Server does not provide Cisco IPsec as a connection service to client machines.

Authentication Options

▸ Password—This option allows an administrator or user to save the user's authentication password. While this is convenient, it is not recommended. (See "Security Considerations" later in this chapter.)

▸ RSA SecureID—RSA provides a onetime password device called SecureID to provide two-factor authentication. This requires an RSA server at the host location to authenticate the generated onetime password on the device.

▸ Certificate—PKI certificates can be issued to devices and installed into their keychains to provide machine-based authentication. Mac OS X provides an application called Certificate Assistant to generate these certificates.

▸ Kerberos—The VPN client can utilize Kerberos for secured single sign-on access to the VPN host if a public Kerberos server from that infrastructure is provided to establish the Kerberos ticket-granting ticket (TGT) and service ticket conversations.

▸ CryptoCard—This provides a onetime password device offering two-factor authentication, which will require a server at the host location to authenticate the generated onetime password on the device.

▸ Shared secret (L2TP and Cisco IPsec only)—This option is used for device-based authentication to the VPN. The secret is separate and distinct from the user's password and is used for device validation, not user authentication.

Additional Considerations

▸ DHCP—When establishing a VPN server at the host location, administrators must provide a contiguous block of IP addresses to be issued to incoming VPN clients, regardless of the protocol or authentication method used. DHCP servers should be set to exclude these addresses to avoid accidental issuance of VPN IP addresses to internal network client equipment.

▸ Host-side firewall—When deploying a VPN server, administrators must ensure that the appropriate ports are open on the firewall to allow communication from the Internet to the VPN server. The ports vary depending on protocol type. Details are provided later in this chapter.

▸ Client-side firewall—In some instances, internal firewalls on clients assume that equipment such as broadband or cable-modem routers will require configuration to allow the traversal of VPN traffic. The ports vary depending on protocol type. Details are provided later in this chapter.

▶ Site-to-site VPN—Mac OS X Server can provide network-to-network authentication connecting remote office locations, but it must be configured solely in the command line. Mac OS X Server currently doesn't provide a graphical interface to configure this functionality.

When deploying a VPN service on OS X Server, administrators must consider several requirements.

If a Mac OS X firewall service or another firewall device is deployed between the Mac OS X server providing the VPN service and the Internet, the ports for that service must be allowed to pass to the VPN service (ports 500, 1701, and 4500 UDP for L2TP; port 1723 TCP for PPTP). If the network infrastructure utilizes NAT for forwarding traffic to the Mac OS X server, the NAT server must support non–UDP/TCP-type forwarding to forward L2TP. Utilizing PPTP may provide a simpler, though less secure, configuration in these network environments.

Client computers behind a firewall that require a VPN connection must configure the firewall to allow traffic on UDP ports 500, 1701, and 4500 for L2TP; or on TCP port 1723 for PPTP.

VPN authentication can be integrated with Open Directory account credentials or Active Directory account credentials for Mac OS X servers bound to an Active Directory or other LDAP version 3–compliant directory service. For additional security, administrators can utilize certificate-based authentication for a user's device (rather than authenticating the user) to ensure that only appropriate assets are connected through the VPN.

NOTE ▶ L2TP and IPsec protocols do not provide authentication. Administrators must apply Internet Key Exchange (IKE), RADIUS, Kerberos, or other authentication technology.

Configuring VPN Service on Mac OS X Server

Mac OS X Server v10.6 can provide L2TP or PPTP VPN services to Mac OS X, Windows, iPhone, or Linux clients. L2TP and PPTP can be provided simultaneously or individually, and can leverage the Remote Authentication Dial-in User Service (RADIUS) on your Mac OS X server or an external RADIUS server to provide user authentication.

Additionally, L2TP VPNs can be load-balanced among multiple servers, and L2TP can provide client machine certificate authentication. Using Server Admin, you can enable or disable L2TP or PPTP services in addition to providing specific configuration information required for each service. In the Client Information tab, administrators can specify DNS servers, network routes, and search domains provided to connecting VPN clients. Finally, administrators can enable verbose logging to support troubleshooting.

Configuring L2TP VPN Service

Mac OS X v10.3 or later, Windows XP, Windows Vista, Windows 7, and Linux distributions all support L2TP, the newer and more secure VPN protocol. L2TP also requires additional firewall and NAT configuration, as well as support from the client's remote access equipment if it provides its own firewall services. PPTP is commonly used for simplified configurations.

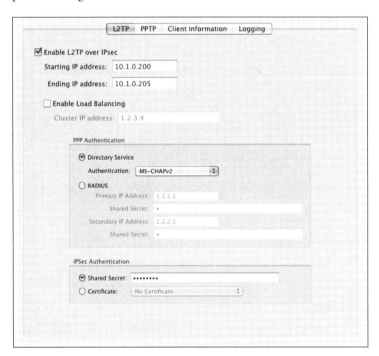

1   In the leftmost pane of Server Admin, click the VPN service name.

2   In the toolbar, click the settings icon and click the L2TP tab.

3   The first two settings set the DHCP range for the incoming VPN clients. Enter a contiguous block of IP addresses that are currently excluded from (or outside the range of) any DHCP service on your internal network. These addresses will be provided to incoming VPN clients' systems so they can communicate with the internal network.

    If you are clustering multiple VPN servers, you can utilize the load-balancing feature, in which case you must specify the cluster IP address. Clustering VPN servers is beyond the scope of this text; more information is available in the "Advanced Networking" white paper provided in the Resources section of Apple's website.

    In the Authentication area, you can select whether the users will authenticate to the VPN service using a directory service (via MS-CHAPv2 or Kerberos) or using an external RADIUS server (via Shared Secret or Certificate).

4   Select Directory Service and choose MS-CHAPv2 (default) from the Authentication pop-up menu.

    For IPsec authentication, you must specify a shared secret, which you will have to provide or *prepopulate* for your users, or select certificate authentication, which entails issuing certificates for each system that will connect to the VPN service.

5   In the Shared Secret field, enter `apple`, which will authenticate the client system configured in the previous examples.

6   Once you've completed and verified your entries, click the Save button located at the lower-right corner of the window.

Configuring PPTP VPN Service

PPTP is the older of the two protocols, and while it is faster, PPTP is also considered less secure. It is used primarily for clients that are connecting from much older operating systems, such as Windows 95 and Mac OS X v10.2, or in situations where firewall configurations cannot be adjusted at either the host or the remote locations to facilitate the L2TP protocol.

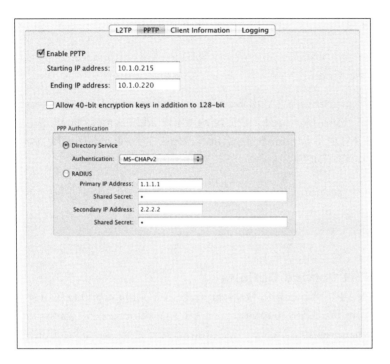

1 In the leftmost pane of Server Admin, click the VPN service name.

2 In the toolbar, click the Settings icon and click the PPTP tab.

3 The first two settings set the DHCP range for the incoming VPN clients. Enter a contiguous block of IP addresses currently excluded from (or outside the range of) any DHCP service on your internal network. These addresses will be provided to the incoming VPN clients' systems so they can communicate with the internal network.

> **NOTE ▶** When you have older client systems that cannot support 128-bit encryption, you can select the "Allow 40-bit encryption keys in addition to 128-bit" checkbox. Do not select this checkbox unless it is necessary and you have older clients that cannot be updated to 128-bit encryption.

In the Authentication area, you can choose whether the users will authenticate against a directory service or an external RADIUS server. If your deployment utilizes a directory service for authentication, you must choose MS-CHAPv2 (default) for PPTP.

4   For this exercise, choose Directory Service and set Authentication to MS-CHAPv2.

5   Once you've completed and verified your entries, click the Save button located at the lower-right corner of the window.

In certain network infrastructures, a RADIUS server may be present. Administrators can leverage this existing infrastructure by specifying the IP address and shared secret provided by the RADIUS administrator. The VPN service will validate the user account with a call to the RADIUS server.

NOTE ▶ Dial-up Internet service providers (ISPs) have widely used RADIUS servers for remote access authentication, and they remain common authentication servers for traditional IPsec environments.

Configuring Other VPN Service Options

Administrators may provide VPN clients with DNS server, search domain, and network routing information to streamline access to internal and external resources. Network routing information is useful when multiple LAN or WAN routes exist at the same location as the host providing the VPN service.

In the Client Information tab shown in the following figure, the DNS Servers field allows the administrator to specify one or more DNS servers for remote users to utilize during a VPN session with the host server. Additionally, one or more search domains can be specified in the Search Domains field.

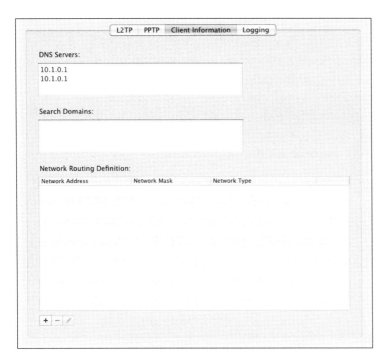

In infrastructures with multiple LAN and WAN segments connected to the host network, the client machines must be provided with routing information that allows them to access resources on those segments. In the Network Routing Definition field, administrators can input information such as IP addresses, subnet masks, and network type (that is, public or private) that can help them further control which computers are able to route traffic through the VPN service.

Using VPN Log Files

The vpn daemon sends log messages to /var/log/ppp/vpnd.log. A sample log with verbose logging turned off looks like this:

```
2009-11-02 01:10:21 EST   Incoming call... Address given to client = 192.168.0.1
Mon Nov  2 01:10:21 2009 : Directory Services Authentication plugin initialized
Mon Nov  2 01:10:21 2009 : Directory Services Authorization plugin initialized
Mon Nov  2 01:10:21 2009 : PPTP incoming call in progress from '166.137.132.125'...
Mon Nov  2 01:10:23 2009 : PPTP connection established.
```

```
Mon Nov  2 01:10:23 2009 : Using interface ppp0
Mon Nov  2 01:10:23 2009 : Connect: ppp0 <--> socket[34:17]
Mon Nov  2 01:10:28 2009 : CHAP peer authentication succeeded for ladmin
Mon Nov  2 01:10:28 2009 : DSAccessControl plugin: User 'ladmin' authorized for access
Mon Nov  2 01:10:29 2009 : MPPE 128-bit stateless compression enabled
Mon Nov  2 01:10:30 2009 : Cannot determine ethernet address for proxy ARP
Mon Nov  2 01:10:30 2009 : local  IP address 69.9.32.234
Mon Nov  2 01:10:30 2009 : remote IP address 192.168.0.1
Mon Nov  2 01:10:39 2009 : LCP terminated by peer (MPPE disabled)
Mon Nov  2 01:10:40 2009 : Connection terminated.
Mon Nov  2 01:10:40 2009 : Connect time 0.3 minutes.
Mon Nov  2 01:10:40 2009 : Sent 0 bytes, received 231 bytes.
Mon Nov  2 01:10:40 2009 : PPTP disconnecting...
Mon Nov  2 01:10:40 2009 : PPTP disconnected
2009-11-02 01:10:40 EST     --> Client with address = 192.168.0.1 has hungup
```

An administrator can track the connection and disconnection process when basic logging is enabled, and can view even more detailed information with verbose logging enabled. In the preceding log, you can see that when the incoming connection (call) is established, an IP address is provided from the contiguous block of addresses specified in the VPN service settings. The appropriate authentication method (directory services, in this example) is engaged, a PPP connection socket is established, and authentication and encryption are started.

Because no proxy is in use, the proxy Address Resolution Protocol (ARP) is undetermined and the address for the remote user is provided.

Then the connection is terminated and the total connection time is displayed, along with the number of bytes sent and received. PPTP is disconnected.

You can turn on verbose logging in Server Admin, or you can use the serveradmin command-line utility.

For example, to enable verbose logging, make the following four serveradmin calls in the command line using the Terminal application:

```
serveradmin settings vpn:Servers:com.apple.ppp.l2tp:Server:VerboseLogging = 1
serveradmin settings vpn:Servers:com.apple.ppp.l2tp:PPP:VerboseLogging = 1
serveradmin settings vpn:Servers:com.apple.ppp.pptp:Server:VerboseLogging = 1
serveradmin settings vpn:Servers:com.apple.ppp.pptp:PPP:VerboseLogging = 1
```

Configuring VPN Server Files

In Mac OS X Server, `launchd` controls the VPN service. When either PPTP or L2TP is enabled, a corresponding plist file is created. When both protocols are enabled, the following two preference list files will be present:

```
/System/Library/LaunchDaemons/com.apple.ppp.l2tp.plist
/System/Library/LaunchDaemons/com.apple.ppp.pptp.plist
```

These files enable one or two (depending on whether one or both services are enabled) `vpnd` daemons with separate command-line arguments. The `vpnd` daemon then reads the specific PPTP or L2TP options from the following file:

```
/Library/Preferences/SystemConfiguration/com.apple.RemoteAccessServers.plist
```

Understanding Mac OS X Client VPN Connections

Mac OS X clients connect to VPN primarily through the Network pane in System Preferences. Mac OS X v10.6 Snow Leopard has integrated Cisco IPsec support, but Cisco provides a downloadable managed VPN client for earlier versions of the operating system.

The Mac OS X VPN client has several options that allow an administrator or user to tailor the experience, the most powerful of which is the VPN on-demand option, which establishes a predefined VPN connection whenever the user attempts to access resources in a specified domain. This feature simplifies managing the VPN client for the end user. Additional options, such as the abilities to disconnect on logout, disconnect on switching users, force all traffic across the VPN, and specify proxy and DNS servers on connection, provide administrators with comprehensive VPN client management tools.

Configuring the PPTP and L2TP VPN Client on Mac OS X

When you want to enable and configure a Max OS X VPN connection from System Preferences, L2TP is the preferred VPN option because of its superior security profile. It requires additional firewall and NAT configuration changes, which organizational policies may not authorize, in which case PPTP is commonly used.

1   Open System Preferences and then click the Network icon.

2   Near the bottom of the Network Interfaces pane, click the Add (+) button.

3   From the Interface pop-up menu, choose VPN and choose a VPN Type.

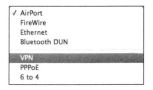

The new VPN interface will appear in the leftmost window with a PPTP designation.

What steps you perform next will depend upon the type of VPN connection you want to establish. For PPTP, complete steps 4 to 7. For L2TP, skip to step 8. For common advanced options, skip to the "Advanced Options" section.

You can create multiple PPTP configurations, potentially for different sites to which your client system would be connecting. In most cases, however, you can leave the Configuration pop-up menu set to Default.

4   In the Server Address field, enter the DNS name or IP address.

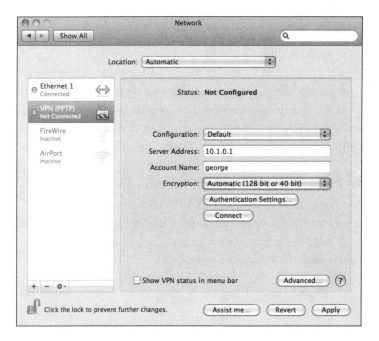

5   In the Account Name field, enter the account name provided to you for remote access through the VPN.

6   The Encryption pop-up menu provides three choices:

     ▶   Automatic—The client will negotiate with the VPN server for the highest level of encryption available.

     ▶   Maximum—The client will connect only with a VPN server providing 128-bit security.

     ▶   None—The client will not require either 40- or 128-bit encryption.

7   Choose Automatic, and click the Authentication Settings button to choose one of five authentication types:

     ▶   Password—The user specifies a password to use for the connection.

     ▶   RSA SecureID—The user must enter the onetime password (OTP) provided by an RSA SecureID hardware token. This infrastructure requires additional software provided by RSA.

     ▶   Certificate—The user selects a certificate preinstalled in his or her keychain, issued by the VPN administrator.

     ▶   Kerberos—A single sign-on is attempted utilizing Kerberos authentication.

     ▶   CryptoCard—Additional hardware and software provided by CryptoCard facilitates authentication.

8   Select the password option and enter *apple* as your password for the purpose of this exercise.

     NOTE ▶ Certificate authentication has become popular in recent years because it allows administrators to utilize certificates issued to specific systems. When an employee loses a system or has left the organization, an administrator need revoke only that certificate rather than reconfiguring all client systems with a new password.

     The new VPN interface will show up in the interface window to the left with an L2TP designation.

9   Verify that the Configuration pop-up menu is set to Default.

You can create multiple L2TP configurations to address the different sites to which your client system may be connecting. However, in most cases, the default value is acceptable.

10   In the Server Address field, enter the DNS name or IP address.

11   In the Account Name field, enter the account name provided to you for remote access through the VPN.

12   Click Authentication Settings to choose one of five user authentication types and two machine authentication options.

The user authentication options are the same as those listed in step 7. The machine authentication options are as follows:

▶   Shared secret—Each remote user receives a predetermined password established by the VPN administrator. This is the least secure option.

▶   Certificate—The administrator issues a certificate to each client system, and it is installed in that system's keychain. The user or administrator selects that certificate when using this option.

▶   Group name (optional)—This option groups computers logically for policy determinations or auditing purposes.

13 Select Shared Secret and then enter `apple` as your shared secret, which you will use in an upcoming exercise.

14 Select the "Show VPN status in menu bar" checkbox to display the VPN connection status in the user's menu bar.

15 In the menu bar, click the newly displayed VPN connection icon, and then click Connect.

You will see an animation in the menu bar, illustrating the connection attempt and authentication process.

16 Once you're connected, click the icon again and choose Disconnect.

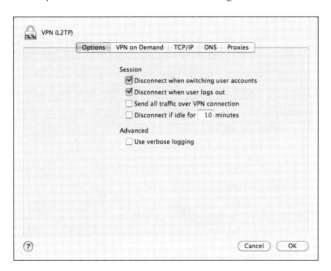

NOTE ▶ Customized VPN configurations can be distributed by administrators to users and conveniently imported by choosing Import Configurations from the Action pop-up menu in Network preferences.

Advanced Options

Clicking the Advanced button displays additional options in five tabs for administrators to further customize their VPN environments. These options vary based on individual infrastructure requirements:

▶ Options—This tab provides behavioral options for the VPN client, such as disconnect on switching users, logout, or disconnect based on idle timeout. You can also choose whether to send all traffic over the VPN connection and turn on verbose logging to help troubleshoot VPN connections.

▶ VPN on demand—This allows the addition of domain names that trigger and launch the VPN connection when the user attempts to access a resource in that domain.

▶ TCP/IP—This provides additional settings for IPv4 and IPv6 configuration, such as static addressing of the VPN client.

▶ DNS—This allows users and administrators to specify the DNS servers used during the VPN session.

▶ Proxies—This option permits users and administrators to specify by protocol or automatically the proxy server(s) used during the VPN session.

   NOTE ▶ When network traffic is allowed to flow over both VPN and local connections, the term split tunnel is often used to describe that connection. This method of VPN connection is discouraged because outside forces may penetrate a protected network via the client system when traffic to other networks is allowed and a system is connected to the VPN. Enabling all traffic over the VPN also presents potential liability issues to the VPN host network responsible for Internet usage policies, and may increase Internet and network bandwidth requirements due to added traffic from VPN clients.

Configuring the Cisco IPsec Mac OS X VPN Client

Some organizations utilize Cisco networking equipment to provide VPN access rather than establishing a dedicated VPN server. Cisco provides a myriad of VPN platforms that scale for small to enterprise organizational sizes. If your organization utilizes Cisco VPN equipment, you can configure its connectivity within Mac OS X v10.6 System Preferences without having to install any additional software.

To enable and configure a Mac OS X Cisco IPsec connection from System Preferences, follow these steps:

NOTE ▶ This exercise assumes that you can connect to a Cisco VPN device.

1 Open System Preferences and click the Network icon.

2 Near the bottom of the Network Interfaces window, click the Add (+) button.

3 From the Interface pop-up menu, choose VPN and choose a VPN type.

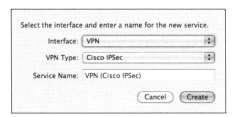

4 From the Service Name pop-up menu, choose IPsec.

The new VPN interface will appear in the window to the left with a Cisco IPsec designation.

5 In the Server Address field, enter the DNS name or IP address of the Cisco VPN device.

6   In the Account Name field, enter the account name provided by your network administrator for remote access through the VPN. For the purpose of this exercise, you can enter your current login name.

7   Click the Authentication Settings button to choose machine-based authentication options:

▶   Shared secret—Each remote user receives a predetermined password established by the VPN administrator. This is the least secure option.

▶   Certificate—The administrator issues a certificate to each client system, and it is installed in that system's keychain. The user or administrator selects that certificate when using this option.

▶   Group name (optional)—This setting logically groups computers for policy determinations or auditing purposes.

8   In the Shared Secret field, enter *apple*.

9   Select the "Show VPN status in menu bar" checkbox to display the VPN connection status in the user's menu bar.

10   Although you won't change the advanced options in this exercise, click Advanced to view the advanced options that are available in two separate tabs:

▶   DNS—This allows users and administrators to specify the DNS servers to be used during the VPN session.

▶   Proxies—This allows users and administrators to specify the proxy server(s) to be used during the VPN session by protocol or automatically.

11   Click Apply to save and apply the changes.

The VPN connection icon will appear in your menu bar. Your VPN connection is now created and ready to connect to the server using a shared secret for machine authentication.

12 Click the VPN connection icon, and select Connect to establish a connection to your Cisco IPsec VPN. When connected, you can click the menu bar icon again and select Disconnect to disable the connection.

Connecting to a VPN allows remote users on the road or around the world to access resources within their organizations as if they were actually sitting in the office. The only limitation they face is the speed of the network connection. Advances in broadband and wireless technologies have made VPN connectivity extremely robust, thereby contributing to the increase in telecommuting and the number of mobile workers.

Understanding iPhone VPN Connectivity

The iPhone OS contains a robust set of VPN client configurations similar to but not as extensive as those of Mac OS X. Many corporate iPhone users need to securely access corporate websites and information when they're away from their offices. The iPhone supports VPN connections over WiFi and cell phone networks using L2TP, PPTP, and Cisco IPsec connections.

Configuring the iPhone VPN Client

The iPhone OS provides an able remote commuting platform that allows users to read documents, spreadsheets, and other business-related information. Additionally, the iPhone OS provides a robust set of VPN options to facilitate secure remote access to corporate resources such as internal websites, email servers, and file sharing.

To enable and configure an iPhone VPN connection, do the following:

1   Touch the Settings Icon to open the iPhone's system settings.

2   In the System Settings main pane, touch General.

3 In the General pane, touch Network.

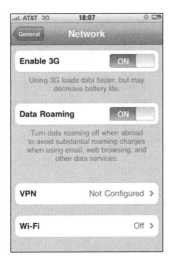

4 Touch the VPN entry, which is set to Not Configured by default.

5 Touch the Add VPN Configuration entry to open the VPN client configuration pane.

6 Touch the desired VPN connection type (L2TP, PPTP, or IPsec).

7   Enter a description, the VPN server's IP address or DNS name, and an account name in the appropriate fields.

8   Enter a password if desired. You could also leave the password blank; you'll be prompted for a password at connection time.

9   For both L2TP and PPTP connections, choose whether an RSA SecurID hard token will be used for authentication. If so, the password option is not needed and does not appear.

10 For an L2TP connection, enter the secret (or shared secret).

    The shared secret is a password provided to VPN clients by their administrators that authenticates the device (but not the user) to the VPN service.

11 For a PPTP connection, set the Encryption Level.

12 For L2TP or PPTP connections, set Send All Traffic to On or Off to choose whether all traffic will be sent through the VPN connection.

13 For an IPsec connection, turn Certificate Authentication on or off. (If you turn it on, you will need to select an installed certificate to use for authentication.) You can also specify a Group Name for the iPhone's machine group in the Cisco VPN Authentication database. Then enter the Secret (the shared secret).

    You can specify whether the VPN connection will utilize a proxy server once connected to the VPN by either clicking the Manual proxy setting at the bottom of the pane and then manually entering the proxy server's information, or clicking Auto to receive the proxy information from the VPN server.

14 Touch Save.

    The new VPN connection now appears in the Choose Configuration list.

    NOTE ▶ The iPhone supports multiple VPN connection settings, allowing users to connect to more than one VPN but not simultaneously. Only a single VPN connection can be engaged at one time.

15 If you created multiple VPN connection configurations, touch the configuration you want to open, and swipe the VPN switch to the On position to open the VPN.

The status indicator will display the state of the attempted or established connection.

After you've created a VPN setting, the Settings main pane will be updated with a VPN icon and switch to allow faster engaging of the VPN (so you don't have to navigate three additional configuration panes).

You can now simply swipe the VPN switch to the On position to utilize your previously specified settings and establish a secure connection to your organization's infrastructure.

The iPhone OS on the iPod Touch and iPhone devices allows secure VPN connections to corporate infrastructures, leveraging many of the same protocols and authentication options as the Mac OS X operating system. Though the configuration on the iPhone may be simple and intuitive, the encryption and VPN technology it provides are secure and robust.

Troubleshooting VPN Clients

The VPN client and VPN services require authentication and configuration information to operate properly. When a remote user attempts a connection to the VPN service, the entire process is recorded in a log file. When troubleshooting VPN clients, follow these steps:

▶ Examine the VPN client log file on OS X:

`/var/log/ppp.log.`

▶ Check the shared secret. The most common client-side error is an incorrect or mis-typed shared secret. Verify your shared secret with the VPN administrator and reenter it. A blank shared secret will provide the following log entry:

`L2TP: no user shared secret found.`

▶ Examine certificates. PKI certificates used for client system authentication are issued with validity dates and can be revoked by administrators. Check the log file for messages regarding the certificate, and check with the administrator regarding the validity, revocation or suspension of the certificate being used.

▶ Ensure domain uniqueness when utilizing VPN on demand to ensure that this feature will function properly. Each domain must have a unique entry.

▶ Verify that each VPN connection has available communication on the appropriate port for each protocol: ports 500, 1701, and 4500 UDP for L2TP; or port 1723 TCP for PPTP. Client computers behind a firewall that want a VPN connection must configure the firewall to allow traffic on UDP ports 500, 1701, and 4500 for L2TP; or on TCP port 1723 for PPTP. Ensure that the port corresponding to your configuration is available.

Troubleshooting VPN Servers

When troubleshooting VPN servers, take the following steps:

▶ Examine the Server Admin configuration for the VPN service and ensure that the service is configured and started. Enable verbose logging during troubleshooting for more detailed information or examine the VPN services log file on Mac OS X Server: /var/log/ppp/vpnd.log

▶ Verify the shared secret. When creating L2TP connections or utilizing RADIUS for authentication, care must be taken to ensure that shared secrets are entered correctly. Additionally, when changing the shared secret on Mac OS X Server, client machines utilizing the VPN will need to be provided with the new shared secret.

▶ Check the IP address range. Client systems connecting to the VPN service will be assigned an IP address from the VPN server. Care must be taken to ensure that:

  ▶ Addresses provided by the VPN service do not conflict with (overlap) addresses provided by DHCP, causing two or more machines to be issued the same IP address.

  ▶ Addresses provided by the VPN service are in the same network range as the desired services to which the client is attempting to connect or the appropriate routing entered in the Client Information setup tab.

▶ Verify port availability. When utilizing firewalls, either external or internal to Mac OS X Server, providing the VPN services, administrators must ensure that the required ports are available (port 1701 for L2TP or port 1723 for PPTP).

Using Other VPN Options

Several other options—besides L2TP, PPTP, and Cisco IPsec—are available in the marketplace for VPN connectivity:

SSH Tunnels

A secure shell tunnel consists of an encrypted tunnel created through an SSH connection. Administrators may set up SSH tunnels to tunnel unencrypted traffic over a network through an encrypted SSH channel. For example, Apple Mail can be configured to use SMTP, by default a nonencrypted protocol (unless deployed in conjunction with SSL). Due to the high volumes of spam traffic on many public venues, the standard SMTP port, TCP port 25, is commonly blocked, which prevents email from reaching these venues. To provide SMTP, you can establish an SSH tunnel that routes all SMTP traffic to the remote Mac OS X server through an encrypted SSH connection. Although the SMTP protocol itself contains no encryption, the encrypted SSH channel through which it travels is secure.

To set up an SSH tunnel, you must pass optional parameters from the command line in the Terminal application when executing the SSH connection to the remote server. The SSH client will forward a specified local port to a port on the remote Mac OS X server. After the SSH tunnel is established, you can connect to the specified local port to access the network service. The local port need not have the same port number as the remote port.

Here is an example of the command-line options to forward local port 2525 to port 25 on the remote host:

```
ssh -L 2525:mail.yourdomainname.com:25 yourusername@mail.yourdomainname.com
```

SSH tunnels can also be used to bypass firewall rules that prohibit specific ports. For example, if your organization prohibits access to Apple Screen Sharing (port 5901) by blocking the port with the firewall, you can create an SSH tunnel through the firewall to forward a specified port on your local machine to port 5901 on the remote server. Doing so allows you to provide remote assistance to a user on the internal network while you are on the road or working from home.

Meerkat, a shareware tool, allows you to more easily configure the tunnels or even trigger them automatically when an application is opened. Meerkat facilitates preconfiguration of the tunnels and automatic launching of tunnels when an application such as Apple Mail is opened.

SSL-VPN

This technology was developed to provide simplified configuration and deployment of VPN technology to larger user communities without requiring the installation or configuration of a VPN client on the remote system. SSL-VPNs display a webpage with a login screen, typically integrated with a directory service, RADIUS, or certificate authentication. After authentication, a Java applet, pushed down to the client, provides VPN connectivity tunneled through the SSL port (TCP port 443). Because most consumer broadband equipment and corporate- or enterprise-grade equipment allows port 443 traffic by default, no user or firewall configuration or intervention is required, which makes this a popular VPN technology. At the time of this writing, vendors that provide Mac OS X support include AEP Networks, Cisco, F5 Networks, Fortinet, Juniper, and SonicWall.

OpenVPN

This open source SSL-VPN provides site-to-site VPN connectivity for bridging networks between two or more remote offices. OpenVPN is available in a free community version or in a paid-support version. TunnelBlick, a freeware utility provided by Google, is commonly used with Mac OS X to provide a simplified interface for opening OpenVPN connections from the menu bar.

Security Considerations

Providing VPN services to users outside an organization's network infrastructure is not a task to be taken lightly. The process opens a gateway, though a secured one, to your organization's internal resources. When considering and deploying this technology, care and planning must be taken to utilize proper security culture among users. They should be clearly educated about the seriousness of opening a VPN connection, with emphasis on the need to protect credentials associated with those connections. Additionally, leveraging two-factor and/or certificate-based authentication increases the security profile of the VPN service provided, further thwarting potential attackers.

▶ When configuring client devices, the interface allows the administrator or user to save a user authentication password. While this may be attractive in terms of ease of use, it allows any individual who has gained login access to the device locally to connect to the VPN without further authentication.

▶ Use L2TP whenever possible. It is substantially more secure than PPTP, which utilizes older cryptographic strategies.

▶ Shared secrets for L2TP and Cisco IPsec provide a level of device authentication for the VPN administrator, but also pose an additional challenge. When a user leaves an organization, all devices must be updated with a new shared secret. This presents an administrative challenge in larger environments.

▶ Using certificates for device authentication is preferable to using shared secrets, as it allows the administrator to revoke an individual device's certificate. Mac OS X provides the Certificate Assistant application to allow administrators to establish a certificate authority and issue these certificates.

▶ When possible, limit the VPN to a single protocol. As a standard security practice, the fewer ports are exposed to the Internet, the less likelihood there is of penetration by threats.

▶ When using Send All Traffic, administrators should augment Internet access with a proxy server to enforce corporate Internet usage policies. This option may also increase the Internet bandwidth required at the host location, due to the added traffic from remote users. This option is preferred to the standard.

What You've Learned

▶ Mac OS X and iPhone each have a built-in VPN client that can connect to Mac OS X servers via L2TP and PPTP protocols, or to any Cisco IPsec VPN server.

▶ Mac OS X Server runs a service called `vpnd` that provides VPN services using either L2TP or PPTP.

▶ Mac OS X can provide on-demand VPN connections when accessing predefined remote domain resources.

▶ L2TP and PPTP offer various security options and levels of encryption to give administrators flexibility in providing secure VPN connectivity to their end users.

▶ The Mac OS X VPN client provides powerful and dynamic remote access for desktop and mobile Mac systems.

▶ The iPhone VPN client provides powerful and dynamic remote access over WiFi or cellular networks.

▶ The Mac OS X Server VPN service can be remotely enabled and disabled by administrators utilizing `serveradmin` commands.

References

For more information, see the following resources:

Administration Guides

Network Services Administration v10.6 Snow Leopard

Apple Training Series: Mac OS X Server Essentials v10.6 Student Guide

Books

Dreyer, Arek, and Greisler, Ben. *Apple Training Series: Mac OS X Server Essentials v10.6* (Peachpit Press, 2010).

Marczak, Edward R. *Apple Training Series: Mac OS X Advanced System Administration v10.5* (Peachpit Press, 2009).

URLs

http://docs.info.apple.com/article.html?artnum=106439.

www.iana.org/assignments/port-numbers

http://images.apple.com/server/macosx/docs/Network_Services_Admin_v10.6.pdf

The Internet Engineering Task Force (IETF) is working on formal standards for L2TP and IPsec user authentication. For more information, see www.ietf.org/ids.by.wg/ipsec.html.

Request for Comments (RFC) documents provide an overview of a protocol or service and details about how the protocol should behave.

If you're a novice server administrator, you'll probably find some of the background information in an RFC helpful.

If you're an experienced server administrator, you can find all technical details about a protocol in its RFC document.

You can search for RFC documents by number at the website www.ietf.org/rfc.html.

For L2TP description, see RFC 2661.

For PPTP description, see RFC 2637.

For Kerberos v5, see RFC 1510.

Chapter Review

1. When supporting Mac OS X v10.2 clients, which VPN protocol must be used?

2. True or false: Mac OS X's VPN client allows on-demand VPN connections that activate when resources for a particular domain are requested.

3. To which types of VPN services can Mac OS X and iPhone VPN clients connect?

4. Can Mac OS X Server provide Cisco IPsec as a VPN service?

5. When enabling a VPN service on Mac OS X Server, must you configure the Mac OS X or the external firewall?

6. What standard Mac OS X Server configuration command is used to enable or disable VPN services remotely?

Answers

1. The PPTP protocol must be used for Mac OS X v10.2 or earlier, Windows 95, and other non–L2TP-compatible systems.

2. True. A Mac OS X VPN client can be configured to initiate the VPN automatically when a particular domain resource is requested and the domain is specified in the VPN on-demand area.

3. Mac OS X v10.6 and iPhone VPN clients support connections to any L2TP-, PPTP-, or Cisco IPsec–compliant VPN server.

4. No, Cisco IPsec services are provided on OS X and iPhone VPN clients for connection to existing Cisco IPsec VPN servers, not to the OS X Server VPN service.

5. Yes. Administrators should ensure that the appropriate L2TP or PPTP ports are open and available to Mac OS X Server to enable the VPN service to operate properly.

6. The serveradmin command can be used to enable or disable the VPN service and check its status by issuing the following commands, respectively:

    ```
    sudo serveradmin start vpn
    sudo serveradmin stop vpn
    sudo serveradmin status vpn
    ```

6

Chapter **6**
Keys and Certificates

SSH (Secure Shell) provides secure remote access from one device to another and offers secure file transfer capabilities and network tunneling, powerful tools for administrators of Mac OS X.

Secure Sockets Layer (SSL) technology ensures encrypted data transfer for services such as iChat, iCal, and Mail. It does so by utilizing certificates to enable encrypted conversation (unlike SSH, which utilizes its own set of cryptography techniques based on the OpenSSH open source project.) While certificates are commonly associated with SSL technology, they can be used for many purposes and are part of the larger public key infrastructure (PKI).

A certificate is defined as an electronic document or file that identifies the owner of the certificate's PKI and organizational information. An independent certificate authority that is trusted by your browser or other software can publicly sign certificates. Your own server can also sign certificates (this is called self-signing), as can a trusted certificate authority that has provided its root public key, has your organization's approval, and is installed on your device.

In this chapter, you'll learn the basics of certificate technology based on PKI, along with several ways to create, install, configure, and use certificates.

Mac OS X uses the x.509 certificate standard, which specifies formats for public key certificates, certificate revocation lists, attribute certificates, and a certification path validation algorithm. Mac OS X Server can leverage certificates for several different purposes; the most common is the end-to-end encryption of data transferred by Mac OS X Server–provided services using Transport Layer Security (TLS) and SSL, such as:

▶ Server administration using Server Admin and Server preferences

▶ User and group management using Workgroup Manager

▶ Address Book service

▶ iCal service

▶ iChat service

▶ Mail service

▶ Open Directory

▶ Podcast Producer

▶ Remote Authentication Dial-in Service (RADIUS)

▶ SSH

▶ Virtual private network (VPN or L2TP)

▶ Web service

Certificates play a crucial role in providing the encryption and protection of the authentication technologies used in these services.

Using SSH and SSH Keys

SSH is a network protocol that establishes a secure channel between your computer and a remote computer. It uses cryptography to authenticate the remote computer. It also provides traffic encryption and data integrity between computers. Though it's an important topic for administrators to understand, be aware that SSH keys do not utilize x.509 certificates or PKI-based keys. SSH generates its own key materials.

SSH is frequently used to log in to a remote system to execute commands, but you can also use it to create a secure data tunnel, forwarding through an arbitrary TCP port. You can use SSH to transfer files using SFTP and SCP. By default, an SSH server uses the standard TCP port 22.

Mac OS X Server uses OpenSSH as the basis for its SSH tools. Notably, it provides portable home directory synchronization via SSH.

Key-Based SSH Login
Key-based authentication is helpful for such tasks as automating file transfers and backups and for creating failover scripts because it allows computers to communicate without requiring a user to enter a password.

Be aware that this approach has its risks. If the private key you generate is compromised, unauthorized users can access your computers. You must determine whether the advantages of key-based authentication are worth the dangers.

Generating a Key Pair for SSH
To set up key-based SSH on Mac OS X and Mac OS X Server, you must generate the keys that the two computers will use to establish and validate their identities. This doesn't authorize all users of the computer for SSH access. Keys must be generated for each user account.

1   In Terminal, verify that an .ssh folder exists in your home folder by entering `ls -ld ~/.ssh`.

2   If .ssh is listed in the output, go to step 3. If .ssh is not listed in the output, run `mkdir ~/.ssh`.

3   Change directories in the shell to the hidden directory by entering `cd ~/.ssh`.

4   Generate the public and private keys by entering `ssh-keygen -b 1024 -t rsa -f id_rsa -P ''`.

    The -b flag sets the length of the keys to 1024 bits, -t indicates to use the RSA hashing algorithm, -f sets the file name as `id_rsa`, and -P followed by two single quotes sets the private key password to be null. The null private key password allows for automated SSH connections.

NOTE ▶ Keys are equivalent to passwords, so you should keep them private and protected.

5   Copy the public key into the authorized key file by entering `cat id_rsa.pub >> authorized_keys2.`

6   Change the permissions of the private key by entering `chmod go-rwx ~/.ssh/.id_rsa.`

7   Set the permissions on the private key so that only the owner can change the file.

8   Copy the public key and the authorized key lists to the specified user's home folder on the remote computer by entering `scp authorized_keys username@remotemachine:~/.ssh/.`

9   To establish two-way communication between servers, repeat this process on the second computer.

The process must be repeated for each user who needs to open key-based SSH sessions. The root user is not excluded from this requirement. The home folder for the root user on Mac OS X Server is located at /var/root/.

Understanding Certificates and PKI Basics

PKI is one of the most pervasive infrastructure technologies, used in modern computing devices ranging from smart phones and computers to printer toner cartridges and e-passport applications. Originally theorized in 1976, PKI was first deployed in 1977, making it one of the most mature technologies still in use.

Comparing Symmetric and Asymmetric Encryption

Before delving into PKI and certificates, you should understand some basics about encryption and cryptographic terminology.

Symmetric encryption, the oldest type of encryption technology, is designed for a simple scenario in which two entities (typically individual users) need to share information without the threat of outside interception. The two entities share a common decoding mechanism, a key that is used to encrypt and decrypt messages.

While symmetric encryption is easy to process, it poses two primary problems. The first issue is how entity A can send the symmetric key to entity B so that the protected information can be transmitted. (Note that an entity in this context can be an individual, an organization, or a device.) The second issue is how entity B can know with certainty that the symmetric key has not itself been intercepted and compromised.

In modern-day e-commerce transactions, these two issues often arise because the entities are frequently unknown to one another prior to a transaction. So how can they encrypt data without previously transmitting a symmetric key?

During World War II, the German armed forces used an encryption device called Enigma to encrypt messages between submarines and other command and control facilities. Each party would have an *Enigma machine*, similar to a typewriter, with interchangeable rotors set according to the codebook in use during that period of time or for a specific message type. This is a good illustration of symmetric encryption. Both parties had to have the machine and the associated codebook in order to decipher the code received via radio transmission.

This shortfall of symmetric encryption is evident in modern-day e-commerce transactions, where the two entities may be unknown to one another prior to a desired transaction. How do they encrypt data without having previously sent each other a symmetric key?

Asymmetric encryption was theorized and developed to solve these two issues and provide additional functionality. Asymmetric encryption requires one entity to generate two cryptographic keys, a public key and a private key. As the name suggests, that entity or its governing organization should protect the private key.

The asymmetric encryption process is simple: Entity A contacts entity B and sends a public certificate that entity B can use to encrypt information sent to entity A. Entity A, which maintains the private key, is the only party that can decrypt messages encrypted with its public key. Further, the private key cannot be derived from the public key. This resolves the issue of encrypting data between two entities without the prior exchange of a symmetric key. It also resolves the threat of interception and discovery of a key, because only the private key can decrypt the encrypted information, and, in this example, only entity A maintains the private key, which it never transmits.

An advanced implementation of the asymmetric process is currently used around the world in e-passport technology. The individual's passport contains a smart card chip, which will authenticate the smart card reader's certificate credentials to ensure that the reader is an authorized device. This prevents unauthorized reading and counterfeiting of passport information.

Asymmetric encryption would seem like a good end-to-end solution for encrypting e-commerce transactions, but it's not ideal because it cats up too much time and too many resources. Asymmetric processing requires more processor power and more processing time, so it is less efficient than symmetric encryption for high-volume transactions such as e-commerce or telephony.

Understanding PKI

The most widely used asymmetric technology is PKI. It's helpful to understand how PKI works as well as the terminology it uses.

Public and Private Keys

Within PKI, public and private keys are created so that keys are mathematically linked: Data encrypted with one key can be decrypted only by the other key, and vice versa. The public key can and should be distributed to other communicating parties. However, the private key remains private to the owner, is not for distribution, and is often encrypted by a pass phrase.

Table 6-1 summarizes the capabilities of public and private keys.

Table 6-1   Comparison of Private and Public Keys

Public Keys Can:	Private Keys Can:
Verify the signature on a message that originated from a private key.	Digitally sign a message or certificate, indicating authenticity.
Encrypt messages so that only the holder of the corresponding private key can decrypt them.	Decrypt messages that were encrypted with the corresponding public key.

For example, if a user named Bob distributes his public key, user Alice can use it to encrypt and return a message. Only Bob may decrypt and read that message because only he has his private key. In this scenario, Alice still has to verify that the public key really came from Bob. If a malicious user posing as Bob sends Alice his own public key, he will still be unable to decrypt Alice's message because he doesn't have Bob's private key.

To verify that the public key comes from Bob, a trusted third party can verify its authenticity. In SSL parlance, this trusted third party is known as a certificate authority (CA). The CA signs Bob's public key with *its* private key, thereby creating a certificate. Anyone can verify the certificate's authenticity using the CA's public key.

Public Key Certificates

Public keys are often contained in certificates. One user can digitally sign messages using a private key, and another user can verify that signature using the public key in the signer's certificate, which was issued by a CA within the PKI.

A public key certificate (sometimes called an *identity certificate*) is a file in a specified format. Mac OS X utilizes the x.509 certificate standard, which specifies formats for public key certificates, certificate revocation lists, attribute certificates, and a certification path validation algorithm. Mac OS X Server can leverage certificates for several purposes. The most common purpose is the end-to-end encryption of data transferred by Mac OS X Server services that use TLS/SSL, such as iCal service, Mail service, Open Directory, and so on. The Mac OS X Server x.509 format contains:

▶ The public key half of a public-private key pair

▶ The key user's identity information, such as a person's user name and contact information

▶ A validity period that specifies how long the certificate can be trusted as accurate

▶ The URL of someone with the power to revoke the certificate (its *revocation center*)

▶ The digital signature of a CA or of the key user

Certificate Authorities

The CA signs and issues digital identity certificates claiming trust of the identified party. In this sense, it is a trusted third party between two transactions.

In x.509 systems, CAs are hierarchical in nature, with CAs referring to other CAs for certification, until you reach a *root authority.* The certificate hierarchy is always top-down, with a root authority's certificate at the top. A root authority is a CA that all of the interested parties trust, or enough of them so it doesn't require yet another trusted third party's authentication.

A CA can be a company that, for a fee, signs and issues a public key certificate to attest that the public key contained in the certificate belongs to its owner, as recorded in the certificate. In a sense, a CA is a digital notary public. A user applies to the CA for a certificate by providing identity and contact information, as well as the public key. A CA must check an applicant's identity so users can trust that the certificates it issues actually belong to the identified applicant.

Identities

Identities, in the context of Mac OS X Server's Certificate Assistant, consist of a signed certificate for both keys of a PKI pair. The keychain makes identities available to the services that support SSL.

Self-signed certificates are certificates that are digitally signed by the private key of the key pair included in the certificate. This is an alternative to having a CA sign the certificate. By self-signing a certificate, you are attesting that you are who you say you are. No trusted third party is involved.

Using TLS and SSL

SSL is a security solution initially developed by Netscape and later refined by the Internet Engineering Task Force (IETF).

> **NOTE ▶** SSL is a common term used for both SSL and TLS v1.0, which was based on the initial work on the SSL specification but solved several security issues and equates to SSL v3.1. In this chapter, we will refer to the combination as TLS/SSL rather than delving into the technical distinctions between the two. For more information, see the "References" section at the end of this chapter.

TLS/SSL provides an elegant combination of asymmetric and symmetric technologies. The initial conversation between client and server applications—for example, a web browser and an e-commerce web server—utilizes asymmetric encryption to establish a secure conversation in which a symmetric key (and additional information) is encrypted and provided for use between the two parties.

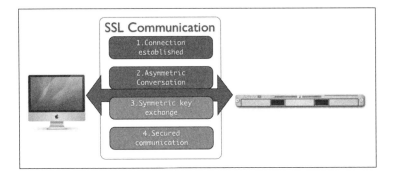

This provides robust security with good performance, but how does it enable the client application (the web browser) to verify the server's identity?

Web browsers and other client applications are often preloaded with a set of trusted certificates provided by several manufacturers (including Apple.) This is commonly referred to as WebTrust, and provides a mechanism by which a party seeking to set up an e-commerce site or other secure service can generate and submit a certificate signing request (CSR) to one of these third parties, which verifies the identity of the requestor and signs the certificate.

The administrator installs this signed certificate onto the server providing the service. When initiating a conversation with that server and service, the client application will receive this certificate, recognize the signature as validly issued by one of its trusted "root" CAs, and proceed with the encryption process without further user intervention.

Organizations are not restricted to using third-party signed certificates. Any organization can create and self-sign its own certificate for use in TLS/SSL communications. There is no difference in the encryption used for a self-signed versus a third-party–signed certificate, but when providing services to unknown entities, an administrator cannot be assured that the unknown entity will trust the self-signed certificate because no independent identity verification has been performed. Therefore a user warning will be displayed.

To avoid this error message for organizational users connecting to their internal resources, administrators can install the root certificate or an appropriate leaf anchor on trusted client systems, which will eliminate this warning message. Details on this process are provided in the "Managing Certificates in the Command Line" section of this chapter.

PKI can also provide additional functionality. CAs publish certificate revocation lists (CRLs) or certificate status online via the online certificate status protocol (OCSP). This information is contained in the certificate and allows client software to validate certificate status prior to conducting encryption or other transactions that rely on a specific certificate. Revocation checking within Mac OS X can be configured to attempt to validate or to require validation of certificates each time they are used. This option is disabled by default and can be enabled by opening Keychain Access > Preferences, clicking the Certificates tab, and specifying OCSP and CRL policies for that client.

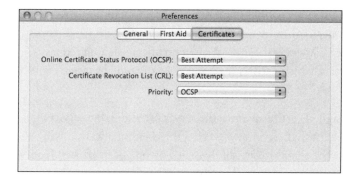

NOTE ▶ Mac OS X Server does not provide CRL or OCSP services.

A commercial product is available from Axway, formerly Tumbleweed (www.axway. com/products-solutions/email-identity-security/identity-security/server-validator).

An open-source OCSP and CA service for Mac OS X is available from www.ejbca.org.

Using Digital Signing

Certificates are commonly used for digital signing, a process that authenticates electronic data using one of several hashing functions. A hashing function takes a block of data, such as a file, and returns a fixed-size hash value. If the data in the file has been modified, the hash function will not return the same value, indicating that the file has changed. Using a combination of this hashing function and certificates, an author can sign a piece of data, such as a PDF or even an application, and the recipient can verify this signature to ensure that the data has not been modified.

Developers commonly use this technology to sign their applications so that users downloading them can be sure they have not been tampered with after creation. Apple requires iPhone developers to sign their applications prior to App Store submission. The process for signing and verification is illustrated in the following figure.

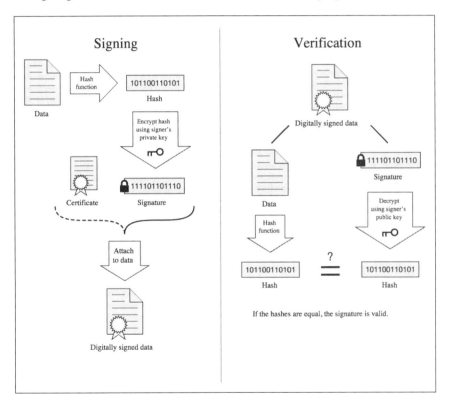

Digital signing also allows users to sign email conversations and common document formats such as PDF, OpenOffice, Microsoft Office, and many others. Utilizing these digital signatures provides the recipient with proof positive that the document or email has arrived unaltered.

NOTE ▶ When using PKI for email or other encryption that requires archival or retrieval at a later time (unlike the packet transmissions of a TLS/SSL session), key management policies should be implemented to protect and save public and private keys to provide for verification of signing or decryption of this information at a later time. Without those keys, encrypted emails and other data cannot be decrypted, nor can digital signatures be verified.

Creating Certificates

Mac OS X systems provide several methods for creating, requesting, and installing certificates. In Mac OS X, you can use Certificate Assistant (which can be opened from the Keychain Access application or /System/Library/CoreServices) to create a new CA, request a certificate from another CA, or sign certificates requested by others. In Mac OS X Server, you can create or request certificates using the Server Admin application. Additionally, command-line tools (security, certtool, and OpenSSL) are available to delete, create, or install certificates and identities on Mac OS X.

Using Certificate Assistant

Server Admin uses Certificate Manager to display certificates and open Certificate Assistant to help you create, use, and maintain identities for SSL-enabled services. Certificate Assistant integrates SSL certificate management in Mac OS X Server for all services that support certificate use.

Certificate Assistant helps create self-signed certificates and CSRs to obtain a certificate signed by a CA. Services that support SSL can access either type of certificate.

Identities that were previously created and stored in SSL files can also be imported into Certificate Assistant, where they are accessible to all services that support SSL. Certificates are stored in the system keychain and located in /Library/Keychains/System.keychain.

Certificate Manager displays the following for each certificate:

▶ The domain name for which the certificate was issued.

▶ Its dates of validity.

▶ Its signing authority, such as the CA entity. If the certificate is self-signed, it reads "Self-Signed."

NOTE ▶ Certificate Manager in Server Admin does not allow you to sign and issue certificates as a CA or a root authority. However, you can perform these functions with Certificate Assistant (see "Creating a CA Using Certificate Assistant" later in this chapter).

When OS X Server is installed, it creates a self-signed certificate, which is initially not trusted, as shown by the red X and the text near the certificate icon. As shown in the lower pane, the certificate information contains the name of the certificate, the authority that signed it (self-signed, in this example), the expiration date, and the trust status. You can view additional information by clicking the Details disclosure triangle.

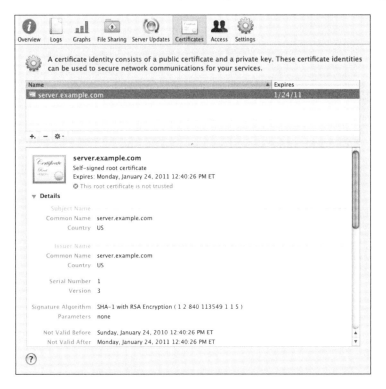

To trust this or other self-signed or intermediate-trusted certificates, you can drag the certificate icon (with the certificate selected) from the lower pane to the desktop and double-click it. Doing so will open Keychain Access and install the certificate. (You may have to authenticate to perform this step.) In the following figure, the certificate is still not trusted, as designated by the red X near the certificate icon on the left.

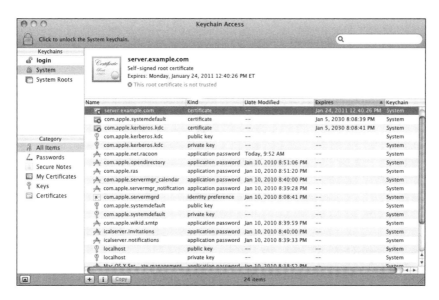

Double-click the certificate, click the trust disclosure triangle, and, from the SSL pop-up menu, select Always Trust. You will be asked to authenticate. Once refreshed, Keychain Access and Server Admin will now reflect the new status of the certificate with a blue plus (+) icon.

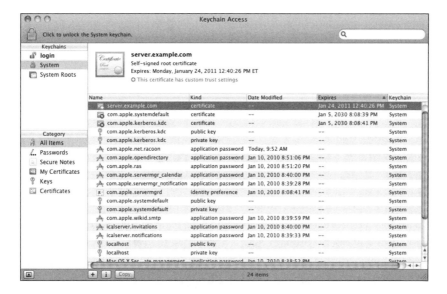

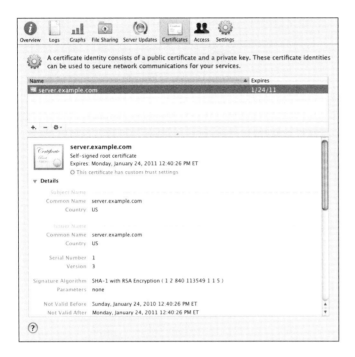

Requesting a Certificate from a CA

Certificate Assistant can help you create a CSR to send to your designated CA. To request a signed certificate, follow these steps:

1 Open Server Admin.

2 In the Servers list, select the server for which you are requesting a certificate, and click Certificates.

3 Click the certificate you want to have signed. Ensure that its DNS name matches the DNS name that client applications will use to engage the service or application.

If the DNS name for the service you are seeking to protect (if different from the server's primary DNS) is not available, you must create a self-signed certificate prior to requesting the signature. See "Creating Self-Signed Certificates" later in this chapter.

4 At the lower left of the certificate list, click the Action button.

5 Choose Generate Certificate Signing Request (CSR).

A dialog showing the CSR request will appear.

6 Click Save to save the CSR request file.

From this point, you will need to follow your CA's directions for uploading or transmitting the request to be signed. These will differ depending on the CA you are utilizing.

7 After you have received the corresponding reply from your CA, click the certificate you had signed by the third party. Then click the Action button again and select "Replace certificate with signed or renewed certificate." Paste the received files into the dialog to complete the process.

Creating a CSR Request from the Command Line

A few powerful command-line tools (`security`, `systemkeychain`, and `certtool`) give you significant control over the creation, request, and management of user and system credentials.

Among those older commands that are still quite helpful when generating and verifing a
CSR or generating raw keys is `certtool` (/usr/bin/certtool).

To create a CSR from the command line, issue the `certtool` command with r to indicate a
request, and then add a filename location where the request file will be created:

```
certtool r ~/Desktop/mycsrrequest.csr
```

The command line will then prompt you for several types of information, starting with
key pair options, information required for a certificate request such as common name,
email contact information, and so on. When completed, the indicated file will contain the
CSR request, which can be sent to a CA for verification and signing.

At the same time that Certificate Assistant creates the self-signed certificate, it generates
the CSR. The CSR is not stored in the keychain, but is written to disk in /etc/certificates/
cert.common.name.tld.csr where common.name.tld is the common name of the certificate that was issued.

Creating Self-Signed Certificates

A self-signed certificate is generated at server setup. Although that certificate is available
for use, you may want to customize it, so you should create a new, self-signed certificate.
This is especially important if you plan to have a CA sign your certificate.

When you create a self-signed certificate, Certificate Assistant creates a public-private key
pair in the system keychain with the key size specified (512 to 2048 bits). It then creates
the corresponding self-signed certificate.

If you're using a self-signed certificate, consider using an intermediate trust for it and
importing the certificate into the system keychain on all client computers (if you have
control of those computers).

1   In Server Admin, select the server with services that support SSL.

2   Click Certificates.

3   Click the Add (+) button and choose "Create a Certificate Identity."

Certificate Assistant opens, populated with the information necessary to generate the certificate.

4   If you override the defaults, choose "Let me override defaults" and follow the onscreen instructions.

5   When finished, click Continue.

6   Confirm the certificate creation by clicking Continue.

Certificate Assistant generates a key pair and a certificate. It encrypts the files with a random pass phrase, puts the pass phrase in the system keychain, and saves the resulting PEM files in /etc/certificates/.

Renewing an Expiring Certificate

Certificates have an expiration date and must be renewed periodically. Renewing a certificate is the same as replacing a certificate with a newly generated certificate that has an updated expiration date.

1   Request a new certificate from the CA. If you are your own CA, create one using your root certificate.

2   In Server Admin in the Servers list, select the server that has the expiring certificate.

3   Click Certificates.

4   Select the certificate identity to renew.

5   Click the Action button and select "Replace Certificate with Signed or Renewed Certificate."

6   Drag the renewed certificate to the sheet.

7   Click Replace Certificate.

Replacing an Existing Certificate

If you change the DNS name of the server or any virtual hosts on the server, you must replace an existing certificate with an updated one.

1   Request a certificate from the CA. If you are your own CA, create one using your own root certificate.

2   In Server Admin in the Servers list, select the server that has the expiring certificate.

3   Click Certificates.

4   Select the certificate identity to replace.

5   Click the Action button, and select "Replace Certificate with Signed or Renewed Certificate."

6   Drag the replacement certificate to the sheet.

7   Click Replace Certificate.

NOTE ▶ After you add a certificate signature, you can't edit the certificate. You must replace it with one generated from the same private key. This is new behavior in Mac OS X v10.6.

Managing Certificates in the Command Line

To modify certificates in the command line, you have several choices of command-line utilities. Because certificates are stored in keychains, keychain manipulation utilities such as `security` and `systemkeychain` can manipulate certificates, as well as other keychain entries. Also, the older `certtool` exists as a certificate-specific utility that manipulates keychains to import certificates, create key pairs, create certificates, and create CSRs.

The `security` tool is capable of importing, exporting, and verifying certificates in keychains. Additionally, it can manage certificate trust anchors. For example, to import a Privacy Enhanced Mail (PEM) certificate into the current user's default keychain, use the `security import` command:

```
$ security import ~/mailcert.pem -f pem
```

The systemkeychain command specifically manipulates the system keychain. This is significant because system identities are stored in the active system keychain. For example, to create a new, empty keychain and establish it as the primary system keychain, issue the following command:

```
# systemkeychain -C
```

The system automatically handles the unlocking of the designated system keychain. If a password is specified after the -C switch, that password can unlock the keychain; otherwise, the keychain has no password, and only the system can unlock it.

The security command-line tool can be used for a variety of certificate- and identity-related functions. For example, to import the certificate certificate.pem into the current user's mycerts keychain file, use this command:

```
$ security import certificate.pem -k ~/Library/Keychains/mycerts
```

The security import command specifies an import operation, and the -k option specifies the keychain to operate on. For more information on command-line certificate manipulation, see the respective man page for each utility.

Using Certificates with Services

When you create a certificate, your intention is to use it for some service or function, such as securing iCal server communications, Mail communications, web server communications, iChat communications, and so on. You can configure a certificate for a specific service in Server Admin by performing a few simple steps.

Enabling SSL for Services

To start, open Server Admin and add the web, iChat, and iCal services to your list of services by clicking each server's name, clicking the service tab, and selecting the checkbox (if it's not already selected) for each service name.

1   In the left pane of Server Admin, select the web service.

2   In the toolbar, click the Sites icon.

3   Select the site for which you would like to enable security.

4   Click the Security tab.

5   Select the Enable Secure Sockets Layer (SSL) checkbox to enable SSL encryption.

A dialog message will appear stating that the port number will automatically change from port 80 to port 443, which is standard functionality. Secure web traffic is executed on port 443, not port 80.

6   Select one of the previously created certificates that match the DNS name you will use to access the website.

7   In Server Admin, click Save.

As seen in the following figure, the server in this example is server.example.com, for which we created a self-signed certificate earlier. Then we created a CSR, sent it to a CA, had it signed, and replaced the self-signed certificate with the CA-signed certificate. Now we are utilizing that certificate for the web service. A single certificate can be utilized for multiple services as long as the DNS name matches the one clients use for access.

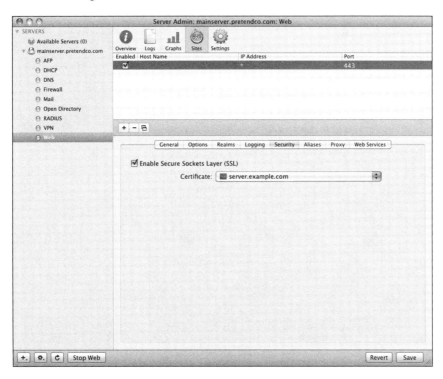

Mail Service

To enable secure communications for the Mail service, you have additional considerations. The Mail service consists of multiple protocols (POP, IMAP, SMTP), and administrators must decide whether to secure inbound and/or outbound communications. Once this policy is established, follow these steps to enable secure SSL communications for inbound and outbound communications with the Mail service.

1   In the left pane of Server Admin, select the Mail service.

2   Click the Advanced tab.

3   In the Advanced pane, click the Security tab.

4   Toward the bottom of the window, from the pop-up menu, select Use, Don't Use, or Require SSL Communications for IMAP/POP and for SMTP. Then, in the pop-up menu next to that selection, choose the certificate to use for securing the communication. Once again, this certificate should match the DNS name that clients will use to connect to the Mail service (it's server.example.com here).

5   In Server Admin, click Save.

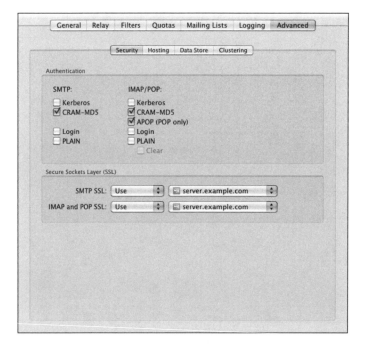

iCal Service

To enable SSL secured communications for the iCal service, do the following:

1   In the left pane of Server Admin, select the iCal service.

2   In the toolbar, click the Settings icon.

3   Click the Authentication tab.

4   From the SSL pop-up menu, choose Use.

5   From the next pop-up menu, choose the certificate that matches the DNS name clients use to connect to the iCal service.

6   Click Save.

    Note that the port number for SSL communications is different than it is for nonsecure communications.

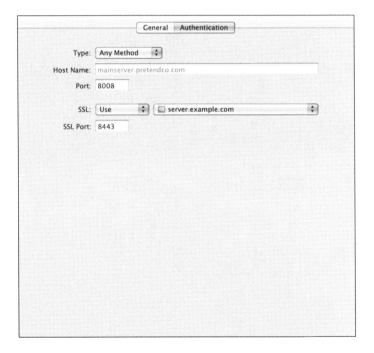

iChat Service

iChat can also utilize SSL to encrypt messaging traffic. The process is similar to that for iCal.

1   In the left pane of Server Admin, select the iChat service.

2   In the toolbar, click the Settings icon.

3   Click the General tab.

4   Select the SSL certificate to utilize for securing communications, which should match the DNS name that clients will use to connect their iChat software to the server.

5   Click Save.

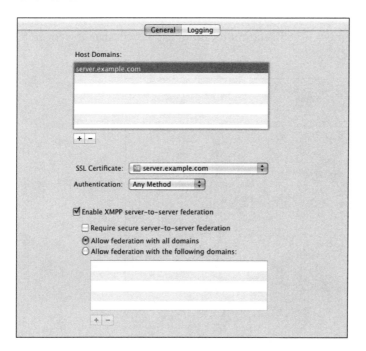

Address Book Service

To enable SSL for the Address Book service, do the following:

1   In the left pane of Server Admin, select the Address Book service.

2   In the toolbar, click the Settings icon.

3   Click the Authentication tab.

4   Click the Security tab.

5   From the SSL pop-up menu, choose SSL encryption.

    Notice that secure communications for the Address Book service take place on a separate port.

6   In the pop-up menu, choose one of the previously created certificates that match the DNS name clients will use to access the website.

7   Click Save.

Creating a CA to Sign Certificates

If your server must communicate using SSL with external computers that you do not control, it is best to purchase SSL certificates from a well-known CA. Once you have obtained the certificates, configuring the services is the same, whether you purchased the certificates from a vendor or signed them with your own CA.

If you are setting up an internal network and only need to encrypt local traffic, set up a CA to sign SSL certificates for the internal network. While the security is only as good as the CA's, in many cases this is sufficient to enable encrypted communication between a web or mail server and its clients.

The basic steps to set up an internal SSL-encrypted network are as follows:

▶   Create a CA. You can use either Certificate Assistant or the command line.

▶   Use the CA to sign the certificates that the servers will use.

▶   Distribute the CA certificates to client systems.

Creating a CA Using Certificate Assistant

Certificate Assistant in Mac OS X v10.6 helps administrators create a CA and provide some basic functionality within a graphical interface. In this exercise, you will create a CA and a self-signed certificate that can be used for several Mac OS X Server–provided services.

1   While in Finder, press Command-Shift-U to open the Utilities folder (a subfolder of your Applications folder).

2   Open Keychain Access.

3   Choose Keychain Access > Certificate Assistant > Create a Certificate Authority.

The Certificate Assistant application opens and prompts you for basic information about the CA you want to create.

4   Enter the name of the CA in the Name field.

5   Select Self-Signed Root CA from the Identity Type pop-up menu.

6   Select SSL Server from the User Certificate pop-up menu.

7   Select the "Make this the default CA" checkbox.

8   Enter an email address for the administrator who will receive CA requests in the Email From field.

9   Click Continue.

After the presentation of an intermediate screen indicating the generation of the required keys, you will see the final information screen pictured below. It indicates that the process is complete and allows you to perform certificate administration functions.

Creating a CA from the Command Line

Creating a CA with Certificate Assistant is the preferred and best practice. However, in some situations the command-line tools enable you to automate and script functionality that is not available using Certificate Assistant.

Again, it is critical that you perform this procedure on a secure computer. The security of your identities, most notably the private key, depends upon the security of the CA. Make sure the computer is physically secure and not connected to any network.

To create the CA using the openssl command, do the following:

1   In Terminal, enter the following commands to create a certificate directory:

```
$ cd /usr/share
$ sudo mkdir certs
$ cd certs
```

2   Generate a key pair using the `openssl` command:

```
$ sudo openssl genrsa -des3 -out ca.key 2048
```

This command generates a Triple Data Encryption Standard–encrypted (TripleDES) RSA private key pair named `ca.key` with a key length of 2048 bits. On creating the key, OpenSSL asks for a pass phrase for it. Use a strong pass phrase rather than a single-word password, and keep it secure. If this pass phrase and ultimately the private key are compromised, it undermines the security of your entire CA.

Storing the CA Private Key

Remember, the CA private key should remain *private*. For added security, you can store the keychain containing the private key on removable media to ensure that the key is unavailable when connected to the network.

Signing a Newly Created CA

After you've created the key pair, the public key is signed to create an SSL certificate ready for distribution to other systems. Later, when you sign other server certificates using your CA private key, any client can use the CA's SSL certificate (containing its public key) to verify those signatures. When a CA signs a server's certificate with its private key, it means that it is vouching for the authenticity of those certificates. Anyone who can trust the CA can trust any certificate that CA signs.

To sign the newly created CA's public key to produce a certificate for distribution, use this command:

```
$ sudo openssl req -new -x509 -days 365 -key ca.key -out ca.crt
```

When prompted, enter a strong pass phrase for the key, as well as filling out these fields:

► Country name
► Organizational unit
► State or province name
► Common name
► Locality name (city)

- ▶ Email address
- ▶ Organization name

Fill out these fields as accurately as possible; leave blank those that do not apply. You must fill in at least one field.

This command sequence creates a self-signed certificate named ca.crt using the key in ca.key, which is valid for a year (365 days). You can set the limit for a longer period of time, but that degrades your security, just as changing passwords infrequently does. You must find a balance between convenience and security.

Creating Folders and Files for SSL

When signing certificates, SSL looks for keys and related information in directories that are specified in its configuration file, openssl.cnf, found in /System/Library/OpenSSL/.

To create the directories and files where SSL expects to find them by default, use these commands:

```
$ cd /usr/share/certs
$ sudo -s
$ mkdir -p demoCA/private
$ cp ca.key demoCA/private/cakey.pem
$ cp ca.crt demoCA/cacert.pem
$ mkdir demoCA/newcerts
$ touch demoCA/index.txt
$ echo "01" > demoCA/serial
```

Now the CA is ready to sign certificates for servers, enabling encrypted communication between servers and clients.

Creating Self-Signed Certificates from the Command Line

In many situations, a self-signed certificate is sufficient. Generating a self-signed certificate from the command line has been greatly simplified by the `certtool` command, which can create a 2048-bit private key, public key, and certificate, and make that certificate immediately available to services configured with Server Admin.

1   Create the private key on the server for which you want a self-signed certificate with the following `certtool` command:

    ```
    sudo certtool C mainserver.pretendco.com u
    ```

2   Replace mainserver.pretendco.com with the DNS name for the certificate you want to create.

    The u option also generates the public-private key pair, and the certificate immediately becomes available in Server Admin.

Refresh Certificate Assistant in Server Admin. The certificate will appear, and other services on that server can use it.

Distributing Server Certificates Using Keychain Access

When utilizing self-signed certificates, client systems must install those certificates to avoid security messages. This can be done using Keychain Access or the command line.

1   Copy the self-signed CA certificate (the ca.crt file) onto each client computer.

    It's preferable to distribute this using nonrewritable media, such as a CD-R, to protect the certificate from corruption.

2   Open the Keychain Access tool by double-clicking the ca.crt icon that appears where you copied the certificate onto the client computer.

3   Drag the certificate to the system keychain using Keychain Access. Authenticate as an administrator, if requested.

4   Double-click the certificate to view the certificate details. In the Details window, click the Trust disclosure triangle.

5   From the "When using this certificate" pop-up menu, choose Always Trust.

    You have now added trust to this certificate, regardless of who signed it.

Distributing Server Certificates Using the Command Line

To distribute certificates to client computers using the command line, do the following:

1   Copy the certificate to the target client computer.

2   Execute this command, first replacing *<certificate>* with the file path to the certificate.

```
sudo /usr/bin/security add-trusted-cert -d -k /Library/Keychains/System. keychain
<certificate>
```

You can use the security tool to save and restore trust settings as well. For more information on using the `security` command-line tool, see the security `man` page.

Using Certificate Assistant to Create an SSL Certificate

Now that you have a valid CA creating certificates for your web and other services, you can see that utilizing the CA is relatively easy. To create the CA certificate, this book will not repeat the entire sequence of operation but rather will focus on the steps specific to the creation of an SSL server leaf certificate.

1   From Keychain Access, choose Keychain Access > Certificate Assistant > Create a Certificate.

2   Select Leaf Certificate from the Identity Type pop-up menu.

3   Select SSL Server from the Certificate Type pop-up menu.

4   Click Continue.

5   From the Issuer list, select the CA certificate that you created in the "Creating a CA Using Certificate Assistant" section.

6   Click Continue.

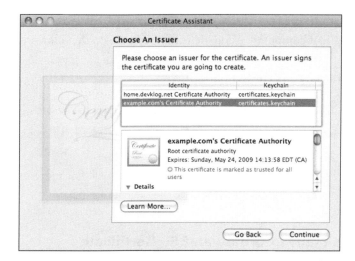

The assistant will display an intermediate screen as it generates the public-private key pair and the certificate, and then installs them into the keychain.

You can now install this certificate onto Mac OS X Server and use it for web, iChat, iCal, Open Directory, or any number of services.

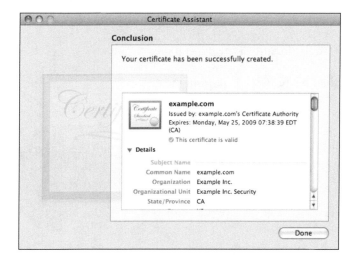

Administrators typically create the CA once on a standalone computer, preferably one that is not connected to a network, and then issue and copy the SSL certificates as needed while deploying servers or additional services. You want to keep this computer off the network for security. If someone acquires your root keys or can access your CA computer, he or she can issue certificates all day long and create bogus websites with security certificates in your organization's name.

Signing and Encrypting Email

Today's computing environment lends itself well to providing secure remote access and communications, but how do organizations verify that email actually originated with the stated sender and, more important, ensure that proprietary or confidential information is not intercepted intentionally or accidentally?

Apple Mail, in conjunction with Keychain Access and PKI certificates, provides a simple solution to this common issue. Organizations can establish their own CA and issue their users certificates with appropriate validity periods that match organizational policies. These certificates can be used to digitally sign and encrypt email communications within an organization or with other trusted organizations. To enable this functionality, do the following:

1   First establish a CA using Certificate Assistant and specify S/MIME (Email) as in the User Certificate in the following figure.

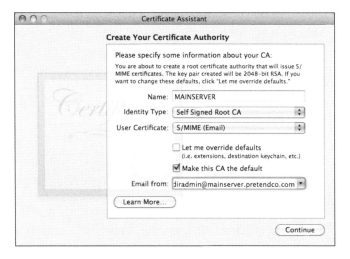

2   Click Continue to accept the defaults and create the CA. This creates a directory that you can access by clicking Show Certificate Authority on the final page.

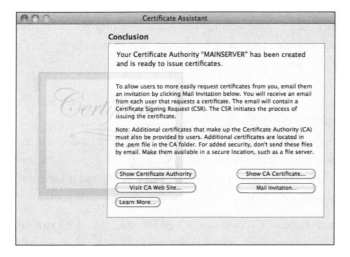

3   Click Show Certificate Authority to prompt the administrator with a certificate request form. Enter the email address for the individual to whom you are assigning the certificate, and select "Emailed to CA" to email the certificate to the email address specified during setup of the CA. You can also choose to save the request to disk and then transfer the file manually.

The administrator will receive an email with the request, and will double-click the attachment to open the signing pane. This signs the certificate request and sends the user an email message regarding the certificate, which is attached.

4   Double-click the attachment and provide credentials on the client system to install the certificate and provide the option to make the issuing CA the default CA for that client.

5   After installation, reopen Mail to see the two new buttons in the Send Mail pane.

The dimmed lock button on the left is the button for enabling encryption. It will become active after entry of a recipient email for which the sender has a valid encryption certificate. Remember that the sender uses the recipient's public key to encrypt the email sent to that recipient. The recipient's private key is the only key that can decrypt that email.

The check-within-the-starburst button is the digital signing option. As part of a digital signature, the sender provides his or her public certificate to enable the recipient to verify the signature.

Apple Mail will apply the options selected and automatically sign or encrypt an email when these options are selected.

NOTE ▶ When utilizing PKI for email or other encryption that requires later archiving or retrieval (unlike the packet transmissions of an TLS/SSL session), key management policies should be implemented to protect and save public-private key pairs to provide for later signature verification or decryption of this information. Without those keys, encrypted emails and other content cannot be decrypted, nor can digital signatures be verified.

S/MIME, used for email and other digital signing tasks, requires that the local part of the RFC822Name (everything to the left of the @ in an email address) be an exact, case-sensitive match for the email address that the message is sent from (for signing) or to (for encryption.) If these addresses do not match, Mac OS X will not sign or allow you to encrypt the message.

Certificates and PKI can be used for a myriad of other functions within Mac OS X—too extensive to enumerate in this book. These purposes include smart card authentication, smart card storage of certificates, SSL client authentication certificates for single sign-on to websites and web applications, digital document signing, application signing, and encryption of other types of services.

Troubleshooting Certificates

The most common error encountered when working with certificates is the expiration of a certificate that is currently in use. All certificates are issued with validity dates, typically encompassing a period of one year, after which time the certificate must be renewed or replaced with a new certificate.

An expired or revoked certificate will appear with a red warning message in both Certificate Assistant and Keychain Access. Double-clicking the certificate will display whether it has expired or been revoked.

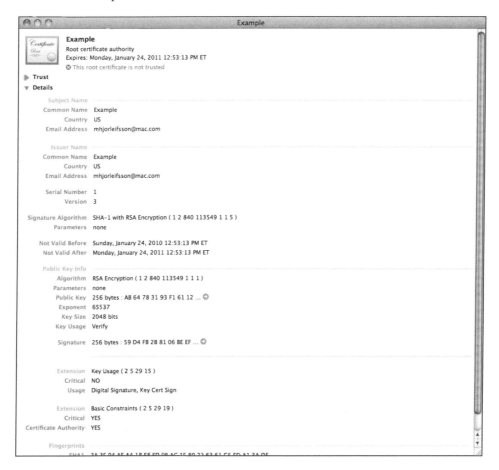

File permissions on CA certificates and key files raise the other common issues that arise in working with certificates. CA private keys should be readable only by an administrator, public keys only by the services that require them. Mac OS X graphical tools such as Server Admin and Certificate Assistant handle file permissions for the administrator and can prevent potential issues when properly used.

Installation of a certificate or trusted chain of certificates on a client machine will prevent the security notifications often associated with self-signed certificates. While it's not an error, end users commonly see the security message as daunting and typically contact help desk personnel. To avoid this, ensure that valid service and personal certificates are properly installed on client systems and migrated when systems are replaced. You can verify a computer's trust chain by selecting the System Roots keychain in Keychain Access.

Using 802.1x Network Authentication

The IEEE 802.1x standard was established to provide a framework for network access control (NAC). 802.1x offers administrators a means of restricting network access to authorized users and devices while leveraging existing authentication mechanisms like Open Directory, RADIUS, Active Directory, and certificates. A simple way to visualize the concept of 802.1x is as a highway, where the user attempting to get on the highway (your network) is stopped at the on-ramp by a police officer (802.1x), and is not allowed access until that officer authenticates him or her.

802.1x is commonly used for wireless implementations but can also be deployed on wired networks and is commonly used at large educational institutions, hotels, and public sector and enterprise organizations. Apple has provided a set of client- and server-side tools to provide client access to 802.1x networks and to activate 802.1x functionality and authentication using AirPort Express and Extreme wireless access points.

Among the inherent benefits of 802.1x is the elimination of unauthenticated access to the actual network, which further protects the resources on that network. Additionally, 802.1x prevents *hubbing*, whereby a user will connect an unauthorized network hub or switch to a single authorized port to add devices to the network. Certain implementations of 802.1x also provide for dynamic virtual LAN capabilities, whereby a user is placed in a holding network until an end-point management tool or other management software can scan his system, and then authenticate it prior to network access. After being cleared, the user is assigned to a specific virtual LAN based on group membership in a directory or RADIUS server. Not all wireless or wired network equipment is compatible with 802.1x. Administrators may need to verify compatibility with the manufacturers of their specific equipment.

The process of 802.1x authentication requires that the client system have a service or software called a *supplicant,* used for negotiation and authentication. When the user connects to a wireless or wired network, the authenticator software in the switch or access point blocks the connection to the network. A security negotiation between supplicant and authenticator is established, and an 802.1x session is created.

The supplicant provides its authentication information to the authenticator, which proxies the information to an authentication server. The authentication server is usually a RADIUS server that may or may not be integrated with the accounts in a directory service such as Open Directory or Active Directory. These steps are commonly referred to as the preauthentication process. After the authentication server authenticates the client, the server initiates the authentication process.

This sends pairwise master keys (PMKs) to the authenticator, which the authenticator in turn proxies to the authenticated client. A four-way handshake between the client and authenticator determines the keys for that session and, once these are established, the client is granted access to the network. These two sets of processes are illustrated in the following diagrams.

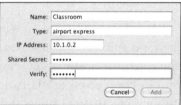

802.1x uses the Extensible Authentication Protocol (EAP) for the previous steps, which can leverage one of several published standards including:

▶ Passwords and certificates

  EAP-TLS (Transport Layer Security)

  EAP-TTLS (Tunneled Transport Layer Security)

  PEAP (Protected EAP)

▶ Cisco published standards

  LEAP (Lightweight EAP)—the original standard, replaced with others

  EAP-FAST (Flexible Authentication via Secure Tunnel)

  EAP-SIM (Subscriber Identity Module)—used for GSM networks and leverages telco authentication technology

▶ For wired networks only

EAP-MD5 (Message Digest Algorithm)

An administrator must take several issues into account when deploying 802.1x. Because the client system has no DNS (it's not yet actually on the network), the supplicant cannot authenticate the server's certificate to its DNS name, so the certificate has to be pre-validated once by an administrator or user. On wireless networks, there is intentionally no correlation between SSID name and RADIUS or domain information, to keep the network obscured from prying eyes. The client system must explicitly trust the server's certificate or a certificate of an issuing authority for that server higher in the trust chain to function properly with 802.1x. A client system can be set up to trust a root CA, but this is not recommended for third-party–signed certificates (such as Verisign). A user from another company that also has a Verisign-signed certificate could gain access to your network because you have trusted the Verisign root, not your intermediate or internal CA.

Understanding 802.1x Implementation in Mac OS X

Apple has implemented 802.1x supplicant technologies into the Mac OS X operating systems and provides an Open Directory–integrated RADIUS server to allow Mac OS X Server to provide 802.1x authentication to AirPort Express, AirPort Extreme, and other standards-based wired and wireless access points.

Mac OS X Server's 802.1x implementation leverages the FreeRADIUS open-source project. Server Admin makes certain configuration assumptions to provide a drastically simplified configuration compared to the configuration file editing required on other UNIX 3.x–compliant operating systems. Command-line configuration is possible using the `radiusconfig` command or by directly editing the configuration (.conf) files, though this is strongly discouraged, due to its complexity.

Mac OS X's supplicant provides four modes of operation to facilitate different environments. User mode requires that a user log in prior to authenticating to the network, which is very difficult in most environments. In System mode, the supplicant enters the mode prior to loading the login window; this mode uses preaccepted certificates.

Login Window mode uses login window credentials and information from System Preferences and the keychain and sends them to the 802.1x authentication session; the device disconnects from the network when a user logs out. While this sounds like a good solution, most administrators provide system maintenance and reporting when users are not logged into their systems, which is not possible in this configuration because the device is no longer network accessible.

Mixed mode, new to Mac OS X Snow Leopard, is a version of System mode that uses a machine certificate for authentication. As such, no user login is needed, but users are then authenticated with Login Window mode, which initiates a new 802.1x session, disconnects it on logout, and returns to System mode.

Configuring Mac OS X Server and AirPort

RADIUS is the primary means of authentication specified in the 802.1x standard. RADIUS is an established technology originally used by remote access and Internet service providers for dial-up access. Mac OS X Server's implementation integrates RADIUS with Open Directory to remove the complexity of maintaining a separate or synchronized authentication database.

Before you can configure RADIUS settings, you must turn on RADIUS service in Server Admin.

1   Open Server Admin and connect to the server.

2   Click Settings, then click Services.

3   Select the RADIUS checkbox.

4   Click Save.

Mac OS X Server v10.6 offers a configuration assistant for RADIUS, which guides you through the process and helps you start RADIUS.

To configure RADIUS using the configuration assistant, do the following:

1   Open Server Admin and connect to the server.

2   Click the triangle at the left of the server.

    The list of services appears.

3   From the expanded Servers list, select RADIUS.

4   Click Overview.

5   Click Configure RADIUS Service.

6   In the RADIUS Server Certificate pane, select one of the following:

    If you select "Choose an existing certificate," choose the certificate you want to use
    from the pop-up menu, and click Continue.

    If you want to create a self-signed certificate, use Certificate Assistant. For more informa-
    tion, see "Using Certificate Assistant to Create an SSL Certificate" earlier in this chapter.

7   From the Available Base Stations list, select the base station you want and click Add.
    Or, at the bottom of the Base Stations list, click the Add (+) button and enter the
    SSID, a descriptive name, the IP address of the AirPort device, and the shared secret.

8   In the Base Station Password field, enter the base station's password and click Add.

9   If you want to remove a base station from the Selected Base Stations list, select it and
    click Remove.

10 Click Continue.

11 In the RADIUS Allow Users pane, you can restrict user access:

    If you select "Allow all users," all users will have access to the base stations you selected.

    If you select "Restrict to members of group," only users of a group can access the base
    stations you selected. This utilizes Max OS X Server's Service Access List (SACL) func-
    tionality to restrict access to the appropriate groups.

12 Click Continue.

13 In the RADIUS setting confirmation pane, verify that your settings are correct. You
    can also print or save your RADIUS configuration.

14 Click Confirm.

Configuring the Supplicant

Configuring the supplicant on Mac OS X is accomplished in the Advanced pane of System Preferences' Networking pane. For this exercise, you will configure an AirPort network interface for Mixed mode 802.1x authentication. Prior to executing these steps, the administrator must install the appropriate certificates on the client device.

1   Open System Preferences.

2   In the left window, select the AirPort network device listed.

3   Verify that AirPort is turned on. If it is not, turn on AirPort, but do not yet join any wireless network.

4   At the lower right of the configuration pane, click the Advanced button, then click the 802.1x tab.

5   From the pop-up menu, choose System Profile.

6   Leave the User Name and Password fields empty.

7   In the Authentication pane, select TLS.

8   Click Configure.

9   Click the Add (+) button, and select the certificate provided by your administrator.

10 Click OK.

11 In the Wireless Network field, enter the SSID of the wireless network you are configuring. Leave the Security Type pop-up menu set to WPA2 Enterprise.

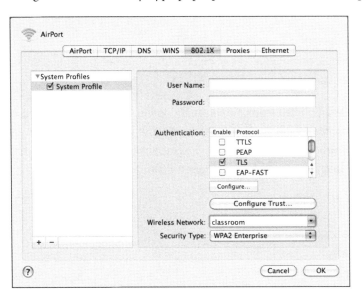

12 In the System Profiles pane, click the Add (+) button and select Login Window.

13 Leave the User Name and Password text boxes blank and, in the Authentication area, select the TTLS and PEAP checkboxes.

14 In the Wireless Network field, enter the SSID of the wireless network you are configuring, and leave the Security Type pop-up menu set to WPA2 Enterprise.

15 Click OK.

16 In the Network Preference pane, click Apply.

17 Log out and attempt to log in again to confirm proper operation.

Configuring RADIUS from the Command Line

Configuration from the command line is available on Mac OS X Server using the `radiusconfig` command. This command has various arguments and options that can be reviewed in its `man` page. The most common command-line tasks include viewing settings, configuring parameters, and configuring certificates. These can be accomplished using the following commands:

```
sudo radiusconfig -appleversion -getconfig -getconfigxml -nascount -naslist
-naslistxml -ver -help -q
sudo radiusconfig -setconfig key value [key value]
sudo radiusconfig -installcerts private-key certificate [trusted-ca-
list [yes | no [common-name]]]
```

Configuring the Mac OS X supplicant from the command line utilizes the `networksetup` command and, unlike server configuration (for which the command line is not recommended), supplicant configuration from the command line is extremely useful when preconfiguring systems for user deployment. The appropriate `networksetup` commands are as follows:

```
networksetup -import8021xProfiles
networksetup -export8021xProfiles
networksetup -export8021xUserProfiles
networksetup -export8021xUserProfiles
networksetup -export8021xUserProfiles
```

To associate an identity to a profile:

```
networksetup -settlsidentityonuserprofile
networksetup -setsidentityonsystemprofile
```

Importing and Exporting 802.1x Profiles

Administrators can create profiles on a test system, then export those 802.1x profiles and use System Preferences to import them manually onto client systems, or apply command-line tools to integrate them as part of their deployment strategy.

From System Preferences, open Network. Select the adapter that contains the 802.1x settings, click Advanced, click the 802.1x tab, and then click the appropriate button to import or export a profile.

In the command line, the networksetup command can be used with various options and arguments, depending on your requirements. For example, to script the deployment of a new system with previously exported profiles, use the following commands:

▶ Import the user or machine identity (certificate and private key):

```
security import -x <identity> -k <system keychain> -f pkcs12 -P passphrase
```

▶ Import and trust the server certificate:

```
security add-trusted-cert -d -r trustAsRoot -p eap -k <system keychain> <server cert>
```

▶ Import the 802.1x system profile:

```
networksetup -import8021xProfiles
```

▶ Associate the identity to the system profile:

```
networksetup -settlsidentityonuserprofile
```

Using 802.1x with the iPhone OS

The iPhone and iPod Touch have an 802.1x-compatible supplicant that's built into the iPhone OS. It provides System mode 802.1x capability, because no login window exists on the iPhone OS to facilitate Login Window or Mixed modes.

The iPhone OS uses profile templates created with the iPhone Profile Configuration Utility (iPCU), which will be discussed in Chapter 7, "Providing iPhone Applications," or it can be manually configured. After the template is pushed to the device, the result is a seamless user login that can be mass-configured and deployed using this method. iPhone configuration profiles can be manually deployed via USB, email, or a secure website.

Troubleshooting 802.1x

Troubleshooting 802.1x can be challenging due to the variety of components involved. Administrators and users tend to focus on the supplicant when troubleshooting, but this is not a good assumption or technique. Start by reviewing the RADIUS logs on Mac OS X Server. They include detailed information regarding the transactions from the access point or network switch to the RADIUS server.

The second area to investigate is the Open Directory logs to verify that the user was able to authenticate after the RADIUS communication took place.

Confirm that DHCP is properly configured and contains enough addresses to accommodate wired and wireless users.

Confirm that the certificates being used have not expired or been revoked.

As a last resort, tcpdump can be used to investigate the actual traffic packets.

Mac OS X can also provide logging. Turn on debug logging using the following command:

```
defaults write /Library/Preferences/SystemConfiguration/com.apple.eapolclient
LogFlags -int 1
```

This will create a log file in which the debugging information is stored:

```
/var/log/eapolclient
```

The iPhone OS also can provide logging. Turn on debug logging using the following command, then sync the device:

```
defaults write
```

Attempt several 802.1x connections and resync. The log files will be downloaded from the device.

Using Smart Cards

Mac OS X has built-in support for smart cards, providing seamless two-factor authentication. Mac OS X supports Common Access Card (CAC), Personal Information Verification (PIV), Japanese PKI (JPKI), Belgian National ID (BELPIC), and any reader that is compliant with the 130 CCID standard. This includes a diverse array of smart card devices such as USB-attached readers, USB keyboards with built-in readers, and USB sticks, to name a few.

When a smart card is inserted, Mac OS X will mount the smart card's information into Keychain Access as a separate keychain, thus allowing any application written to utilize Mac OS X's security framework to access the materials contained on the chip. For instance, Apple Mail will match the appropriate field in a certificate to the email address used in the mail account to provide digital signing and encryption using the identities contained on the smart card.

The iPhone uses a smart card chip based on the GSM standard to provide various security authentication options for the telecommunications providers that provide iPhone services.

Several whitepapers and video tutorials about smart cards are available on Apple's website in the business resources section. See www.apple.com/business/resources and www.seminars.apple.com.

Applying Multifactor Authentication

Multifactor authentication requires a user to provide credentials and other information depending on the number of authentication components requested. Most users are familiar with single-factor authentication, which consists of a user name (the credential) and a password (the component). But many regulatory bodies, such as the Securities and Exchange Commission and the Payment Card Industry (PCI), now require that organizations utilize a minimum of two-factor authentication.

Two-factor authentication requires something an entity (or user) has—a smart card, for example—and something that the entity knows, such as a pin number. A common two-factor authentication application is an ATM card issued by the banking industry. Other examples in the information technology industry include a keychain device (referred to as a *key fob*) that randomly generates a code based on proprietary mathematical calculations, smart cards, USB token devices, and so on. Three-factor authentication adds a third component:

who you are. This authentication requires biometric information such as a fingerprint or an iris scan to provide a unique or nearly unique basis for identity verification.

Several multifactor authentication options are available for the Mac OS X operating system, such as smart cards and third-party devices provided by companies including Aladdin, Charismathics, RSA, ActivIdentity, VASCO, Sony, Athena, and MultiFactor.

Employing Disk Encryption

Apple's FileVault provides encryption for users' home directories, but some organizations mandate full-disk encryption as part of their security policy. Several third-party and open source options are available to meet this requirement. Full-disk encryption encrypts the entire hard drive or specific volumes on a hard drive at the hardware or volume layer rather than inside the operating system.

PGP, Check Point, Knox, Bloombase, Apricorn, and WinMagic provide full disk encryption and/or management solutions compatible with Mac OS X. Also available is an open source project called TrueCrypt.

The iPhone's storage is encrypted by default and requires no additional Apple or third-party tools for encryption.

Using Security on iPhone OS Devices

The iPhone OS provides three segments of security in its operation: device oriented, network oriented, and on the platform itself. The iPhone OS provides for passcode strength, time-out policies, and restricted camera access. Protecting data stored on an iPhone is essential in any environment with a high level of sensitive corporate or customer information. In addition to encrypting data in transmission, the iPhone 3GS provides hardware encryption for data stored on the device.

Additionally, data backed up to a user's computer with iTunes can be encrypted. When an encrypted configuration profile is stored on the user's device, this capability is enforced automatically.

If a device is lost or stolen, it's important to be able to deactivate and erase it. It's also a good idea to have a policy in place that will wipe the device after a defined number of failed passcode attempts, a key deterrent against attempts to gain unauthorized access to the device.

The iPhone 3GS offers hardware-based encryption using AES 256-bit encoding to protect all data.

Encryption is always enabled, and users cannot disable it, nor does it require any additional settings or configurations. It's always on for all users of the iPhone 3GS. Because the iPhone uses hardware encryption, it is enabled regardless of battery or performance issues.

Mobile users must be able to access corporate information networks from anywhere in the world, yet it's also important to ensure that users are authorized and that their data is protected during transmission. The iPhone OS includes proven technologies to accomplish these security objectives for both Wi-Fi and cellular data network connections. The iPhone OS supports strong network authentication methods, as well as two-factor token authentication.

The iPhone OS integrates with a broad range of commonly used VPN technologies through support for Cisco IPsec, L2TP, and PPTP. Support for these protocols ensures the highest level of IP-based encryption for transmission of sensitive information. The iPhone OS supports SSL v3 as well as Transport Layer Security (TLS) v1, the next-generation security standard for the Internet. Safari, Calendar, Mail, and other Internet applications automatically start these mechanisms to enable an encrypted communication channel between iPhone and corporate services.

The iPhone OS also supports WPA2 (Wi-Fi Protected Access 2) Enterprise to provide authenticated access to your enterprise wireless network. WPA2 Enterprise uses 128-bit Advanced Encryption Standard (AES) encryption, giving users the highest assurance that their data will remain protected when they send and receive communications over a Wi-Fi network connection.

The iPhone OS is a platform designed with security at its core. It takes a "sandbox" approach to application runtime protection and requires mandatory application signing to ensure that applications cannot be tampered with. The iPhone OS also has a secure framework that facilitates secure storage of application and network service credentials in an encrypted keychain. For developers, it offers a common crypto architecture that can be used to encrypt application data stores.

Security Considerations

SSH

SSH services are a valuable tool to administrators, allowing them to access their systems remotely with an efficient, secure, and fast tool. Because of the popularity of SSH access, many crackers will attempt dictionary or other attacks against a server or client machine running SSH. To thwart these attempts, administrators can take precautions such as editing the sshd configuration file to change the port used by SSH, enabling access controls using Server Admin or System Preferences, and enabling SSH key-only authentication by modifying the configuration file.

Certificates

Certificate technology based on PKI is ubiquitous in today's cell phones, computers, security devices, credit cards, and so on. As such, care must be taken when accepting certificates from third parties to ensure that the delivering party and the party identified on the certificate are indeed the same. Examination of a CA's CPS or CPD policies (typically available on the web) will inform administrators as to the processes and procedures the CA uses to validate identity prior to issuance of certificates or identity. Furthermore, these documents will detail the security, both physical and digital, that is implemented to protect these identities and certificates.

When creating your own CA or providing certificate signature requests, care must be taken to protect the key materials (private and public keys) generated during the process. If someone can copy these files, that person can request additional certificates as if he or she were you or a member of your staff.

Utilizing certificates for digital signing and encryption has become a more and more popular use for the technology. Administrators should take steps to store keys used for digitally signing any official correspondence or documents to ensure that validity can be established at any later time. More important, when keys are used for encryption, private-key escrow and storage procedures must be invoked to ensure that documents and correspondence can always be decrypted.

Policies and procedures detailing the issuance requirements, storage protection requirements, and peripheral procedures should be created and maintained.

802.1x Network Authentication

802.1x network authentication provides a robust method for ensuring the identity of devices and/or individuals attempting to connect to the network.

802.1x leverages certificate technologies, so the same prudence should be exercised in issuance and verification as for the other methods detailed above.

Log files and Internet-based resources should be reviewed on a consistent basis to ensure that no attempted penetrations or published vulnerabilities become apparent for supplicants, authenticators, or authentication server technologies.

Disk Encryption

Of note to administrators of systems that are deployed with full disk encryption is the management of the keys used for the encryption or password and the user role policies for accessing those protected devices. Administrators should establish policies and procedures that allow for the recovery of organizational data from these devices in the case of lost user passwords or a user's departure from the organization.

What You've Learned

This chapter discusses certificates, basic cryptography, and PKI that provide administrators with the tools to secure communications for Mac OS X Server services. You have learned the following:

- ▶ The difference between symmetric and asymmetric keys
- ▶ How to create a certificate utilizing the Certificate Assistant portion of Server Admin
- ▶ Utilizing Certificate Assistant to create a CA
- ▶ How to create a CA utilizing the command line
- ▶ Installing self-signed certificates for use on the server utilizing the command line
- ▶ Deploying self-signed certificates to client systems via the command line
- ▶ Creating CSR requests to third-party CAs and installing the corresponding certificates
- ▶ How to create S/MIME certificates for email signing and encryption

References
The following documents were useful in the development of this chapter.

Administration Guides
Network Services Administration v10.6 Snow Leopard

Advanced Server Administration Guide v10.6 Snow Leopard

Mac OS X Server Essentials v10.6 Student Guide

Books
Dreyer, Arek, and Greisler, Ben. *Apple Training Series: Mac OS X Server Essentials v10.6* (Peachpit Press, 2010).

Marczak, Edward R. *Apple Training Series: Mac OS X Advanced System Administration v10.5* (Peachpit Press, 2009).

URLs
http://images.apple.com/server/macosx/docs/Network_Services_Admin_v10.6.pdf

http://images.apple.com/server/macosx/docs/Advanced_Server_Admin_v10.6.pdf

http://smartcardservices.macosforge.org

www.ejbca.org

www.checkpoint.com

www.bloombase.com

www.winmagic.com

www.apricorn.com

www.pgp.com

www.truecrypt.org

www.knoxformac.com

The Internet Engineering Task Force (IETF) provides several standards for various uses of PKI and certificate technologies. For more information, see www.ietf.org/dyn/wg/charter/pkix-charter.html.

Request for Comments (RFC) documents provide an overview of a protocol or service and details about how the protocol should behave.

If you're a novice server administrator, you'll probably find some of the background information in an RFC helpful.

If you're an experienced server administrator, you can find all technical details about a protocol in its RFC document.

You can search for RFC documents by number at the website www.ietf.org/rfc.html.

For S/MIME description, see RFC 2785.

For TLS v1.1 description, see RFC 4346.

For x.509 v3 certificates, see RFC 2459.

For 802.1x description, see RFC 3580.

For SCEP description, see draft-nourse-scep-20.txt.

Chapter Review

1. Can digital signing be used to encrypt messages between email sender and recipient?
2. Which graphical application tool provided via Keychain Access allows administrators to create their own CA?
3. Which command-line tool can be used to generate and install a self-signed certificate on Mac OS X server for use in Server Admin?
4. Which command-line tool can be used to install a self-signed certificate to a user's keychain on a client system?
5. Do software developers use digital signatures with software updates and installation packages to ensure encryption of the conversation between a website and the end user?

Answers

1.   No. Digital signing confirms that a message has not been tampered with since the sender signed it and verifies the sender's identity. It is not used to encrypt emails.

2.   Certificate Assistant.

3.   certtool can create a self-signed certificate, which is automatically installed in Server Admin to provide for web, Mail, iChat, iCal, and other services.

4.   security is the command-line tool used on Mac OS X to provide import, export, or verification of certificates.

5.   No, software developers utilize digital signing of applications and updates to ensure that no tampering of the respective application or update has taken place.

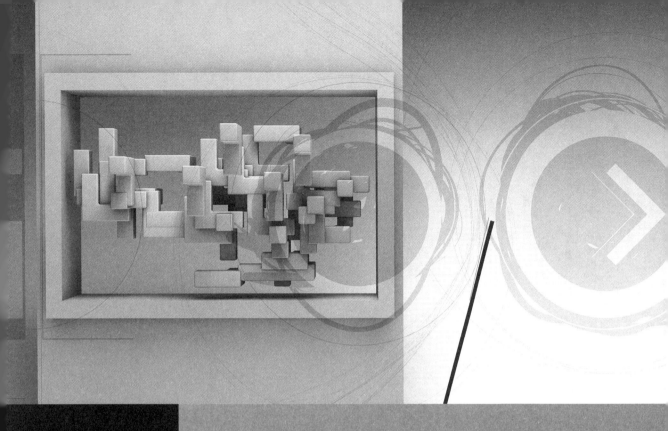

Part 3 Working with Mobile Devices

7

Time

This lesson takes approximately 120 minutes to complete.

Goals

Access the iPhone SDK

Create simple iPhone web and native applications using SDK utilities

Understand the benefits of deploying an iPhone web application or a native iPhone application

Set up native application installation on an iPhone

Deploy a native iPhone application within an organization

Understand provisioning profiles

Access iPhone Configuration Utility

Use iPhone Configuration Utility to create, distribute, and manage iPhone configuration profiles

Distribute and install a configuration profile on an iPhone

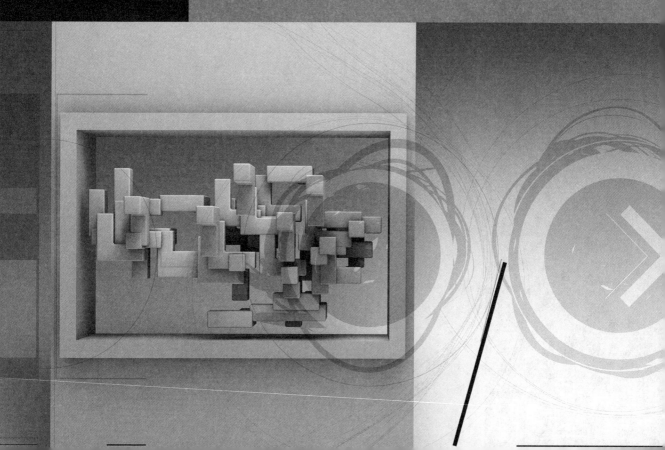

Chapter **7**
Providing iPhone Applications

With the addition of the Mobile Access Server (MAS) to Mac OS X Server v10.6, Apple has provided a secure method for system administrators to provide intranet service access to external users. Although most users will access those services through desktop or laptop systems, more and more people are accessing them via a smart phone. With enterprise-level customers adopting the iPhone in ever-increasing numbers, system administrators must have a deeper understanding of the iPhone and how to communicate with it.

To that end, this chapter focuses on the development and deployment of iPhone applications in an enterprise environment, and the Apple support and tools available to manage the iPhone on your intranet. Although this chapter is not intended to provide all of the information you'll need to become an iPhone development guru, it should leave you with a better understanding of the issues involved in developing and deploying iPhone applications.

Using the iPhone Developer Program

Developers can participate in iPhone development at three levels. Apple Developer Connection (ADC) members (including those with free online membership) can log into the iPhone Dev Center website using current credentials. They will be prompted to agree to the iPhone Software Development Kit (SDK) guidelines, and then they will be able to download the iPhone SDK and access most of the iPhone Dev Center. The primary disadvantage to this level of membership is that the developer cannot install applications on an iPhone OS device, but must instead test code on iPhone Simulator. Also, members at this level cannot submit applications to the App Store. To install code on an iPhone OS device, the developer must join the iPhone Developer Program.

The iPhone Developer Program is a paid program sponsored and managed by Apple to serve individuals interested in developing applications for the iPhone OS. The program provides a complete, integrated process for developing iPhone and iPod Touch applications. Participants are provided access to tools that will help them develop, test, and distribute applications.

You can participate at the Standard or Enterprise levels. The Standard program is for developers who are creating free and commercial applications and want to distribute applications on the App Store. Membership in this program costs $99 a year.

The Enterprise program serves companies with 500 or more employees who are creating proprietary in-house applications. Enterprise-level membership costs $299 a year.

The specific benefits of these programs are available at http://developer.apple.com/iphone/program/apply.html.

Both levels will give you access to the following tools:

- ▶ iPhone SDK
- ▶ iPhone Dev Center Resources
- ▶ iPhone Developer Program Portal
- ▶ Testing on iPhone and iPod Touch
- ▶ Code-level technical support
- ▶ Apple Developer Forums (in beta at the time of this writing)
- ▶ Ad Hoc Distribution

Only the Standard program includes the ability to sell applications on the App Store. In-house application distribution is available only with the Enterprise program.

After becoming a member of the iPhone Developer Program, you have access to the iPhone Developer Program Portal in the iPhone Dev Center. The Program Portal is a restricted-access area of the iPhone Dev Center that allows you to configure and manage devices to test your iPhone applications.

Understanding the iPhone SDK

The iPhone SDK 3.1.2 comes with all of the frameworks, tools, and resources necessary to develop iPhone applications on your Intel-based Macintosh computer. The SDK downloads as a disk image (DMG) and installs, by default, in the Developer directory at the root level of your boot drive.

In this section, you will explore the iPhone SDK in relation to its components: frameworks, tools, and resources. Depending on whether you are developing local or web-based applications for the iPhone, you may or may not use all of these tools.

Using Frameworks

Apple delivers most of its system interfaces in packages called *frameworks*. A framework is a directory that contains a dynamic shared library and the necessary resources (such as header files, images, helper applications, and so on) to support that library. To use frameworks, you link them into your application projects just as you would any other shared library. Linking them to your project gives you access to the features of that framework and tells the development tools where to find header files and other framework resources.

In addition to providing frameworks, Apple delivers some technologies in the form of standard shared libraries. The interfaces for these technologies are available in the standard library and interface directories.

Using Developer Tools

The iPhone SDK includes several key components that are beneficial for the successful development of iPhone applications:

▶ Xcode—This integrated development environment (IDE) manages your application projects and lets you edit, compile, run, and debug code. Xcode integrates with many other tools and is the main application you use during native application development.

▶ Interface Builder—A powerful tool for visually designing user interfaces, Interface Builder allows you to rapidly prototype and build your interface to reflect a true Mac OS X experience.

▶ iPhone Simulator—This Mac OS X application simulates the iPhone technology stack, allowing you to test iPhone applications locally on your Intel-based Macintosh computer.

▶ Instruments—You can use this runtime performance analysis and debugging tool to gather information about your application's runtime behavior and identify potential problems.

▶ Dashcode—This is an integrated development environment for building iPhone OS web applications and Dashboard widgets.

Xcode

To create a new iPhone application, you start by creating a new project in Xcode. A project manages all of the information associated with your application, including the source files, build settings, and rules for assembling all of the pieces. The heart of every Xcode project is the project window, which provides quick access to all of the elements of your application. In the Groups & Files list, you manage the project files, including source files and the build targets created from those source files. In the Toolbar, you access commonly used tools and commands. In the Detail view, you configure a space for working on your project. In the Text Editor, you add further customizations. The Status Bar provides feedback on the status of processes.

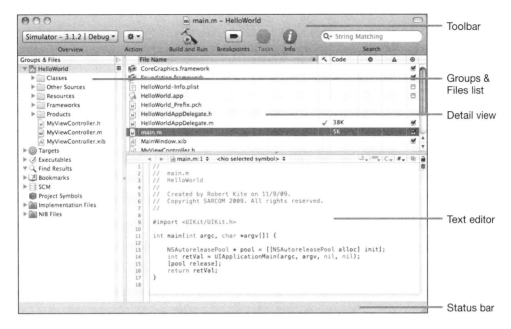

From within Xcode, you can create the majority of the components necessary for building an iPhone application. However, you will probably use Interface Builder for creating your interface.

Interface Builder

Using Interface Builder, you assemble your application's interface by dragging preconfigured components onto the View window. The View window is a representation of the screen of an iPhone or iPod Touch.

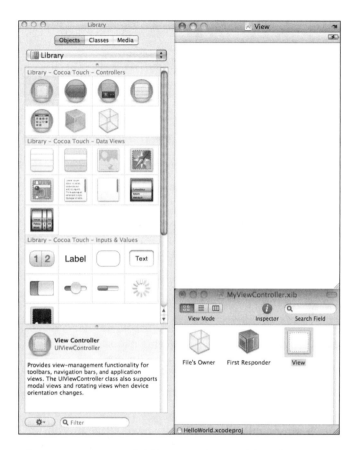

The components available in Interface Builder include standard system controls such as switches, text fields, and buttons, in addition to custom views to represent the views your application provides. After you have placed the objects on the window's surface, you can position them in the interface, configure their attributes using the inspector, and establish the relationships between those objects and your code. When the interface looks the way you want it, you save the contents to the nib file of your project.

NOTE ▶ Although an Interface Builder document may have a .xib extension, historically the extension was .nib (an acronym for NeXT Interface Builder). As a result, they are commonly referred to as nib files.

Overall, using Interface Builder saves a tremendous amount of time in creating your application's user interface. Interface Builder can replace hand-coding to create, configure, and position interface objects. Because it is a visual editor, you see exactly how your interface will look at runtime.

iPhone Simulator

When you build an application in Xcode, you have the choice of building it for iPhone Simulator or for a device. iPhone Simulator allows you to run and debug applications without connecting an iPhone or iPod Touch. iPhone Simulator implements the iPhone API and provides an environment that resembles the actual iPhone environment. Both native and web application developers can realistically preview behavior on an iPhone while running their applications locally on a development machine.

> **NOTE ▶** iPhone Simulator is not a perfect analog of an iPhone OS device. Not all features of such a device are available in the Simulator and some features may not work as expected.

After you are satisfied with your application's behavior, you can tell Xcode to build your application and run it on an actual iPhone or iPod Touch connected to your computer.

Instruments

To ensure that you deliver the best user experience, the Instruments environment lets you dynamically trace and profile your application's code in real time. Instruments gathers data from an application running on a simulator or on actual hardware and graphically display that data in the *timeline*. You can monitor many aspects of your application, including memory usage, disk activity, network activity, and graphics performance. This tool allows you to see exactly where you could increase code efficiency because it displays types of information side by side. So you can analyze the overall performance of your application, and not just the performance of a specific area.

In addition to providing the timeline view, Instruments includes tools to analyze the application's behavior over time. Instruments can store information from multiple program runs, helping you determine whether the adjustments you have made are having the desired results.

Dashcode

Dashcode's integrated environment allows you to lay out a web application's user interface, write code, and even test web content without any other applications or tools. Dashcode's layout tools, composers, and editors simplify the process of creating all the resources necessary for an iPhone web application. It also includes handy tools that help you manage and debug any code you write for Safari and iPhone.

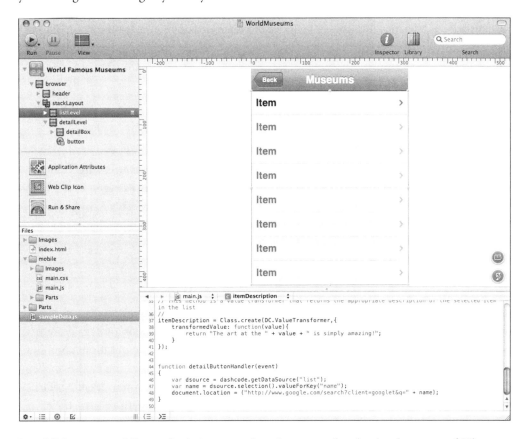

In addition to providing a single integrated environment for the development of iPhone, iPod Touch, and Safari web content, Dashcode is also the tool of choice for developing Dashboard widgets.

Accessing Resources

Many useful resources address iPhone OS application development, including the iPhone Reference Library, Apple's World Wide Developers Conference, and the iPhone Dev Center. Although not all of these resources are provided free of charge, a great deal of free material is available on the iPhone Dev Center website at http://developer.apple.com/iphone.

▶   iPhone Reference Library—The iPhone SDK includes the iPhone Reference Library. Installed by default, this library includes the reference documentation for the iPhone OS. At the current time, over 750 documents are available on topics ranging from performance to security. Although it's available through Xcode, the library is also available online and is updated independently of Xcode.

▶   Apple World Wide Developers Conference—The WWDC offers lectures and hands-on labs specifically tailored to iPhone developers and presented by Apple engineers.

▶   iPhone Dev Center—Although the iPhone Reference Library can be accessed from within Xcode as part of the iPhone SDK, additional tools and resources are available through the iPhone Dev Center. If you have purchased an iPhone developer membership, you have access to Apple Developer Connection on iTunes. This is an invaluable resource as you actually get to see and hear experts discussing iPhone development technologies, techniques, and best practices.

Creating Web Applications

Depending on the types of services, games, or utilities you have on your iPhone, you may be unknowingly using web applications all the time. iPhone web applications are really web-sites that have been optimized for use with Safari on the iPhone. The applications combine HTML, Cascading Style Sheets (CSS), and JavaScript code to implement interactive applications that live on a web server, are transmitted over the network, and run inside the Safari browser. These sites will display well on the iPhone or iPod Touch screens because their navigational tools and interface design are customized for those display environments.

Dashcode is only one of the Apple tools that allows you to ensure, before deployment, that you've optimized your website's interface and navigation. In this section, you will explore the benefits of web applications, and then create one of your own.

Evaluating the Benefits of Web Applications

Of the two types of applications you can deploy for the iPhone and iPod Touch, the web application is probably the easiest and least time consuming to deploy. Among the benefits of creating web applications for the iPhone and iPod Touch are the following:

▶   You can use your existing knowledge. If you are currently serving websites, you probably have most of the knowledge necessary to create a web application. You can rely on your ability to code in HTML, CSS, and JavaScript, with little modification, to create an effective iPhone and iPod Touch web application and your servers can provide content to iPhone and iPod Touch web applications just as they currently provide content to desktop users.

▶   Excellent development tools already exist. In addition to the tools already discussed in this chapter, Apple provides WebKit, a Mac OS X framework that lets developers embed a web browser in their Cocoa applications. WebKit has a JavaScript and Objective-C interface to access a webpage's Document Object Model (DOM). Dashboard, Mail, and many other Mac OS X applications also use WebKit as an embedded browser. WebKit is available as an open source project from http://webkit.org.

While providing browser functionality, WebKit also implements extensions to HTML proposed in the HTML5 standards, CSS, and JavaScript, including several Safari-specific extensions, such as CSS animation and transform properties, and JavaScript database support. Safari on the iPhone OS also includes JavaScript Multi-Touch event support.

▶   You can instantly deploy web applications.

If you've already optimized your websites and servers for use with Safari on the iPhone OS, you can publish your web application by simply publishing the URL for its website. When you want to update the web application's content, you need only update the content on the web server.

If you want to provide information that is internal to your company, family, or organization, you can secure that site using firewall rules, virtual private network (VPN), Secure Sockets Layer (SSL), or even the Mobile Access Server. These tools allow you to control access to your site via user authentication and authorization.

Build a Simple Web Application

To understand how easy it is to develop a web application, you'll now build one. Although this example may not provide you with all of the information, tools, or experience necessary to go into business building web applications, it will familiarize you with the process and show you how you might use web applications in your workplace.

In this example, you will modify Dashcode's standard Browser template to create an interactive list of world-famous museums. The Browser template provides a mobile Safari web application that displays some built-in information and supports page-based navigation.

The information built into the Dashcode template relates to U.S. National Parks. You will replace this with details about museums. Let's begin:

1   Open Dashcode from the /Developer/Applications/ folder.

2   Select the Browser template and deselect the "Develop for: Safari" checkbox.

3   Click Choose.

A project window opens, displaying the first page of a new mobile Safari web application based on the Browser template.

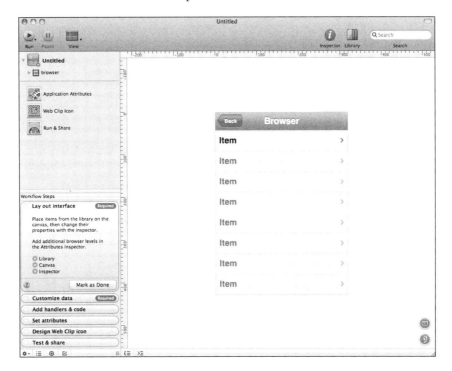

4   Double-click Browser and change the title to Museums.

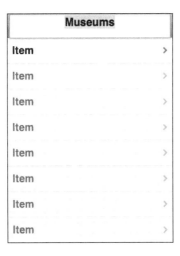

5   At the top of the navigator, double-click Untitled and change the name to World Famous Museums, then save the project to your desktop as WorldMuseums.

Although you will replace the template information, now is a good time to make sure that everything is running as expected and that iPhone Simulator is working correctly.

6   In the Dashcode toolbar, click the green Run button.

iPhone Simulator opens and displays the following screen:

Notice that the title of the site is World Famous Museums and the title of the first page is Museums. However, you will also note that the items listed—Acadia, Bryce Canyon, and so forth—are not museums. We will fix this shortly.

7   Click Acadia.

You will see the details for Acadia National Park.

Now that you have confirmed that the application is behaving as expected, you will replace the park information with museum information.

8   In the Dashcode toolbar, click the blue View button, and then choose Files.

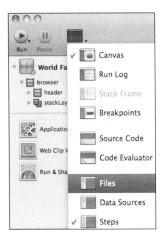

The bottom of the navigator column now lists the files associated with this application. At the bottom of the list is a JavaScript file called sampleData.js. This file contains the information you will replace.

9   Select sampleData.js.

You will notice that the file contents appear in the source code editor to the right.

```js
// sampleData.js
1  {
2      title: 'National Parks',
3      items: [
4          { name: "Acadia", location: "Maine, USA" },
5          { name: "Bryce Canyon", location: "Utah, USA" },
6          { name: "Carlsbad Caverns", location: "New Mexico, USA" },
7          { name: "Cuyahoga Valley", location: "Ohio, USA" },
8          { name: "Death Valley", location: "California, USA" },
9          { name: "Denali Preserve", location: "Alaska, USA" },
10         { name: "Grand Canyon", location: "Arizona, USA" },
11         { name: "Haleakala", location: "Hawaii, USA" },
12         { name: "Joshua Tree", location: "California, USA" },
13         { name: "Kings Canyon", location: "California, USA" },
14         { name: "Mesa Verde", location: "Colorado, USA" },
15         { name: "Shenandoah", location: "Virginia, USA" },
16         { name: "Yellowstone", location: "Wyoming, USA" },
17         { name: "Yosemite", location: "California, USA" }
18     ]
19 }
```

You are going to replace the parks and locations in this file with information about the museums.

10   Edit the sampleData.js file to resemble the image below. Save your changes.

```js
// sampleData.js
1  {
2      title: 'Famous Museums',
3      items: [
4          { name: "Metropolitan Museum of Art", location: "New York, USA" },
5          { name: "British Museum", location: "London, United Kingdom" },
6          { name: "Tate Museum", location: "London, United Kingdom" },
7          { name: "Vatican Museums", location: "Rome, Italy" },
8          { name: "Museo Nacional del Prado", location: "Madrid, Spain" },
9          { name: "Hermitage", location: "St. Petersburg, Russia" },
10         { name: "Smithsonian", location: "Washington, DC, USA" },
11         { name: "Louvre", location: "Paris, France" },
12         { name: "Guggenheim", location: "Bilbao, Spain" },
13         { name: "Uffizi", location: "Florence, Italy" }
14     ]
15 }
```

11 Open iPhone Simulator again to verify your changes.

So far, so good. However, if you click on British Museum, you will see the following information:

You ought to change the text to something more appropriate for a museum.

12 In the file list at the bottom of the navigator, select main.js.

In the source code editor, you will see the contents of the file. You are going to change only one line:

```
39       return "The scenery in " + value + " is amazing this time of year!";
```

13 Change the text in line 39 to match the string in the following figure, and then save.

```
39       return "The art at the " + value + " is simply amazing!";
```

Now that you have edited the template to better suit the subject matter, you can add a button on the detail page to perform a Google search on that museum. If you had your own website containing information about these museums, you could also point the button to that site.

NOTE ▶ Web browsers, including Safari on iPhone, implement a security model known as "same source." This means that webpages are not allowed to request information from Internet domains other than the one from which they came. You are able to test this on iPhone Simulator because Dashcode is simulating running this site on that server.

To add a button, you will use a button *part*. Parts are controls and views used in a web application's user interface. Dashcode lists the available parts in a Library.

14 In the navigator, select the detailLevel layout to display the detail screen in the canvas.

15 From the Window menu, choose Library.

16 Drag the Push Button part into your detail page on the canvas.

17 Double-click the button and change the name to More Info.

Now you want to tell the button what to do when it is clicked.

18 On the detail page, select the button, and in the menu bar, click the Inspector button.

The Inspector opens.

19 Double-click in the Handlers column next to the onclick event name.

20 Enter the name of a new function, detailButtonHandler, and press Return.

Notice that the source code editor now displays the source code for detailButtonHandler. You should also notice that line 46 reads // Insert Code Here.

21 Select line 46, and enter the following three lines of code:

```
var dsource = dashcode.getDataSource("list");
var name = dsource.selection().valueForKey("name");
document.location = ("http://www.google.com/search?client=googlet&q=" + name);
```

The results should resemble this:

```
44 function detailButtonHandler(event)
45 {
46     var dsource = dashcode.getDataSource("list");
47     var name = dsource.selection().valueForKey("name");
48     document.location = ("http://www.google.com/search?client=googlet&q=" + name);
49 }
```

22 Save the project and open iPhone Simulator.

23 Click British Museum, and then click the More Info button.

Google.com opens with information related to that museum.

Now that you have completed a very basic web application, you understand a few of the capabilities associated with web applications. Dashcode is a powerful tool, and you have only scratched its surface.

> **MORE INFO** ▶ For more detailed information on Dashcode and web application development, see the iPhone OS Reference Library.

Creating Native Applications

The iPhone SDK also provides the tools and resources needed to create native iPhone applications. Unlike a web application, which runs in Safari, a native application runs as a standalone application on an iPhone OS–based device. Native applications have access to all the features that make the iPhone and iPod Touch unique, such as the accelerometers, location services, and Multi-Touch interface. A native application can also save data to the local file system and communicate with other installed applications via custom URL schemes. Native applications are installed directly on an individual device and can run without a network connection.

Under the iPhone OS, you develop native applications using the UIKit framework. This framework provides fundamental infrastructure and default behavior to create a functional application in a matter of minutes. Even though the UIKit framework (and other frameworks on the system) provides a significant amount of default behaviors, it also provides hooks that you can use to customize and extend those behaviors.

Understanding the Benefits of Native Applications

Although web applications are easy and less time-consuming to build and deploy, they are limited in terms of the ability to be available anytime and anywhere. Imagine developing a game that runs on a website rather than on a standalone device. Now imagine that you lose Internet access. The application no longer works.

With a native application, you can offer a user the best of both worlds. Your application can benefit from user interface elements, such as 3D, that are not available on the mobile version of Safari, and can also include components that connect to the Internet for advanced features or information.

Further, native applications can generate revenue for you, your organization, or your company when you offer them for sale on Apple's iTunes App Store.

In the next section, you will build a simple native application. This exercise won't make you an iPhone software wizard, but it will give you a grasp of the tools and processes associated with building a native iPhone application.

Building a Simple Native Application

For this exercise, you will use the Hello World application from Apple's *Your First iPhone Application* document. The location of this document is listed in the Resources section at the end of this chapter.

When you developed a web application, you used Dashcode. For this example, you will use Xcode. The result will be an iPhone application that incorporates multiple components to demonstrate some of the basic features of an iPhone application.

> **NOTE ▶** As you perform this exercise, you will encounter terms and statements that you may not know. It is not the intention of this exercise to provide all of the information necessary for you to become an iPhone developer. Rather, it is intended to introduce some of the steps involved in creating an iPhone application and familiarize you with the process. If you decide that you want to further pursue native application development for the iPhone, you should join the iPhone Developer Program.

Creating the Project

You begin the process by opening Xcode and creating the project.

1   Open Xcode, then click "Create a new Xcode project."

The New Project window appears.

2   Verify that Application is selected under iPhone OS in the source list, then select "Window-based Application" and click Choose.

3   Save the application to your desktop as HelloWorld.

After saving the file, your new project window should look like this:

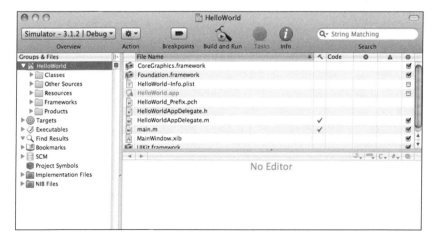

Adding a View Controller

The existing template provides the basic information for this application. However, you must add a *view controller* class. In addition to controlling how the device screen looks to the user, the view controller also helps with navigation and memory management. For this exercise, you will use only the view controller's ability to manage the user interface.

1   From the top of the Groups & Files list, select HelloWorld.

2   From the File menu, choose New File.

3   Select the Cocoa Touch Class group, then select the UIViewController subclass. Be sure to select the "With XIB for user interface" option.

> **NOTE ▶** Selecting "With XIB for user interface" means that Xcode creates a nib file to accompany the view controller, and adds it to the project.

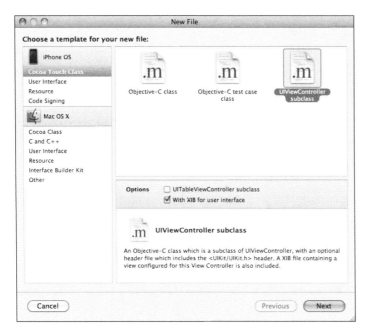

4   Click Next.

Now you will name the controller and make sure that both the .m and .h files are created.

5   In the File Name field, type `MyViewController.m`.

6   Select the "Also create 'MyViewController.h'" checkbox, and click Finish.

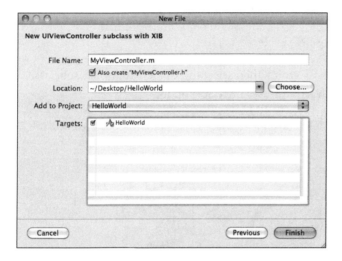

Now that you have a view controller added to your project, you can add a view controller property.

NOTE ▸ Remember, more information on these terms and files is provided in the iPhone Reference Library. This lesson is intended only to provide you some familiarity with the tools used to create a native application.

7   Click the disclosure triangle next to the Classes group, then select the HelloWorldAppDelegate.h file.

The text editor now shows the contents of that file.

8   Edit the file by making the following changes in the text editor:

Insert `@class MyViewController;` above the line beginning `@interface`.

Insert `MyViewController *myViewController;` below the line beginning `UIWindow`.

Insert `@property (nonatomic, retain) MyViewController *myViewController;` below the line beginning `@property`.

When you have finished, your text editor should resemble this figure:

```
// 
//  HelloWorldAppDelegate.h
//  HelloWorld
// 
// 

#import <UIKit/UIKit.h>

@class MyViewController;

@interface HelloWorldAppDelegate : NSObject <UIApplicationDelegate> {
    UIWindow *window;
    MyViewController *myViewController;
}

@property (nonatomic, retain) IBOutlet UIWindow *window;
@property (nonatomic, retain) MyViewController *myViewController;

@end
```

You will now create an instance of the view controller and set it as the value for the property.

9   In the Groups & Files list, select the HelloWorldAppDelegate.m file.

The text editor now displays the contents of that file.

10 In the text editor, insert the following text changes below the line beginning `(void)applicationDidFinishLaunching`:

```
MyViewController *aViewController = [[MyViewController alloc]
    initWithNibName:@"MyViewController" bundle:[NSBundle mainBundle]];
[self setMyViewController:aViewController];
[aViewController release];
```

You have created the instance of the view controller. Now you'll set up the view. The view controller is responsible for managing and configuring the view when asked. This next set of statements asks the view controller for its view and adds that view as a subview for the window.

11 Below the line beginning [aViewController release]; add the following lines:

```
UIView *controllersView = [myViewController view];
[window addSubview:controllersView];
```

You are almost done with this file. You have only three more tasks to complete: Import the view controller's header file, synthesize the accessor methods, and make sure the view controller is released in the dealloc method. (This statement releases the view controller in the first statement.)

12 Import the header file for MyViewController by inserting the following line immediately above the line that begins #import: "HelloWorldAppDelegate.h"

```
#import "MyViewController.h"
```

13 Tell the compiler to synthesize the accessor methods for the view controller in the @ implementation block of the class by inserting the following line immediately below the existing @synthesize statement:

```
@synthesize myViewController;
```

14 Release the view controller in the first statement in the dealloc method by inserting the following line immediately above releasing the window:

```
[myViewController release];
```

When you have completed steps 9 through 14, your HelloWorldAppDelegate.m file should look like this:

```
//
//  HelloWorldAppDelegate.m
//  HelloWorld
//
//

#import "MyViewController.h"
#import "HelloWorldAppDelegate.h"

@implementation HelloWorldAppDelegate

@synthesize window;
@synthesize myViewController;

- (void)applicationDidFinishLaunching:(UIApplication *)application {

    MyViewController *aViewController = [[MyViewController alloc]
                                initWithNibName:@"MyViewController" bundle:[NSBundle mainBundle]];
    [self setMyViewController:aViewController];
    [aViewController release];

    UIView *controllersView = [myViewController view];
    [window addSubview:controllersView];
    [window makeKeyAndVisible];
}


- (void)dealloc {
    [myViewController release];
    [window release];
    [super dealloc];
}

@end
```

15 Save your project.

Configuring the View

Now you'll configure the user interface and define how interface elements interact with each other. To configure the user interface, you'll use Interface Builder. You access Interface Builder from within Xcode, and you'll move between the two as you proceed.

1   In Xcode, double-click the view controller's XIB file (MyViewController.xib) to open the file in Interface Builder.

You should see a group of windows similar to those in the following figure. The View window will be blank at this point.

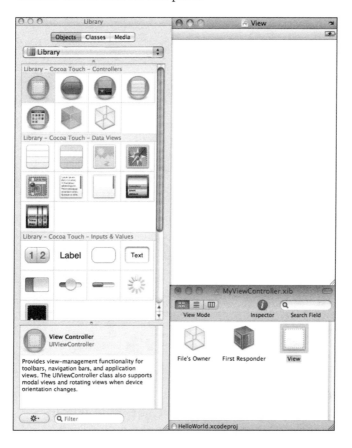

2   From the Library window, drag three objects into the view: a text field (UITextField), a label (UILabel), and a button (UIButton).

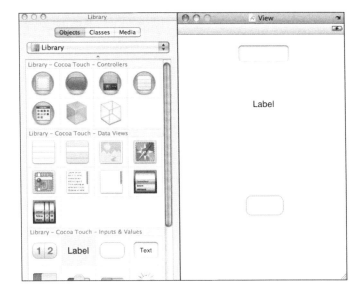

3   Arrange the elements so they look like this:

4 Add a placeholder string, Your Name, to the text field by double-clicking in the text field and typing Your Name.

5 Resize the label so that it extends to the margins (blue dotted lines on either edge of the view window).

6 Delete the text (Label) from the label by double-clicking the label and pressing the Delete key.

7 Add a title to the button by double-clicking the button and typing Hello.

8 Select the text field. Then, from the Tools menu, select the Attributes Inspector.

9 Set the Alignment of the text field to centered.

10 From the Capitalize pop-up menu, choose Words.

11 From the Return Key pop-up menu, choose Done.

When you have finished with all of these modifications, you should have a view that looks like this:

Connecting the View in Xcode

The interface elements are arranged just as they should look when users launch the application, but you still have to connect the view controller to that user interface. To accomplish this, you will edit the MyViewController.h file in Xcode.

First, let's add instance variables for the text field and label elements in the user interface:

1   In Xcode, in the list under Groups & Files, select the MyViewController.h file.

    The contents of that file appear in the text editor.

2   Create instance variables for the text field label within the `@interface` block by entering the following statements immediately prior to the closing bracket of that block:

    ```
    UITextField *textField;
    UILabel *label;
    NSString *string;
    ```

3 Create property declarations for the instance variables by inserting the following statements between the closing bracket of the `@interface` block and the `@end` statement:

```
@property (nonatomic, retain) IBOutlet UITextField *textField;
@property (nonatomic, retain) IBOutlet UILabel *label;
@property (nonatomic, copy) NSString *string;
```

4 Create a declaration for the `changeGreeting:` action method by inserting the following text directly below the last entry of the previous step:

```
- (IBAction)changeGreeting:(id)sender;
```

Third, ensure that the view controller acts as a delegate for the text field.

5 Specify that the `UIViewController` object adopts the `UITextFieldDelegate` protocol by adding `<UITextFieldDelegate>` after `UIViewController`.

After you have edited the MyViewController.h file, it should look like this:

```
//
//  MyViewController.h
//  HelloWorld
//
//

#import <UIKit/UIKit.h>

@interface MyViewController : UIViewController <UITextFieldDelegate> {
    UITextField *textField;
    UILabel *label;
    NSString *string;
}
@property (nonatomic, retain) IBOutlet UITextField *textField;
@property (nonatomic, retain) IBOutlet UILabel *label;
@property (nonatomic, copy) NSString *string;
- (IBAction)changeGreeting:(id)sender;
@end
```

6 Save the file so that Interface Builder will recognize the changes.

To test your progress, you'll edit the MyViewController.m file to implement a stub `changeGreeting:` method.

7 In Xcode, select the MyViewController.m file in the list under Groups & Files.

The contents of that file appear in the text editor.

8 After the `@implementation` MyViewController line, add the following:

```
- (IBAction)changeGreeting:(id)sender {
}
```

Connecting the View in Interface Builder

Now that you have defined how the view controller responds to various actions, you will establish the connections in the nib file, working within the Interface Builder.

1   In Xcode, double-click the MyViewController.xib file.

Interface Builder should come to the front of the screen and you should see the view exactly as it was when last viewed. The first task is to connect the label and text-Field outlets.

2   Control-click File's Owner to display a translucent panel that shows all the available outlets and actions.

3   Starting at the circle to the right of the label outlet, drag to the label in the View window.

4   From the circle to the right of the textField outlet, drag to the textField in the View window.

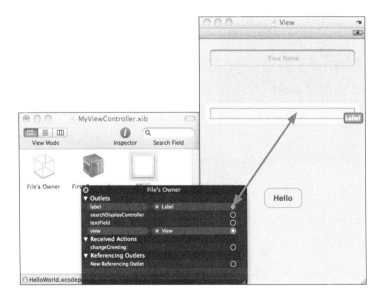

Second, you can set the button's action method.

5 Control-click the button to open the Inspector.

6 From the circle to the right of Touch Up Inside, drag to the File's Owner icon in the MyViewController.xib window.

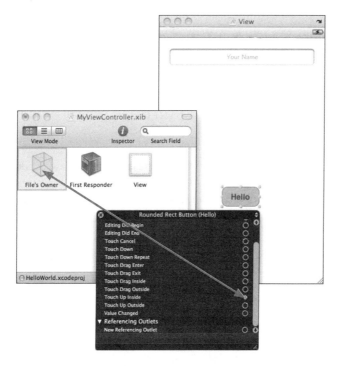

7 Select changeGreeting: in the translucent panel that appears over File's Owner.

Third, you must set the text field's delegate to be the File's Owner (the view controller).

8 From the text field in the View window, Control-drag to the File's Owner icon in the MyViewController.xib window.

9 In the translucent panel that appears, select "delegate."

10 Save the project.

Implementing the View Controller

When implementing the view controller, you must ensure that the properties for the instance variables are configured and that instance variables are released from memory before the application closes completely. You will implement the `changeGreeting:` method and ensure that the keyboard is dismissed when the user taps Done.

Tell the compiler to synthesize the `accessor` methods.

1   In Xcode, select the MyViewController.m file.

The contents of that file appear in the text editor.

2   Add the following statement after the `@implementation MyViewController` line:

```
@synthesize textField;
@synthesize label;
@synthesize string;
```

Now you should relinquish ownership in the `dealloc` method because all of the property declarations specify that the view controller owns the instance variables.

3   Update the `dealloc` method to release the instance variable before invoking the super's implementation. To do so, add the following statements before the super's implementation:

```
[textField release];
[label release];
[string release];
```

Next, you must implement the `changeGreeting:` method so that when the button is tapped, it sends a `changeGreeting:` message to the view controller. The view controller should then retrieve the string from the text field and update the label.

4   To complete the implementation of the changeGreeting: method, insert the following statements between the brackets of the line beginning - (IBAction):

```
self.string = textField.text;


NSString *nameString = string;
if ([nameString length] == 0) {
    nameString = @"World";
}
NSString *greeting = [[NSString alloc] initWithFormat:@"Hello, %@!", nameString];
label.text = greeting;
[greeting release];
```

Finally, you must implement a method for the text field that allows the keyboard to be dismissed when the user taps Done.

5   Implement the textFieldShouldReturn: method by inserting the following statements after the last bracket of the changeGreeting block:

```
- (BOOL)textFieldShouldReturn:(UITextField *)theTextField {
    if (theTextField == textField) {
        [textField resignFirstResponder];
    }
    return YES;
}
```

When you have completed these changes, your MyViewController.m file should look like this:

```
#import "MyViewController.h"


@implementation MyViewController

@synthesize textField;
@synthesize label;
@synthesize string;

- (IBAction)changeGreeting:(id)sender {

    self.string = textField.text;

    NSString *nameString = string;
    if ([nameString length] == 0) {
        nameString = @"World";
    }
    NSString *greeting = [[NSString alloc] initWithFormat:@"Hello, %@!", nameString];
    label.text = greeting;
    [greeting release];
}

- (BOOL)textFieldShouldReturn:(UITextField *)theTextField {
    if (theTextField == textField) {
        [textField resignFirstResponder];
    }
    return YES;
}


- (void)didReceiveMemoryWarning {
    // Releases the view if it doesn't have a superview.
    [super didReceiveMemoryWarning];

    // Release any cached data, images, etc that aren't in use.
}

- (void)viewDidUnload {
    // Release any retained subviews of the main view.
    // e.g. self.myOutlet = nil;
}


- (void)dealloc {
    [textField release];
    [label release];
    [string release];
    [super dealloc];
}


@end
```

NOTE ▶ The text between /* and */ (which consists of comments) has been removed for ease of reading.

Building and Debugging a Native Application

Now that you have everything in nearly final form, let's build and debug the project before testing it on iPhone Simulator.

1   From the Xcode toolbar, choose Build and Debug.

You may be asked if you want to save changes to files, and so on. You do. After the building and debugging process, iPhone Simulator will open and you will see your application.

2   Type your name and test the functionality of your application.

You should find that the button works. (It highlights when you click it.) You should also find that if you click in the text field, the keyboard appears and you can enter text.

Deploying an Application

So you have an application that you've tested on iPhone Simulator, and you are ready to test it on an actual iPhone or iPod Touch. Before you can move to this stage of the development process, you should complete a few more tasks.

In this section, you will add your development devices to the iPhone Developer Program and configure your computer for development. You will discover which options are available for deploying a native iPhone application within an organization.

Preparing Devices for Development

To test your application on a device, you must configure your computer and that device for iPhone OS development.

To begin, you first create or obtain the following digital assets:

▶ Certificate signing request—A certificate signing request (CSR) contains personal information used to generate your development certificate. You submit this request to the iPhone Developer Program Portal.

> **NOTE ▶** The Program Portal is visible only to members of the iPhone Developer Program. To become an iPhone Developer Program member, visit http://developer. apple.com/iphone/program.

▶ Development certificate—A development certificate identifies an iPhone application developer. After the CSR is approved, you download your developer certificate from the portal and add it to your keychain.

▶ Provisioning profile—A provisioning profile associates one or more development certificates, devices, and an iPhone application ID (a unique identifier for the iPhone applications you or your organization develop under an iPhone Developer Program contract).

To install iPhone applications signed with your development certificate on a device, you must install at least one provisioning profile on that device. This provisioning profile must identify you (through your development certificate) and your device (by listing its unique device identifier). If you are part of an iPhone developer team, other members of your team, with appropriately defined provisioning profiles, may run applications you build on their devices.

In summary, your computer and device must meet the following requirements:

▶ Your computer must have your development certificate in your keychain.

▶ Your device must contain at least one provisioning profile that contains your developer certificate and identifies your device.

▶ Your development device must have iPhone OS 2.0 or later installed.

▶ To meet these requirements, perform the following steps:

1 Specify your application ID.

2 Register your device with the Program Portal.

3 Install the iPhone OS on your device.

4 Obtain your development certificate.

5 Add your development certificate to your keychain.

6 Obtain your provisioning profile.

7 Add your provisioning profile to Xcode.

8 Install your provisioning profile on your device.

Publishing Applications for Testing

After testing and tuning your application internally, it is always a good idea to perform wider testing with a representative sample of your application's potential users. Such testing may reveal issues that surface only with particular usage patterns. Incorporating a few non-developer users in your testing strategy lets you expose your application to a variety of usage styles and, if that usage produces crashes in your application, allows you to collect the crash reports (also known as crash logs) to analyze and resolve those execution problems.

An iPhone application in development can run only on devices with provisioning profiles generated by the application developer. As iPhone Developer Program members, you and your fellow team members install these files on your devices as part of your development process.

To include users that are not part of your team (also known as testers), you must add them as part of your team in the Program Portal. After you've added them, you can issue them test-provisioning profiles (also known as ad-hoc provisioning profiles), which allow them to install applications on their devices that have not been published to the App Store.

To prepare your application for external distribution and testing, follow these steps for best results:

1   Add testers to your team.

Before any of the testers can install your application on their devices, they must be part of your team with their devices registered. To accomplish this, each tester needs to send you his or her device ID so you can register that device.

2   Add iTunes artwork to your application.

If you do not create your own iTunes artwork for your application, iTunes will use generic artwork. If testers are currently reviewing multiple applications, it may be hard to distinguish one application from another without actually launching each one.

3   Prepare your application for distribution.

Before sending your application to a tester, build it using the Release build configuration. To find the directory containing your binary, within Xcode, go to the Groups & Files list, find the application in the Products group, and choose Reveal in Finder.

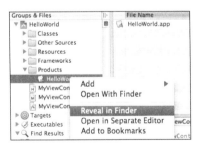

4   Distribute your application.

After identifying the location of the application binary file, you are ready to distribute the application to your testers. Send your application binary and the tester's provisioning profile to the tester. When the tester receives the files, he or she will need to install those files in iTunes.

When the tester receives the two files, he or she drags both the provisioning profile and the application to the iTunes Library group. The application then appears in the Applications list and the tester synchronizes the device. If the iPhone OS on the device is earlier than the iPhone OS for which you prepared the application, the tester will need to update the OS on his or her device.

Deploying Finished Applications

After you have successfully tested and debugged your application, you are ready to distribute it within your organization. You can distribute an application in two ways: You can publish your application on the App Store, at which point it will be available to the world; or you can distribute the application yourself.

Applications from the online App Store work on the iPhone and iPod Touch without requiring any additional steps. If you develop an application that you want to distribute yourself, it must be digitally signed with an Apple-issued certificate. You must also provide your users with a distribution provisioning profile that allows their devices to use the application.

The process for deploying your own application is as follows:

1   Register for enterprise development with Apple.

2   Get a distribution certificate.

3   Sign your applications using your distribution certificate.

4   Create an enterprise distribution provisioning profile that authorizes devices to use applications you have signed.

5   Deploy the application and the enterprise distribution provisioning profile to your
    users' computers.

6   Instruct users to install the application and profile using iTunes.

You could also use iPhone Configuration Utility to preload applications on devices for users.

Working with Profiles and iPhone Configuration Utility

iPhone Configuration Utility lets you easily create, encrypt, and install configuration
profiles; track and install provisioning profiles and authorized applications; and capture
device information, including console logs. To create configuration profiles for devices
with iPhone OS 3.1 or later, you need iPhone Configuration Utility 2.1 or later.

iPhone Configuration Utility requires at least one of the following:

▶   Mac OS X v10.5 Leopard

▶   Windows XP Service Pack 3 with .Net Framework3.5 Service Pack 1

▶   Windows Vista Service Pack 1 with .Net Framework 3.5 Service Pack 1

iPhone Configuration Utility operates in 32-bit mode when used with 64-bit versions
of Windows.

> **MORE INFO** ▶ You can download a copy of iPhone Configuration Utility for any of
> the platforms listed above at www.apple.com/support/iphone/enterprise.

When you run iPhone Configuration Utility, a window similar to the following figure will appear:

The main section of the window changes as you select items in the sidebar.

The sidebar displays the Library, which contains the following categories:

▶   Devices—Shows a list of iPhone and iPod touch devices that have been connected to your computer.

▶   Applications—Lists the applications that are available to install on devices attached to your computer. A provisioning profile might be needed for an application to run on a device.

▶ Provisioning Profiles—Lists profiles that permit the use of the device for iPhone OS development, as authorized by ADC. Provisioning profiles also allow devices to run enterprise applications that are not distributed using the iTunes Store.

▶ Configuration Profiles—Lists the configuration profiles you've previously created, and lets you edit the information you entered, or create a new configuration that you can send to a user or install on a connected device.

The sidebar also displays a Connected Devices list, which displays information about the iPhone or iPod Touch currently connected to your computer's USB port. Information about a connected device is automatically added to the Devices list, so you can view it again without having to reconnect the device. After a device has been connected, you can also encrypt profiles for use on that device only. When a device is connected, you can use iPhone Configuration Utility to install configuration profiles and applications on it.

Creating and Distributing Configuration Profiles

A configuration profile is a single file that configures specific (single or multiple) settings for the iPhone or iPod Touch. This profile consists of payloads that represent individual collections of specific setting types, such as VPN settings, within the configuration profile.

Although you can create a single configuration profile that contains all of the payloads you need for your organization, consider creating one profile for certificates and another one (or more) for other settings so that you can separately update and distribute each type of information. Doing so also allows users to retain the certificates they've already installed when installing a new profile that contains VPN or account settings.

Many of the payloads allow you to specify user names and passwords. If you omit this information, multiple users can use the profile, but the user will be asked to enter the missing information when the profile is installed. If you do personalize profiles for each user and include passwords, you should distribute the profile in encrypted format to protect its contents.

To create a new configuration profile, click the New button in the toolbar of iPhone Configuration Utility. You add payloads to the profile using the payloads list. Then you edit the payloads by entering and selecting options that appear in the editing pane. Required fields are marked with a red arrow. For some settings, such as Wi-Fi, you can click the Add (+) button to add configurations. To remove a configuration, click the Delete (–) button in the editing pane.

After you've created a profile, you can connect a device and install that profile using iPhone Configuration Utility.

Alternatively, you could distribute the profile by email, or by posting it to a website. When users use their devices to open an email message or download the profile from the web, they're prompted to start the installation process.

You can directly install configuration profiles to a device that has been updated to iPhone OS 3.0 or later and is attached to your computer. You can also use iPhone Configuration Utility to remove previously installed profiles.

Distributing Configuration Profiles via Email

When you distribute a profile via email, users can install it by receiving the message on their devices, then tapping the attachment to install it.

1   Click the Share button in the iPhone Configuration Utility toolbar, and in the dialog that appears, select a security option:

     None—This creates a plain-text .mobileconfig file that can be installed on any device.

     Sign Configuration Profile—This signs the .mobileconfig file so it won't be installed by a device if it's altered. Once installed, the profile can be updated only by a profile that has the same identifier and is signed by the same copy of iPhone Configuration Utility.

     Sign and Encrypt Profile—This option signs the profile so it cannot be altered, and encrypts all of the contents so the profile cannot be examined and can only be installed on a specific device. If the profile contains passwords, this option is recommended. Separate .mobileconfig files will be created for each of the devices you select from the Devices list. If a device does not appear in the list, it either hasn't previously been connected to the computer so that the encryption key could be obtained, or it hasn't been upgraded to iPhone OS 3.0 or later.

2   Click Share.

     A new Mail (Mac OS X) or Outlook (Windows) message opens with the profiles added as uncompressed attachments. The files must be uncompressed for the device to recognize and install the profile.

Distributing Configuration Profiles via the Web

You can distribute configuration profiles using a website. Users download and install the profile using mobile Safari on their devices. To easily distribute the URL to your users, you can send it via SMS.

1   Click the Export button in the iPhone Configuration Utility toolbar.

In the dialog that appears, select a security option:

None—This option creates a plain-text .mobileconfig file that can be installed on any device. You should make sure that when you put the file on your website, it's accessible only to authorized users.

Sign Configuration Profile—This signs the .mobileconfig file so it won't be installed by a device if it's altered. Once installed, the profile can only be updated by a profile that has the same identifier and is signed by the same copy of iPhone Configuration Utility. You should make sure that when you put the file on your website, it's accessible only to authorized users.

Sign and Encrypt Profile—This signs the profile so it cannot be altered, and encrypts all of the contents so the profile cannot be examined and can only be installed on a specific device. Separate .mobileconfig files will be created for each of the devices you select from the Devices list.

2   Click Export, then select a location in which to save the .mobileconfig files.

The files are ready for posting on your website. Don't compress the .mobileconfig file or change its extension, or the device won't recognize or install the profile.

Installing a Configuration Profile with iPhone Configuration Utility

Installing a configuration profile with iPhone Configuration Utility may be the simplest way to configure your device. However, if you have many devices, doing so will take a long time. To configure your device(s) using the utility, follow these steps:

1   Connect the iPhone or iPod Touch to your computer using a USB cable. After a moment, the device appears in the Devices list in iPhone Configuration Utility.

2   Select the device, and click the Configuration Profiles tab.

3   Select a configuration profile from the list, and click Install.

4   On the device, tap Install to install the profile.

When you install directly onto a device via USB, the configuration profile is automatically signed and encrypted before it's transferred to the device.

Installing a Downloaded Configuration Profile

You can provide your users with a URL where they can download the profiles onto their devices, or you can email the profiles to an account that your users can access using the device before it's set up with your enterprise-specific information.

When a user downloads a profile from the web or opens it in an email attachment, the device recognizes the .mobileconfig extension as a profile and begins installation when the user taps Install.

During installation, the user is asked to enter any necessary information, such as passwords that were not specified in the profile, and any additional information required by the settings you specified.

If configured to use Exchange, the device also retrieves the Exchange ActiveSync policies from the server, and will refresh the policies, if they've changed, with every subsequent connection. If the device or Exchange ActiveSync policies enforce a passcode setting, the user must enter a passcode that complies with the policy in order to complete the installation.

Additionally, the user is asked to enter any passwords necessary to use certificates included in the profile.

If the installation isn't completed successfully—perhaps because the Exchange server was unreachable or the user cancelled the process—none of the information the user has entered is retained.

Users may want to change how many days of messages are synced to the device and which mail folders other than the inbox are synced. The default values are "three days" and "all folders." Users can change these in Settings > Mail, Contacts, Calendars > *Exchange account name*.

Removing and Updating Configuration Profiles

Configuration profile updates aren't pushed to users. You will need to distribute the updated profiles to your users for them to install. As long as the profile identifier matches and, if signed, has been signed by the same copy of iPhone Configuration Utility, the new profile replaces the profile on the device.

Settings enforced by a configuration profile cannot be changed on the device. To change a setting, you must install an updated profile. If the profile was signed, it can be replaced only with a profile signed by the same copy of iPhone Configuration Utility. The identifier in both profiles must match in order for the updated profile to be recognized as a replacement.

> **NOTE ▶** Removing a configuration profile removes policies and all of the Exchange account's data stored on the device, as well as VPN settings, certificates, and other information, including mail messages, associated with the profile.

If the General Settings payload of the profile specifies that it cannot be removed by the user, the Remove button won't appear. If the settings allow removal using an authorization password, the user will be asked to enter the password after tapping Remove.

What You've Learned

▶ The iPhone SDK tools that are most useful for the development of web applications for the iPhone OS are Dashcode and iPhone Simulator.

▶ The iPhone SDK tools that are most useful for the development of native applications for the iPhone OS are Xcode, Interface Builder, iPhone Simulator, and Instruments.

▶ To gain access to the iPhone SDK, you must be a member of the iPhone Developer Program.

▶ To install a native application for testing on an iPhone, you must have a development certificate in the keychain on your computer, a provisioning profile, and iPhone OS 2.0 or later installed on the device.

▶ You have two options for deploying an application within your organization. You can use the App Store, or you can distribute the application yourself.

▶ When deploying the applications yourself, you can predeploy applications using iPhone Configuration Utility or have the users install the applications and provisioning file themselves.

▶ The benefits of a web application as opposed to a native application include ease of deployment, the use of existing knowledge, and the use of existing tools.

▶ The benefits of deploying a native application as opposed to a web application include its availability anytime and anywhere, as well its potential to generate revenue from iTunes App Store distribution.

▶ A provisioning profile associates one or more development certificates, devices, and an iPhone application ID (a unique identifier for the iPhone applications you or your organization develop under an iPhone Developer Program contract).

▶ You install a provisioning file by dragging the file to the user's Library group within iTunes.

▶ iPhone Configuration Utility can be used to create, distribute, and manage iPhone configuration files.

References
For additional information, see these resources:

Administration Guides
iPhone OS Enterprise Deployment Guide for v3.1 or Later, 2nd Edition

Presentations
"Integrating iPhone into the Enterprise—Session 601, Apple World Wide Developers Conference 2009"

"iPhone Web Applications from Start to Finish—Session 206, Apple World Wide Developers Conference 2009"

URLs

iPhone OS Technology Overview: http://developer.apple.com/iphone/library/
documentation/Miscellaneous/Conceptual/iPhoneOSTechOverview/Introduction/
Introduction.html

Your First iPhone Application: http://developer.apple.com/iphone/library/documentation/
iPhone/Conceptual/iPhone101/Articles/00_Introduction.html

iPhone Application Programming Guide: http://developer.apple.com/iphone/library/
documentation/iPhone/Conceptual/iPhoneOSProgrammingGuide/Introduction/
Introduction.html

iPhone Development Guide: http://developer.apple.com/iphone/library/documentation/
Xcode/Conceptual/iphone_development/100-iPhone_Development_Quick_Start/iphone_
development_quick_start.html

Safari Web Content Guide: http://developer.apple.com/iphone/library/documentation/
AppleApplications/Reference/SafariWebContent/Introduction/Introduction.html

Dashcode User Guide: http://developer.apple.com/iphone/library/documentation/
AppleApplications/Conceptual/Dashcode_UserGuide/Contents/Resources/en.lproj/
Introduction/Introduction.html#//apple_ref/doc/uid/TP40004692-CH1-SW1

Videos

iPhone Getting Started Videos

Introduction to the iPhone SDK, John Geleynse (Director, Software Technology Evangelism,
Apple), 2008

iPhone Development Tools Overview, Michael Jurewitz (Developer Tools Evangelist, Apple),
2008

iPhone SDK for Web Developers, Mark Malone (iPhone and Internet Technologies
Evangelist, Apple), 2008

Key Practices for iPhone Application Development, Vicki Murley (Safari Technologies
Evangelist, Apple), 2008

Chapter Review

1. What are the system requirements for installing the iPhone SDK?

2. In addition to web applications, what else can you create with Dashcode?

3. When using Dashcode, you would click Run to open iPhone Simulator and display your application. In Xcode, how do you open iPhone Simulator and display your application?

4. If you are developing a native application for external distribution on the App Store for a company with more than 500 employees, which iPhone Developer program should you join, Standard or Enterprise?

5. Before you can receive a development certificate from the Program Portal, what must Apple accept?

6. If you need to be positive that your application would work without network access, which type of application should you develop?

7. How do you change the payload of a VPN configuration profile that has already been deployed?

Answers

1. You must install the iPhone SDK on an Intel-based Macintosh computer. The iPhone SDK is not supported on Power PC systems.

2. You can also use Dashcode to create Dashboard widgets.

3. In Xcode, you click "Build and Debug" to open iPhone Simulator and display your application.

4. You should join the Standard Program as you are developing applications for distribution on the App Store, not solely for internal distribution.

5. Before it can provide a development certificate, Apple must approve your CSR (certificate signing request).

6. You should develop a native iPhone application.

7. To update any changes within any of the payloads that make up a profile, you must replace the entire profile.

8

Time   This lesson takes approximately 60 minutes to complete.

Goals   Understand the Mobile Access service on Mac OS X Server

Learn the benefits of using Mobile Access service as compared to VPN

List the services to which the Mobile Access service provides proxy access

Use Mobile Access service to provide access to private resources

Use certificates with proxied services

Identify the client OS requirement to allow computers to access services on the private network via the Mobile Access service

Define forward and reverse proxy and compare to Mobile Access Server

Chapter **8**

Using Mobile Access Server

Mobile Access Server (MAS) provides a secure method for sharing internal resources with external clients by enabling access to IMAP, SMTP, and HTTP protocols (such as web service), as well as CalDAV— all behind a corporate firewall and without the need for a virtual private network (VPN). This is accomplished by sending requests for mail, web, Address Book, and iCal services to a server that acts as a reverse proxy to the actual servers (called *origin servers*) providing the services.

In a typical forward proxy situation, clients on the LAN forward their requests (generally for webpages, but potentially for other services) to a proxy server on the LAN. The proxy server then makes the request to the Internet server, downloads the results, and returns them to the requesting client. The proxy may perform additional tasks such as caching or content filtering.

A reverse proxy basically reverses the data flow. A client on the Internet makes a request to the proxy server. The proxy server analyzes the request, forwards it to the appropriate internal server, obtains the result, and returns it to the Internet-based client. Typical uses for a reverse proxy are to protect the LAN-based servers from direct access from the Internet and for load balancing across multiple servers. The Mobile Access service functions in the security capacity of a reverse proxy.

To use MAS, the client only needs to have appropriate client software (web browser, calendar client, and so on). However, depending upon the specific configuration of origin servers and SSL certificates, client limitations may adversely impact your ability to access some origin servers.

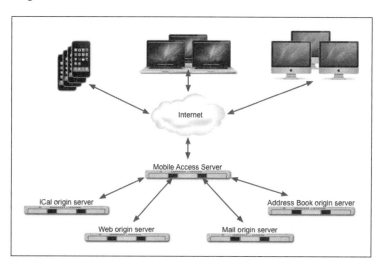

The Mobile Access service runs on a server that is accessible from the public (Internet) and private (intranet) networks. This server acts as the gateway through which connections are made from the Internet to origin servers located on the private intranet. Proxy service access is available to the Mail, iCal, Address Book, and web services hosted on various origin servers.

To access these services via MAS, the client computers' operating system must be capable of running a CalDAV client, a mail client, and any modern web browser.

> **NOTE** ▶ Contrary to some public documentation, MAS is compatible with the wikis hosted on Mac OS X Server v10.6.

When properly configured, MAS provides the following benefits:

▶ There's no need to open ports in the firewall to allow connection to specific LAN servers.

▶ MAS is more secure than VPN because MAS allows access only to specific services, not to the entire LAN.

▶ MAS does not host any sensitive data, which makes it less vulnerable to exploits.

▶ MAS limits which users can authenticate and which services authenticated users can access.

▶ MAS utilizes Secure Sockets Layer (SSL) to hide sensitive data over the Internet.

Understanding MAS

MAS uses a combination of SSL certificates, split DNS, and proxied authentication mechanisms to provide a secure, robust access solution for mobile users.

Using SSL and MAS

To ensure that data transferred through MAS is encrypted, an SSL certificate is required. SSL uses a public key infrastructure (PKI) to create and manage certificates used by SSL-enabled services.

Access to origin services provided over web-based protocols (such as web, iCal, and Address Book) is always performed using SSL. The mail protocols work differently, but do support SSL. This is always enabled for IMAP and can be initiated by the client for SMTP.

You can employ two methods to use certificates for proxied services. The first is to create a separate certificate for each host name. The second is to create a single wild card certificate that all SSL-enabled services can share.

You also need to implement certificates on the origin server(s). On the origin server(s), you have four options. You can use the same host name-specific certificates used on MAS, or you can get new certificates specific to each host name on the origin server(s). You can also choose to use the same wild card certificate used on MAS, or get a new wild card certificate for the origin server(s).

When using certificates, follow these guidelines:

▶   Use CA-issued certificates, not self-signed ones. With self-signed certificates, users will be asked to accept an invalid certificate, which will train your users to always click Continue in this dialog and may open them up to exploitation on other sites.

▶   If you do use self-signed certificates, you can import the Root Certificate using iPhone Configuration Utility for your iPhone or iPod Touch device, or using Keychain Access on Mac OS X.

▶   Use wild card certificates on MAS or import certificates from all of your origin servers.

For more information about certificates, refer to Chapter 6, "Keys and Certificates."

Using Split DNS and MAS

Split DNS resolves a fully qualified domain name (FQDN) to multiple IP addresses, which permits internal users to communicate directly with a particular server while external users are directed to MAS.

For example, www.pretendco.com could have a DNS record on an Internet-facing DNS server with an IP address of 17.153.27.53. The DNS record for the same domain name—www.pretendco.com—on an intranet-facing DNS server could have an IP address of 10.1.0.6.

When a user attempts to connect to the www.pretendco.com server from the public network, he or she will be directed to a server with the IP address 17.153.27.53. When a private network user attempts to connect to www.pretendco.com, the user will be routed to a server with the IP address 10.1.0.6.

One of the main user benefits of this DNS configuration is that bookmarks and shortcuts created using the domain name of a specific server will work whether the user is on the public or private network.

MAS uses split DNS to allow users on private and public networks to refer to different servers by the same names. Your bookmarks and configurations will work regardless of which network you are accessing. MAS is multihomed, meaning that it has interfaces on multiple networks, the public network, and the private network. Any public network connection request for a proxied service goes through MAS before it is routed to the origin server. However, any connection request on the private LAN connects directly to the origin server and bypasses MAS. The mail services work a little differently and will be discussed later in this chapter.

In Mac OS X Server v10.6, MAS is based on a reverse proxy server. It provides access from the Internet to an intranet. If a user authenticates with MAS and has authorization to use the requested service, MAS reissues the request to the origin server, which may also require authentication.

Using MAS Authentication Mechanisms

MAS always authenticates access. It uses one of three techniques to do so, depending on the service the client is accessing. In the case of web service, MAS will use a session-based approach (through a webpage) to initially authenticate to the server. If a user chooses, MAS can remember him or her and not prompt that user again for 14 days. The origin server may additionally authenticate the user, potentially resulting in multiple prompts to authenticate for internal websites.

The Address Book and iCal services work a little differently. These services have their own authentication and authorization methods. Rather than implement these same methods in an additional service (MAS), the Mobile Access service uses the origin server's authentication process to authenticate the user.

The mail services work in a third way. The Mobile Access service stands in for the mail service and authenticates the user directly using typical mail authentication techniques.

> **NOTE ▶** MAS does not support Kerberos authentication directly or as a pass-through for proxied services. For example, it will not support access to an internal website that is protected using Kerberos.

When MAS proxies an origin server, that server is limited to specific authentication mechanisms. For instance, when Address Book and iCal are proxied, they support only basic or digest authentication over an SSL session through MAS. Local clients may still use Kerberos to access them. The Kerberos-only authentication option for the services does not allow access through MAS.

Consider the following authentication methods when servers are proxied:

- Web
  - Basic
  - Digest
  - Session-based
- Address Book and iCal
  - Basic
  - Digest
- Mail (SMTP)
  - None
  - PLAIN
  - LOGIN
  - CRAM-MD5
- Mail (IMAP)
  - CLEAR
  - PLAIN
  - LOGIN
  - CRAM-MD5

Access through MAS requires authentication to either Open Directory (OD) or Active Directory (AD). Based on the users and groups created in OD or AD, you organize a whitelist of authorized users and groups by service type: iCal, Address Book, mail, and web. After authentication, the user credentials are validated against the whitelist to verify that the user has been granted access to the particular service.

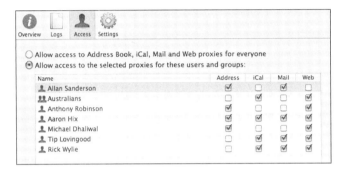

Controlling Access to Web Services

The following figure illustrates a typical communication process between an external host, MAS, and the HTTP origin server.

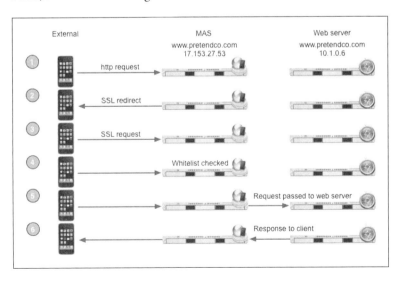

1. The external client requests an HTTP connection with a web server (www.pretendco. com in this example). Based on the DNS information the client has, www.pretendco. com resolves to 17.153.27.53. This IP address has been assigned to MAS; therefore, all external requests to www.pretendco.com will go to MAS.

2. MAS redirects the client to a secure connection (HTTPS).

3. The client again requests connection to www.pretendco.com, this time as an HTTPS request. This and subsequent conversations with MAS will be wrapped in a secure connection.

4. MAS sends the client a login webpage and the user is asked to log in. MAS authenticates the user against Directory Services, and then checks the user against a whitelist for that service. If the user is authenticated and on the whitelist, MAS will proxy requests to the origin server(s). If the user is not authenticated or not on the whitelist, the user receives an Access Denied URL and is given the opportunity to try again.

NOTE ▶ You can change both the icon and the text in the login dialog. The icon can be changed in /Library/Preferences/com.apple.securityproxy_http.plist. The text can be changed in /usr/share/collaboration/css/proxy/strings/en_lproj/Localizable.strings.

5.   After the user clicks the "Log in" button, the options to log out or open the page appear.

6.   If the user chooses to open the page, MAS requests the page from the origin server
     (possibly over SSL) and then sends the requested content to the client over SSL.

     NOTE ▶ After the user has successfully logged into MAS, the "Keep me logged in" ses-
     sion ID is valid for 14 days by default. This value can be modified in Server Admin in
     the Settings pane of the Mobile Access service.

An administrator can remove access to a user or group at any time because the headers
are constantly examined to verify that the user is on the whitelist.

Now, suppose you have three web servers, each of which hosts a completely separate site. From
the public side of your network, all web traffic is routed to your MAS, regardless of the origin
server's host name. For example, www.pretendco.com routes to 17.153.27.53. However, the
same address applies to www1.pretendco.com, www2.pretendco.com, and so on.

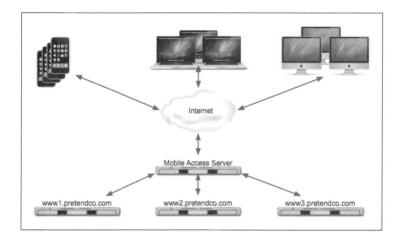

The method of controlling access to web services illustrated in the preceding figure works well when only one web server is proxied. If more than one web server is proxied, you'll have a conflict between the host header (which tells MAS which origin server should receive the request) and the SSL certificate used to encrypt the traffic.

The host header is an HTTP header and as such is encrypted by the SSL wrapper. If these three hosts use different SSL certificates, MAS doesn't know which certificate to use when decrypting the request because it cannot access the host header without first decrypting that request.

Prior to Mac OS X Server v10.6.2, the process worked until step 5 of the access model, when MAS loaded the requested URL from the origin web server. Prior to v10.6.2, if more than one web server was on the intranet, MAS did not know which server should receive that request.

When the external client creates the request, it knows the host name to which it wishes to connect. It attempts to tell MAS by placing the name in the host header. However, because the communication with MAS is over an SSL connection, the information in the host header is encrypted and can be decrypted only with the correct certificate. If each website uses a different certificate, Apache cannot determine which origin server should fulfill the URL request.

Prior to Mac OS X Server v10.6.2, you had a few methods for addressing this situation:

▶ You could use the same wild card certificate on MAS for all web origin servers. This allows MAS to view the host header and forward the URL request to the correct origin server.

▶ You could specify a different port number for each origin server.

▶ Although it wasn't recommended, you could edit the virtual host config files to be IP specific.

These solutions work on later versions of Mac OS X, too, but with the arrival of Mac OS X Server v10.6.2, they became unnecessary because Apple adopted Apache 2.2.13, which supports Server Name Indication (SNI).

SNI allows a client to include the requested host name in step 3 of the access model. This allows MAS to determine the correct host name of the origin server from the beginning of the connection and then use the correct certificate to decrypt the request from the client and issue the same request to the correct origin server.

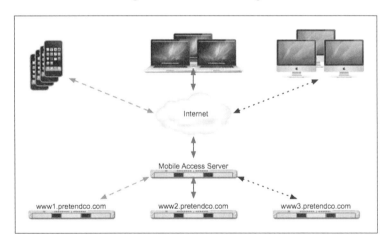

With Apache 2.2.13, you no longer need a certificate to view the host header of the request. However, you do need the certificates to create an SSL connection. Also, you don't need to specify a different port number for each origin server because all such requests can be routed via the host name of the origin server.

NOTE ▶ Although many modern browsers support SNI, most Windows XP–based browsers do not. If you have a large Windows XP installed base that will be accessing sites through your MAS, you may want to choose a different solution.

Controlling Access to iCal and Address Book Services

Previously, you learned that MAS uses three authentication mechanisms. For websites, it prompts the user for credentials and then checks the user against its whitelist. A particular website on a LAN may not require authentication because it can assume all users are trusted. When MAS is introduced, that assumption is no longer valid, but the site still may not have an authentication mechanism. As a result, MAS imposes the mechanism you just learned about.

iCal and Address Book services are always authenticated. As a result, MAS does not need to implement any authentication for these services. It can simply allow the service to perform the authentication. However, not all users may be allowed to access their calendar or address book from outside the LAN. As a result, MAS does maintain a whitelist for these services and checks user access through MAS against it.

The following figure illustrates a typical communication process between an external host, MAS, and a CalDAV server (origin server). Because the processes for controlling access to the iCal server and the Address Book server work the same way, the figure illustrates both services running on the same server. However, running both services on the same server is not a requirement, nor is it a limitation. CalDAV and CardDAV services can be run on separate servers.

NOTE ▶ Unlike web service proxies in MAS, CalDAV and Address Book server HTTP connections are not redirected to HTTPS. Most clients do not support this redirect functionality. They simply fail to connect through MAS. Therefore, the client must be configured to use SSL for access to work through MAS.

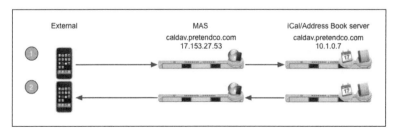

1. The external client requests an HTTPS connection with the CalDAV server (caldav.pretendco.com). In DNS available to the client, caldav.pretendco.com resolves to 17.153.27.53. This IP address has been assigned to MAS, so all requests to caldav.pretendco.com are sent to MAS. When MAS receives a request to authenticate to caldav.pretendco.com, it passes that request directly to the origin server for authentication. The origin server uses its normal authentication and authorization methods to determine if the user is allowed access. The response is returned to MAS.

2. MAS examines the response from the origin server to find the identity of the user. Then it examines its whitelist to see if the user is authorized to use MAS. If the user is not on the whitelist, a response indicating that the user is not authorized is substituted for the response from the origin server.

Controlling Access to Mail Services

The final access control mechanism comes into play with mail services. The mail protocols are not HTTP derived, so the Mobile Access service needs to take a different approach when dealing with mail.

The following figure illustrates a typical communication process between an external host, MAS, and a mail server (origin server).

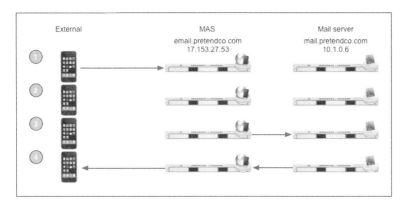

1. An external user requests connection to a mail server (email.pretendco.com) over IMAP with SSL. Unknown to the client, email.pretendco.com is actually a proxy server for mail.pretendco.com.

    NOTE ▶ If the client is not using SSL, the connection will fail.

2.   MAS authenticates the user against Directory Services, and then authorizes the user based on a whitelist.

3.   If the user is authenticated and authorized, MAS forwards the request to the mail server, mail.pretendco.com. MAS uses the user's credentials to log into the mail server on the user's behalf.

4.   The mail server allows the user to retrieve mail via proxied mail commands. The proxied transactions are transparent to the client.

Note that the user's client is configured to access mail from email.pretendco.com, not from mail.pretendco.com. DNS will resolve email.pretendco.com to MAS on both the public Internet and the private LAN. In short, for users allowed to use MAS, email access will always be proxied, regardless of whether it originates on the LAN or outside the firewall.

Configuring MAS

Configuring MAS is fairly straightforward. First you must enable the service on your server. Then you have to configure each service and its origin. Finally you configure MAS, based on the configurations of the services on your origin servers.

Before you can configure any available services to use MAS, you will add Mobile Access to the list of services in Server Admin.

1   Open Server Admin and connect to the server.

2   Click Settings, then click Services.

3   Select the Mobile Access checkbox, and click Save.

Configuring Mobile Access

With Mobile Access enabled, you can configure MAS to act as a proxy for Address Book, iCal, mail, and web services.

1   If necessary, open Server Admin and connect to the server.

2   Click the disclosure triangle to the left of the server to display the services list.

3   From the expanded services list, select Mobile Access. Then click Settings.

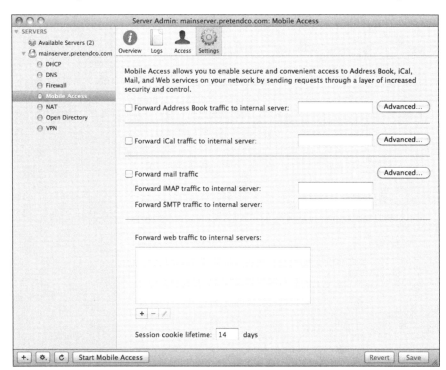

You are now ready to configure the Mobile Access settings.

NOTE ► The proxy server gracefully restarts when you save certain changes. If the changes require a full restart, you are prompted to approve it.

MAS—Web

You use Server Admin to indicate the internal web origin server(s), to set the external and internal ports, and to configure the SSL settings for MAS.

If you are using authentication on your web origin servers, you must use basic, digest, or session-based authentication. Kerberos authentication is not supported.

To configure Mobile Access service web settings, do the following:

1 While viewing the Settings pane of the Mobile Access service, click the Add (+) button below the "Forward web traffic to internal servers" list.

2 Enter the fully qualified domain name of your internal web server.

   NOTE ▶ Don't forget to establish the same name in the public DNS, with the name resolving to the public IP address of your MAS.

3 Select the server you just added, and click the Edit button.

4 You will notice that the external connection requires an SSL certificate. From the SSL Certificate pop-up menu, choose a certificate, if the correct one is not already chosen. If no certificates are listed, or if you do not see the correct certificate, refer to Chapter 6, "Keys and Certificates," for more information.

5 Configure the other settings. If you are going to use port numbers to differentiate various internal websites, configure the appropriate numbers.

6 Click OK, and then click Save.

   If more than one web server exists on your site, repeat steps 1 through 6 to add those servers to the list.

7   With the Mobile Access service still selected, click the Start Mobile Access button at
the bottom of the Servers list.

MAS—iCal

You use Server Admin to indicate the internal iCal origin server, set the external and internal ports, and configure the SSL settings for MAS.

When configuring MAS to proxy iCal, you must use basic or digest authentication on the iCal server. Kerberos authentication is not supported.

1   From the Settings pane of the Mobile Access service, select the "Forward iCal traffic to internal server" checkbox.

2   In the "Forward iCal traffic to internal server" field, enter the fully qualified domain name of the iCal server.

3   Click Advanced. You have several options to configure. However, unless you modified settings in the firewall, need to use a service-specific certificate, or want to use SSL internally, click OK. Otherwise, enter the appropriate values.

4   After you have confirmed that the settings are correct, click OK.

5   Click Save.

6   Verify that the iCal server's configuration matches what you specified for MAS: For example, if the iCal server listens on port 8443, MAS should try to talk to it on port 8443.

Remember that you can use only basic or digest authentication. Also, confirm that the port numbers and SSL settings are the same on MAS and the origin server, and that the client is configured to use SSL.

MAS—Address Book

You use Server Admin to indicate the internal Address Book origin server, set the external and internal ports, and configure the SSL settings for MAS.

When configuring MAS to proxy Address Book, you must use basic or digest authentication because, once again, Kerberos authentication is not supported.

1   From the Settings pane of the Mobile Access service, select the "Forward Address Book traffic to internal server" checkbox.

2   In the "Forward Address Book traffic to internal server" field, enter the fully qualified domain name of the Address Book server.

3   Click Advanced. You have several options to configure. However, unless you modified settings in the firewall, need to use a service-specific certificate, or want to use SSL internally, click OK. Otherwise, enter the appropriate values.

4   After you have confirmed that the settings are correct, click OK, and then click Save.

5   Make sure you have configured your Address Book server to match the configuration of your internal connections.

Remember that you can use only basic or digest authentication. Also, confirm that the port numbers and SSL settings are the same on MAS and the origin server, and that the client is configured to use SSL.

MAS—Mail

You use Server Admin to indicate the internal mail origin server, to set the external and internal ports, and to configure the SSL settings for MAS. When configuring a mail proxy, your MAS and origin mail server must have unique DNS names. You cannot use the same DNS name for both servers.

When configuring MAS to proxy a mail service, SMTP and IMAP clients accessing MAS must authenticate using clear text (CLEAR, PLAIN, or LOGIN) or CRAM-MD5 password authentication over an SSL session. The client must use SSL. Kerberos is not supported.

1   From the Settings pane of the Mobile Access service, select the "Forward mail" checkbox.

2   In the "Forward IMAP traffic to internal server" field, enter the fully qualified domain name of the IMAP server.

3   In the "Forward SMTP traffic to internal server" field, enter the fully qualified domain name of the SMTP server.

4   Click Advanced. You have several options to configure. However, unless you modified settings in the firewall, need to use a service-specific certificate, or want to use SSL internally, you should click OK. Otherwise, enter the appropriate values.

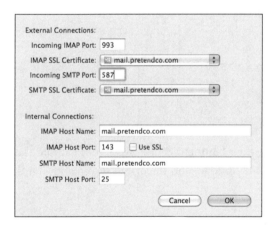

5   After you have confirmed that the settings are correct, click OK, and then click Save.

6   Make sure your mail server is configured correctly.

7   Verify that all mail clients that will use the proxy are configured to connect to the public interface, or that a split DNS is configured to point the internal client to the internal interface of MAS. Proxied mail users should always use the proxy server, even when connected to the LAN.

Troubleshooting MAS

MAS is dependent on the accurate configuration of the services for which it serves as proxy. Therefore, the majority of the issues discovered while using MAS are not necessarily problems with the server, but often lie with the iCal, Address Book, mail, or web service configurations on the origin servers. A description of these specific configuration procedures is beyond the scope of this book. For more information, refer to *Apple Training Series: Mac OS X Server Essentials v10.6* (Peachpit Press, 2010).

How do you know when your troubleshooting issues are not related to the services configuration on the origin servers? In the next section, you'll learn about some common problems and troubleshooting methods.

Troubleshooting a MAS Configuration

Many dependencies must be satisfied for a successful implementation of MAS:

► MAS must be bound to either the OD or the AD service. If the server is not bound to a directory service, you will be unable to add users or groups to the whitelist, and the server will be unable to authenticate or authorize access to services.

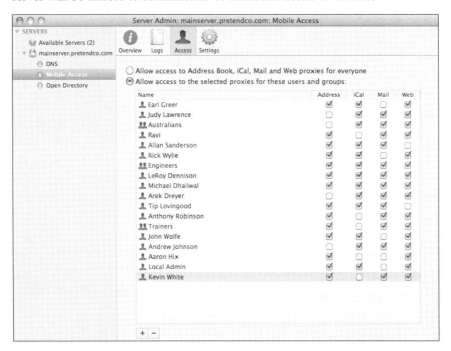

▶ MAS must be able to resolve both public and private domain names for each of the origin servers for which it serves as proxy. You can do this by placing one DNS server on the Internet and another on the intranet. For information on various DNS configurations, see Chapter 1, "Understanding the Domain Name System."

▶ MAS must have a valid SSL certificate. You can create a single wild card certificate to use on MAS. The origin servers may use the same certificate(s), or you can create certificates for each proxied origin server. While you can leave the origin servers unprotected by SSL, it is not considered best practice to do so. The origin server certificates can be imported into MAS and specified for the appropriate service in the MAS settings in Server Admin.

Troubleshooting MAS

When MAS is not behaving as you expect and you have confirmed that the origin server configuration is correct, examine the Overview pane of the Mobile Access service. The Overview pane displays detailed information on the proxies currently running on the server and the internal servers with which those proxies are associated. If everything looks correct, review the logs.

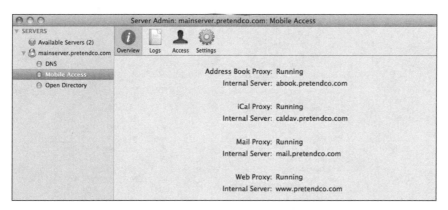

Reviewing the Logs

The logs will help you track down whether your problem is with the server configurations, the client configuration, the client connectivity to MAS, or between MAS and the origin servers. Each of the proxied services has at least one log. The mail and web services each have two.

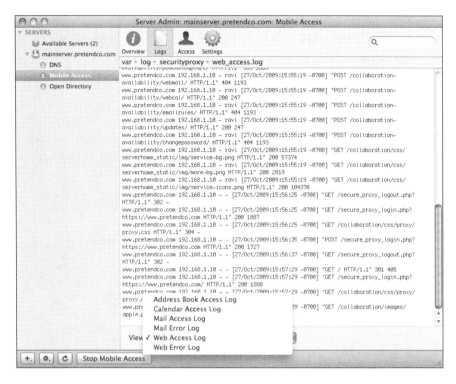

To view Mobile Access service logs, take the following steps:

1   With the Mobile Access service selected in the Servers list, click Logs.

2   From the View pop-up menu, choose the log you want to review.

    You can view mail access and error logs, Calendar access logs, Address Book access logs, and web access and error logs.

Although you can access this information using Console.app or System Profiler, the Logs pane in Mobile Access displays information related only to Mobile Access and to the specific services for which it serves as a proxy.

Troubleshooting MAS—Web

Although the web proxy of MAS works with most websites, some web applications and links might require additional configuration to function.

Consider the following issues when setting up proxies for your website or web applications:

▶ If your web application requires the addresses of the remote clients, your application must obtain the client address through the X-Forwarded-For header, which contains the actual IP address for the client. The more typical REMOTE_ADDR header will contain the IP address of MAS for proxied clients.

▶ If possible, keep web links relative, because your scheme might be HTTP internally, but will be HTTPS externally.

▶ If you have links to hosts within your intranet that are not proxied, the links do not function through the proxy.

▶ The whitelist either allows access to web services or it doesn't. It is not granular enough to allow access to some proxied web servers, but not others.

What You've Learned

▶ The basic function of the Mobile Access service on Mac OS X Server is to provide proxied access from the Internet to specific services hosted on origin servers on a private network.

▶ Using the Mobile Access service is more convenient and can be more secure than using VPN access. When a user authenticates, MAS checks the user's authorization and directs requests to the appropriate origin server. MAS is more secure than VPN because MAS allows connections only to specific servers for specific services on the private intranet, whereas VPN generally allows access to the entire intranet. VPN, on the other hand, provides more flexible access to resources on the protected network.

▶ The Mobile Access service provides proxied access to iCal, Address Book, mail, and web services. It functions as a reverse proxy.

▶ To provide access to private resources on the intranet, MAS requires authentication through Directory Services as well as authorization through a whitelist. Further, the entire transaction with an external client is through SSL.

▶ MAS supports two methods for using certificates with proxied services. First, a certificate can be obtained for each origin server and imported into MAS. Second, a single wild card certificate can be obtained and used on any server for any service.

References
For additional information, consult these sources:

Administration Guides
Address Book Server Administration v10.6 Snow Leopard

Advanced Server Administration v10.6 Snow Leopard

iCal Server Administration v10.6 Snow Leopard

iPhone OS Enterprise Deployment Guide for v3.1 or later, 2nd Edition

Mail Service Administration v10.6 Snow Leopard

Network Services Administration v10.6 Snow Leopard

Books
Albitz, Paul, and Liu, Cricket. *DNS and BIND,* 5th Edition (O'Reilly Media, Inc., 2006).

Dreyer, Arek, and Greisler, Ben. *Apple Training Series: Mac OS X Server Essentials v10.6* (Peachpit Press, 2010).

White, Kevin M. *Apple Training Series: Mac OS X Support Essentials v10.6* (Peachpit Press, 2010).

Presentations
Apple World Wide Developers Conference 2009: Session 617—Deploying Mobile Access Server

RFC Documents
Access the RFC (Request for Comment) documents at: www.faqs.org/rfcs/rfc#### (#### = RFC Number).

RFC 2616—Hypertext Transfer Protocol—HTTP/1.1

RFC 3040—Internet Web Replication and Caching Taxonomy

RFC 3143—Known HTTP Proxy/Caching Problems

RFC 4366—Transport Layer Security (TLS) Extensions

URLs
BIND 9 Administrator Reference Manual: http://oldwww.isc.org/index.pl?/sw/bind/arm94/index.php

DNS for Rocket Scientists: www.zytrax.com/books/dns

Chapter Review

1. MAS is based on what type of proxy service?
2. When would VPN be a better solution for intranet access by external clients?
3. Why would you assign specific port numbers, such as www.pretendco.com:8000, to external web server host names?
4. By what mechanism does MAS confirm that a user is authorized to access the intranet for specific services?
5. Why is a self-signed certificate not recommended for use on MAS?

Answers

1. MAS is based on a reverse proxy.
2. VPN would be a better solution for remote access when the specific user requires access to services or resources that are not available via Mobile Access.
3. When using a version of Mac OS X Server prior to v10.6.2, you would assign port numbers to external web server host names if you had more than one web server on the intranet. This solution circumvented the issues related to virtual hosts and SSL certificates. However, with the release of v10.6.2, Apple has implemented SNI, and this workaround often is no longer necessary.

4. MAS uses the whitelist to determine authorized users.

5. When using a self-signed certificate, users are prompted to accept a certificate from an untrusted site. Training users to accept such a certificate may condition them to accept certificates in other situations in which they should not do so for security reasons (for example, when the certificate failed validation for legitimate security reasons).

Index